Deer of
the world

By the same author

Deer and Their Management in the Deer Parks of Great Britain and Ireland
The Deerstalking Grounds of Great Britain and Ireland
The Deer of Great Britain and Ireland
The Ancient White Cattle of Britain and Their Descendants
The Wild Goats of Great Britain and Ireland
Deerstalking in Scotland

Pampas deer

G. Kenneth
Whitehead

Deer of
the world

A Studio Book
The Viking Press New York

Published in 1972 by The Viking Press, Inc.
625 Madison Avenue, New York, N.Y. 10022

SBN 670–26612–4
Library of Congress catalog card number: 72–81680

Printed in Great Britain by
The Anchor Press Ltd
Tiptree, Essex

Contents

Illustrations

(b) Altai Wapiti *Cervus canadensis songaricus* (Drawn by J. Smit.)

(c) Thorold's deer stag *Cervus albirostris* (Drawn by J. Smit)

10(a) Japanese Sika deer *Cervus nippon nippon* during the rut

(b) Japanese Sika deer stag in February (front view)

(c) Japanese Sika deer stag in February – rear view – showing the white caudal patch and light-coloured gland patches about the hocks

11(a) Kerama Sika deer stag *Cervus nippon keramae*

(b) Manchurian Sika deer stag *Cervus nippon mantchuricus*

12(a) Formosan Sika deer stag *Cervus nippon taiouanus* in the autumn

(b) Formosan Sika deer stag *C.n. taiouanus* in July

(c) Dybowski's Sika deer *C.n. hortulorum*

(d) Shou or Wallich's deer *Cervus elaphus wallichi*

13(a) Eld's deer *Cervus eldi eldi*

(b) Siamese Eld's deer *C.e.siamensis*

(c) Schomburgk's deer *Cervus schomburgki*

14(a) Swamp deer hind *Cervus duvauceli duvauceli*

(b) Swamp deer stag *C.d.duvauceli*

(c) Chital or Axis deer stag *Axis axis axis* in San Diego Zoo

15 Chital or Axis deer *Axis axis axis* at Whipsnade Zoo

16(a) Hog deer stag *Axis porcinus porcinus*

(b) Hog deer stag *A.p.porcinus*

17(a) Kuhl's deer or Bawean deer stag *Axis kuhlii*

(b) Kuhl's deer or Bawean deer hind *Axis kuhlii*

18(a) Ceylonese Sambar stag *Cervus unicolor unicolor*

(b) Group of Ceylonese Sambar stags *C.u.unicolor*

(c) Malayan Sambar stag *C.u.equinus*

(d) Skull and antlers of Calamian deer *Axis calamianensis*

19 Moluccan Rusa deer *Cervus timorensis moluccensis*

20(a) White-tailed deer buck *Odocoileus virginianus borealis*

(b) Albino White-tailed deer doe *Odocoileus virginianus* in Douglas County, Wisconsin

(c) White-tailed deer buck *O.v. virginianus* (Museum specimen)

21(a) Mule deer buck *Odocoileus hemionus hemionus*

(b) Mule deer does *O.h.hemionus* in deep snow

22(a) Pampas deer *Ozotoceros bezoarticus* in the Field Museum of Natural History, Chicago

(b) Pampas deer doe *O.b.celer*

(c) Marsh deer *Blastocerus dichtomus* – mounted group in the Field Museum of Natural History, Chicago

23(a) Huemul or Guemal *Hippocamelus bisulcus*

(b) Huemul doe *Hippocamelus bisulcus*

(c) Brocket deer *Mazama americana* in the Field Museum of Natural History, Chicago

24(a) Pudu deer buck *Pudu pudu* in the Field Museum of Natural History, Chicago

Maps

NOTE

It is to be understood that although deer occur within the limits of the area outlined they do not necessarily occupy every part of the shaded area, but only those which are suitable for them.

Localities mentioned are only approximate and are intended to designate centre of distribution.

Acknowledgment is made to the following for the use of photographs

Manuel de Anchorena 22(b), F. W. Bond 12(d), *Chorley Guardian* 32(b), Francisco Erize frontispiece, E. P. Gee & World Wildlife Fund 28(a), Mrs. Gourley & World Wildlife Fund 12(b), A. Grosse 23(a), G. Hallström & The Nordic Museum, Stockholm 30(d), James Hancock & World Wildlife Fund 23(b), Roy A. Harris & K. R. Duff 8(a), 10(a), 15, 19, 26(a) and (b), 28(b), 29(c), 31(a), (b), (c) and (d), Peter Jackson & World Wildlife Fund 13(a), Dr. F. Kurt & World Wildlife Fund 18(a) and (b), K. H. Lundin 5(a) and (b), R. van Nostrand, San Diego Zoo 14(c), C. J. Ott & Bruce Coleman Ltd 7(a) and (b), F. Vollmar & World Wildlife Fund 12(a), 16(a) and (b), 17(a) and (b) and 28(c), Fritz Walther & World Wildlife Fund 29(b), Department of Mines & Resources 6(b), Field Museum of Natural History, Chicago 22(a) and (c); 23(c) and 24(a), National Film Board of Canada 4(b), 20(a) and 21(b), National Museum of Canada 4(a), 9(a), 20(c) and 21(a), Munich Zoo 27(b), Wisconsin Natural Resources Dept. 20(b). Parc Zoologique, Paris 13(b), Opel-Freigehese 3(a) and (b).

Acknowledgment is also made to Messrs. Rowland Ward, Ltd., for permission to use photographic reproductions of three coloured plates by J. Smit that originally appeared in *Deer of All Lands* (1898) by R. Lydekker – namely 9(b) and (c) and 29(a).

Apart from 8(b) (original watercolour by W. H. Riddell in the author's possession), 32(a) (Sketch by Winfred Austen); 13(c) and 18(c) (both by unknown photographers), all the remaining photographs have been taken by the author.

18(d) has been copied from Heude, P(1888) *Cerf des Philippines et de l'Indo-Chine*.

Introduction

It is over seventy years since R. Lydekker compiled *The Deer of All Lands* (1898) – a book that is now extremely scarce and expensive, with few good copies being available much under £100.

Since that date no book of comparable scope has been written by any author in Britain or elsewhere, apart from, perhaps, K. K. Flerov's *Musk Deer and Deer* (1952), which in its original form was published in the Russian language, but has since (1960) been translated into English by the Israel Program for Scientific Translations, and N. E. Holten's *Hjortevildt i alverdens lande* (1970).

There have, of course, been a number of comprehensive monographs on individual genera and species, such as Taylor's *The Deer of North America* (1956), Banfield's *A Revision of the Reindeer and Caribou, Genus Rangifer* (1961), Murie's *The Elk of North America* (1951) and Petersen's *North American Moose* (1955) etc., and reference to these books has been invaluable in the compilation of this present volume.

Not all the world's deer have been so closely studied as the deer of North America and Europe, and indeed information regarding the deer of the Far East and South America is sadly deficient. However, as a result of considerable correspondence with authorities and hunters in these remote lands I have been able to make a reasonably up-to-date assessment of the present status and classification of the world's deer.

Although Australasia – which includes Australia, New Zealand and New Guinea – is deficient in any indigenous deer, no fewer than ten species have, during the past century, been introduced to these countries and have been completely acclimatised, the majority of them having had to change their breeding habits by as much as six months to suit the change in season. A chapter on the 'Introduced Deer of Australasia' has, therefore, been included.

Lydekker, in 1898 (*The Deer of All Lands*) proposed eleven genera, consisting of fifty-seven species and forty-eight subspecies. Seventeen years later the same authority increased the number to fifteen genera, fifty-eight species and one hundred and fifty-five subspecies, with a number of races *incertae sedis*. (*Catalogue of the Ungulate Mammals in the British Museum. (Nat. Hist.*)) In this present work although the number of genera has been increased by two due to the fact that both Fallow deer and Pampas deer have been designated separate status – *Dama* and *Ozotoceros* respectively – the number of species has been reduced by about a third to forty. Unfortunately, the reverse has been the case with the subspecies, which have been increased to almost two hundred, the majority of these increases being referrable to the North and South American genera *Odocoileus* and *Mazama,* which include no fewer than forty-nine and twenty-six subspecies respectively, and the world-embracing *Cervus*, with sixty-five subspecies.

There is, undoubtedly, room for a reduction, but this must not be achieved by extermination, as has apparently happened to Schomburgk's deer of Thailand, but by a more rational assessment and realisation that environment and insular isolation play a decisive role in the size of both animal and antler development – two features that have so often been used to create a new race. I am glad, therefore, that Banfield (1961) has been able to reduce the number of species in *Rangifer tarandus* (Reindeer/ Caribou) from nineteen to nine, and also that modern opinion now considers the Reindeer of the Old World and Caribou of the New World as one species, *tarandus.* I have never, however, been entirely happy that the Wapiti of North America and eastern Asia should be grouped with the Red deer of Europe and the Middle East, as one species *Cervus elaphus,* for I believe there is ample justification in classifying the Wapiti as *Cervus canadensis*. This I have done.

Wherever possible I have endeavoured to arrange each chapter so that it covers the complete range of any particular genus, and although this has been nearly possible in so far as the American deer are concerned, a certain amount of overlapping of range has of necessity occurred when trying to separate the deer of Europe and northern Asia from those of southern Asia and the Far East

ACKNOWLEDGMENTS

In order to complete this work, I have had to correspond with many people in many parts of the world. To list them all here would be both tedious and unnecessary. Nevertheless I am indeed grateful for all the assistance that has been so freely given.

I would like, however, to make a special acknowledgement to Mr R. W. Hayman of the British Museum (Natural History) for his advice in the preparation of the classification of the *Cervidae* which has been quite invaluable.

G. KENNETH WHITEHEAD

1

What is a Deer?

Deer belong to the order ARTIODACTYLA, which is divided into a number of sub-orders, one of which is sub-order *Ruminantia*, the ruminants. This sub-order includes the deer family known, technically, as the *Cervidae*. This family is a very extensive one and consists of no fewer than seventeen genera, forty different species and over one hundred and ninety subspecies.

The distribution of the *Cervidae* is world wide, except that in an indigenous state it is absent from Australia, New Zealand and practically the whole of the African continent except the extreme north. Because of introductions, however, a number of different species of deer have, during the past century or so, been introduced to Australia and New Zealand where they are now well established in a wild state (see pages 134 and 142).

Ruminants are animals which ruminate or chew the cud. These animals, which include antelopes, cattle, sheep and goats, are characterised by the absence of incisors or cutting teeth in the upper jaw. Instead of incisors they have a callous pad against which the cutting teeth or incisors of the lower jaw can press, and in this way the food, during grazing or browsing, can be ripped off. Each mouthful, instead of being completely masticated, or chewed up, is immediately swallowed and passed into the lobe of the stomach known as the rumen. Here it remains to soften and soak. The animal continues to feed in this fashion until its hunger is appeased. It then lies down, and the process of ruminating commences.

In order to ruminate, deer possess a stomach of four cavities through which the food must pass before it is finally digested. When a deer, after feeding, has lain down, the rumen is contracted and some of the food – now called the cud – is returned to the mouth. This time the cud is thoroughly chewed up with the back teeth or grinders (molars and premolars), with a slow and continuous movement of the lower jaw until the mouthful has been reduced to a pulp, when it is again swallowed. Bypassing the rumen, it is now digested in other parts of the stomach. Another mouthful of unchewed food is then brought up, and the chewing process repeated until that and the rest of the food that has been taken during feeding has been masticated.

The normal dentition of all *Cervidae* is either 32 or 34 teeth, as follows (*one side only*):

Incisors	Canines	Pre-molars	Molars	Total	(half mouth)
$\dfrac{0}{3}$	$\dfrac{0}{1}$ or $\dfrac{1}{1}$	$\dfrac{3}{3}$	$\dfrac{3}{3}$	$\dfrac{6}{10}$ or $\dfrac{7}{10}$	$= 16$ or 17

In the lower jaw the canines are invariably present, though modified in such a way as to resemble lateral incisors. In the upper jaw canines are present in a number of deer, which include Red deer, Wapiti, Père David's deer, Tufted deer, the Muntjacs, Musk deer and Chinese Water-deer. In the last four deer, and in particular Musk deer and Chinese Water-deer, the canines of the males have developed into tusks and project outwards and downwards to a considerable length. In the case of the Musk deer and Chinese Water-deer, neither of which ever grow antlers, these tusks are the primary offensive weapons used when fighting other males or as defence against a predator. The canines on the Muntjacs and Tufted deer, although well developed, do not extend to quite the same length as on the two previously named deer, and since the males of both carry small antlers, these small tusks seem to be used as secondary weapons only, particularly when fighting their own kind. However, when attacked by dogs, there are several recorded instances of the severe wounds a cornered Muntjac has been able to inflict on its attackers with the sharp canine teeth.

The tusks of the male Muntjac are only about a third of the length of the Chinese Water-deer's, measuring about 22 mm ($\frac{7}{8}$ inch) in length.

Some species of deer, such as the Roe deer, in which the upper canine is normally absent, *very* occasionally do possess them, but in the majority of cases, when upper canines are present it is, I believe, generally an immature animal, for by the time the beast becomes adult, these small teeth have been dislodged. I have also seen upper canines present on a three-year-old Fallow buck, but such instances with this species must be extremely rare.

The grinders consist of three molars and three premolars top and bottom on each side, and are so formed that their surfaces wear down unevenly by the lateral movement to which they are subject during the process of chewing.

Each tooth is composed of alternate layers of enamel – dentine and cementum – which, being of different degrees of hardness, are differently affected by the grinding action. Eventually, however, in aged animals the grinders, particularly those in the centre, will become worn down almost to the level of the gums.

Not all the deer develop their full mouth of permanent teeth in the same period of time. All deer at birth have six incisors and two lower canines – all milk teeth. The replacement of these milk teeth and development of the full mouth depends very much on the species. The Red deer, for instance, requires some thirty months whilst the full mouth of the Roe will be complete in about thirteen months.

Another characteristic feature in ruminants is that they are four-toed, for unlike the primates, they have neither thumbs nor great toes. Instead, the feet are so arranged that the axis of the limb falls between the two middle toes, whilst the inside and outer toes are much reduced in size – indeed, in some animals, such as the camel and giraffe, they are completely lost. The two middle toes of the ruminants make up what is generally known as a cloven hoof.

Apart from size, of course, the shape of the cloven hoof varies according to the type of terrain which the deer normally inhabits. Thus the hooves of the Reindeer and Caribou, which are designed for travel over snow, are much flatter and splayed out than those of, say, the Red deer or Wapiti. The hooves of the weird Père David's deer – about the only large mammal which no person living or dead has ever reported as having seen alive in the wild state – are also rather splayed, thus suggesting that its original home was on snow or soft ground (see page 101). In most species of deer the front hooves are noticeably larger than the hind feet.

All deer possess pre-orbital glands or face glands, but in some, such as the Muntjacs and Père David's deer, they are more developed than in others. They are situated just in front of the eye and consist of sacs which open on the skin surface, usually by a slit-shaped cavity, and discharge a strong-smelling secretion. There have been many theories as to what useful purpose these glands serve. The Reverend Gilbert White, in his *Natural History of Selborne,* called them 'spiracula' or breathing places, which he said enabled the deer, when thirsty, to plunge its nose very deep under water, and continue drinking for a considerable time without fear of suffocation! White, usually a most painstaking naturalist, had been misled on this occasion. Stags and hinds do not completely submerge their noses when they drink. They only lightly touch the water with their lips and gently suck it up, leaving their nostrils free for breathing and smelling. And even if they did plunge their snouts well below the surface, they still could not use these glands for breathing, for anatomical investigation has shown that there is no communication between these cavities and the nostrils. Moose, when feeding on submerged aquatic plants, however, will sometimes submerge themselves so completely that not a ripple will remain on the water where they went down. Complete submergence sometimes lasts for thirty to fifty seconds.

Mr Dugald Macintyre, author and naturalist, writing in *The Field* on the 5th April 1947, ventured the opinion that the facial gland might be an escape valve for bile and that it was a necessity because deer have no gall-bladders.

There is, however, no sort of connection between the facial gland and the gall-bladder. The facial gland is an elaboration of the open tear duct leading from the eye. It is glandular, and is possibly a sex-scent gland.

Another theory is that the strong-smelling secretion contained in the pre-orbital cavity is rubbed off on rocks and trees, and in this way the deer are able to recognise each other's presence and keep contact with each other. With so many other methods of maintaining contact with their fellow deer, such as by scent, urination and cropped herbage, this latter theory seems the least likely. I, personally, have never seen a deer expressly rub the facial gland against anything, but the males of many species will open it widely when angry or excited. This is particularly noticeable in the case of Père David's deer.

In addition to these facial glands most deer have interdigital or foot glands, situated in the cleft of the cloven hoof, and these doubtless leave scent upon the ground over which the owner has passed. Some deer have a gland situated on the hind leg, the position of which is indicated by tufts of hair longer than the surrounding hair and often of a contrasting colour. In a number of species, such as the Sika deer, these glands are situated high up on the cannon bone, whilst in others, such as the White-tailed deer, the gland is near the lower extremity of the cannon bone.

Deer are distinguished from other ruminant animals by the existence of antlers, which are present in the male sex of all the living genera except two, namely *Moschus* – the Musk deer, and *Hydropotes* – the Water-deer. As already noted, both these genera have well-developed upper canines which are used for fighting. The genera *Elaphodus*, Tufted deer, and *Muntiacus*, the Muntjacs, are similarly equipped with well-developed upper canines, but the males of both these deer carry small antlers – those of the former being extremely small and devoid of branches, whilst those of the Muntjac are larger, recurved and generally possess a small brow tine.

Apart from the genus *Rangifer* – the Reindeer or Caribou – the females of all the deer are generally lacking in antlers, but on occasions the females of some genera such as *Capreolus* – Roe deer – will grow small antlers. In the case of female Roe, the existence of small antlers does not seem to affect their breeding capacity, and does with small antlers, or well-developed pedicles, have been seen with kids at foot.

With regard to the origin of antlers, it should be remembered that the earliest known deer were devoid of these appendages, and that when they first made their appearance they were of simple fork formation. It is only in more recent times that the more complicated patterns of our existing forms have been developed.

The antlers, which are produced and shed annually, are true bone, and are grown from two outgrowths of the frontal bone which are known as pedicles. In most species of deer the new antlers begin to grow as soon as the old ones are discarded, and during growth they are covered with a furry skin known as velvet. One of the exceptions to this pattern is the Reindeer or Caribou, the fully adult males of which shed their antlers shortly after the autumn rut, although growth of the new antler does not commence until the following spring. For further details about the growth and shedding of antlers, see Chapter 3.

All the deer, with the exception of the Musk deer, possess a liver without a gall-bladder. The genus *Moschus,* Musk deer, does have a gall-bladder whilst the males also of this genus have a large glandular pouch situated on the abdomen, which secretes the musk from which these animals take their name.

All the deer, with the exception of the genus *Rangifer* – Reindeer and Caribou – have some portion of the muzzle devoid of hair, although in *Alces* – the Moose or Elk – this naked area is reduced to a very small triangular-shaped patch. In the case of *Moschus,* Musk deer, however, the naked portion of the muzzle is large and completely surrounds the nostrils.

The Elk or Moose, and in particular the Alaskan form, is the largest living deer in the world today, a good bull measuring up to 7 feet (213 cms) at the shoulder, and weighing some 1,800 lbs (816 kilograms). In former times an even larger deer was found in northern Europe, namely the Giant Deer *Megaceros giganteus* – often and quite erroneously referred to as the Irish Elk – but this great animal, the antlers of which frequently measured over 10 feet (305 cms) in spread, has now been extinct for several thousands of years. At the other end of the scale, the Pudu of South America is the smallest living deer, the males of which measure only some 14 or 15 inches (38 cms) high at the shoulder, and weigh about 18–20 lbs (9 kilograms). True, the Mouse-deer or Chevrotain is even smaller, but this small mammal although a member of the *Ruminantia* is not a *Cervidae* but belongs to the family *Tragulidae* and is, therefore, not a true deer, having only three compartments to its stomach. Another feature which serves to distinguish the deer from the Chevrotains is that in the former the metacarpal and metatarsal bones (small bones of the foot) supporting the small lateral toes are always incomplete; that is to say they are represented only by their upper and lower extremities. In the Mouse-deer or Chevrotain these bones are always complete.

The female deer – which is variously described as hind, doe or cow, according to species (see page 31) – has four teats. Females of some species, such as Red deer, normally only have a single calf (also called fawn or kid, according to species) whilst others, such as the Roe deer, Elk and White-tailed deer frequently have twins and occasionally triplets. The diminutive Chinese Water-deer, however, may have four fawns, and five are not unknown.

During the year two changes of the pelage take place, the one in spring which is inclined to be protracted, and the other in the early autumn. In some species such as the Roe there is a marked difference between the summer and winter coat, whilst in those deer which are normally spotted in summer – such as the Fallow deer and Sika deer – the tendency is for these spots to disappear in winter as the coat darkens. However, in the Indian Chital or Axis deer the spots are permanent and there is little change in colour between the winter and summer coat.

Colour abnormalities occur in most species of deer, such as albinos or melanistic strains, but of all the species of deer the Fallow deer undoubtedly displays the greatest range of colour variation. Originally there were probably only three main colour types, the black, the white and the typical fallow which is a rich fawn with large spots in summer pelage, and a uniform greyish brown, with little or no spotting, in winter. Today, as a result of much inbreeding and crossing, there are many aberrant colour forms to be seen in deer parks and elsewhere as a result of escapism. These colour types include menil or spotted, sooty-dun, blue or silver-grey, and sandy. In parts of Europe, and in particular in eastern Netherlands, a melanistic strain of Roe deer occurs, whilst in other parts of Europe there is a white strain (as distinct from albino which are pink-eyed) of Red deer. Other colour abnormalities such as white or coloured saddle-backs, or a white blaze on the face, generally referred to as bald-faced, also occur.

The young of most species of deer – there are a few exceptions – are spotted at birth and retain these spots for about three months when the young animal assumes its first winter coat. Included among the exceptions are the Moose or Elk and the Sambar of India although the young of the Malayan Sambar does show slight spotting on the flanks.

The tail of all the species of deer except one is either short or medium short,

B

the exception being the unique Père David's deer, the tail of which measures some 26 inches (66 cms) in length to the end of the hairs. In the Chinese Water-deer it is extremely short, whilst in the Roe to all outward appearances the tail is completely lacking. However, a rudimentary tail is present which is only discernible when a dead specimen is examined closely. During the winter months, however, the Roe doe grows a prominent anal tush – a tuft of long hair which is sometimes mistaken for a tail. This 'tail', however, is a very useful guide to distinguish the sexes when the bucks have just cast their antlers in winter. It is surprising, nevertheless, how many artists of the eighteenth and nineteenth centuries depicted their Roe with tails!

2

Economic Uses of Deer

From a commercial and economical point of view deer are of more importance than is often considered the case. To the Lapps of Scandinavia and tribes of the northern USSR the Reindeer is indispensable, for it is the basis of existence for these nomadic people, providing, as it does, food, clothing and transport.

The Caribou of North America is similarly essential to the survival of the northern Indian and Eskimo – for without the herds of Caribou to supply their daily needs they would perish. Indians of the Tinne tribe are known as 'Caribou-eaters', whilst Eskimos of the Barren Grounds of northern Canada are often referred to as 'Caribou-Eskimos'. Although these people of North America do not domesticate the Caribou in the manner in which the northern races of Europe do, they make use of every part of the animal they kill. The flesh is consumed, the bones crushed for marrow, the blood often goes into soup. A favourite cut of meat is one taken from the rump, whilst the back fat is a valuable addition to the larder, being added to lean meat to provide carbohydrates for energy. Even the contents of the stomach, which consist mainly of reindeer moss *Cladonia rangiferina* – a lichen which forms the staple diet of the Reindeer and Caribou and which, in its original form before digestion by the deer, would be indigestible to man – is eaten with relish by some of the northern tribes. It is called *nerrocks* or *nerrokak*. The tips of the antlers whilst still in velvet are sometimes used for food, whilst from the hardened antlers fish hooks are fashioned. From the shin bones knives are made and a strong thread can be produced from the tendons.

Wild or domesticated, the Reindeer has had a long association with man. It was, in fact, the 'Reindeer Age' that marked the dawn of human history, for in that period, about twenty-five to thirty thousand years ago, the artists of the day, the 'Reindeer Men' of the late Stone Age, painted their animal pictures which included the Reindeer, on the walls of the caves. Whether or not those men of the late Stone Age ever domesticated any of the animals they drew, and in particular the Reindeer, is not known but there is a reference from a Chinese source dated about AD 499 to domesticated Reindeer.

It has been said of the Lapps who inhabit the Reindeer countries of Norway, Sweden and Finland that the Reindeer is more important than they are themselves, for the animals could get on very well without the Lapps but the Lapps could not survive without their Reindeer.

Although the Lapps 'herd' their Reindeer, herding is not driving the animals in a direction in which the deer do not want to go. Normally the Reindeer prefer to travel into the wind. The Lapps *follow* their herds from their summer feeding grounds to their wintering grounds and *vice versa*, their aim being, as far as is possible, to maintain the animals in a 'semi-wild' state. In some ways it might be comparable to cattle herding on a ranch system.

Herding Reindeer is a comparatively modern science with the Lapps (*c.* 1800). The herders ensure that the deer are on the right pasture at the right time of the year. They also see that the females are undisturbed during calving, although no human aid is necessary at birth. Other jobs include the marking of calves, gelding of bulls destined for slaughter and, later, the slaughtering of them. In Scandinavia the majority of Reindeer are slaughtered in October and November, but slaughtering occasionally takes place in January, and still more rarely in July when the Lapps only kill what they require for their own use.

At the present time in Scandinavia there are far more 'domestic' Reindeer than wild ones – indeed there are no truly wild ones left in Sweden today, although there may be some individuals which have become separated from herds and have 'gone wild', but their numbers are, in any event, negligible. About 1950, the domestic Reindeer herds of the Lapps in Norway, Sweden and Finland were estimated at almost half a million animals, but this was only half the number said to exist on the Russian collective farms.

In northern Russia much of the Reindeer breeding is done in connection with collective farms. One of these farms, the Kharp collective farm, grazes its Reindeer herds during the summer on the Vangureyskiye uplands near the shores of the Barents Sea. By the sea it is fresher and cooler and the sea breezes help to keep the mosquitos and gad flies away from the herd. The 'pedigree' deer of the Kharp herd always summer here, but in the winter the herds move south. In the autumn about 4,000 Reindeer of the Kharp herd will be slaughtered, but none from the pedigree animals which will be dispersed to improve the stock of other herds.

The Kharp collective farm was formed in 1930 as an association for Reindeer breeding. About 1938 some twenty Nenets families (formerly Samoyeds) banded together, having altogether a combined stock of some 3,000 Reindeer. During the years that followed the Reindeer stock increased, but the collective farm, as a business concern, just could not get going as the amount of goods to be marketed was pitifully low, quite apart from the fact that there were too many people about with no work to do. Herds of Reindeer, however, had to be slaughtered to provide food for them.

The Soviet authorities, therefore, saw that the only way to combat this state of affairs was to develop a many-sided economy – such as cattle and fur-bearing animal breeding, fishing and hunting – but Reindeer farming was still to remain the principal industry. How was this to be done? The Reindeer had to be herded from place to place. Fish, worth marketing, could only be caught along the Pechora River and on the coast. The answer was to be found in the formation of a number of organised bases. Thus the little township of Koryagovka, lying on the left bank of the Pechora River, was selected as the settlement for the Kharp farms. Here the people lived in huts; here there were farm buildings for their cattle and a fish farm for salmon. A silver-fox farm was also started, with a nucleus introduction of seventy foxes obtained from Archangel'sk. Now, every member of the community had some useful work to do, whereas before only the Reindeer herder did any real work. This was a significant change in the way of life of the Nenets people. In 1940, income of the collective farm was 138,000 roubles. Ten years later it had increased to 720,000 roubles. This is the history of just one collective farm in Russia. There are others, such as the Naryan-Ty, the Stalin, the Gor'kiy and the Vyucheyskiy.

During the late summer and autumn Reindeer milk, which is rich in protein, fat and vitamins, is available, but the quantity is only very small, about 0·2–0·3 litres (about ½ pint) per day, or a total of 4·0 to 4·5 litres (about 7 to 8 pints) during the lactation period of a female Reindeer. The butter fat content of Reindeer milk varies according to the month of lactation, and analysis has shown that during the fifth month the fat content averages about 20·80 per cent, with a range of 18·75 to 22·95 per cent.

Small as the quantity is, it will be seen that Reindeer milk is about four times as rich in butter fat as ordinary cows' milk. It is also used for making into cheese, butter and yoghourt. Few figures are available for the butter fat content of the milk from other species of deer, but a few samples from shot deer taken *immediately* after death were sent to the University of Glasgow (Department of Veterinary Pathology) for analysis, and these showed that for Red deer hinds the average butter fat content is about 14 per cent, with one figure as high as 16 per cent. The milk from four Fallow does was examined and gave an average butter fat content figure of 11·5 per cent with the highest at 15·9 per cent from a three-year-old.

Reindeer meat is popular with the general public in Scandinavia, and the comparatively small amount that has reached the shops in London has been well received by people who don't like Red deer venison. On average, a four-year-old male Reindeer (gelded) will weigh about 220 lbs (100 kilograms) and yield some 110 lbs (50 kilograms) of meat.

Reindeer and Caribou meat is, of course, the staple diet of many northern peoples of Europe and North America. It is eaten fresh, smoked or dried, and will keep well for long periods. The flavour is described as intermediate between beef and mutton. Young females and calves, naturally, produce the better venison, but all Reindeer are edible except the bulls during the rutting season.

Although there is comparatively little demand for venison in Great Britain today, it is much appreciated in many countries of Europe and elsewhere. Every year about 1,200 tons (1,219,200 kilograms) of venison, representing an export value of about £425,000, are exported from Scotland to Germany, whilst in 1964 over 1,150 tons (1,168,400 kilograms) of venison, valued at about £354,322, were exported from New Zealand, the majority of which (about 1,116 tons or 1,133,856 kilograms) went to West Germany and the Netherlands. Other countries importing small quantities of New Zealand venison were Switzerland (about 24 tons or 24,384 kilograms), and the USA (about 16 tons or 16,256 kilograms), whilst smaller quantities were sent to France, Sweden, Hong Kong and Malaya.

A correspondent who has spent many years in northern Europe told me (*in litt.*) that when in Russia and Finland before 1914 he never ate any Reindeer meat as joints 'but only as a delicatessen such as tongues'. At one time there was, according to Lydekker (1898), a considerable trade in Reindeer tongues, but at the time of writing had 'almost ceased on account of the low prices obtained in England'.

As with cattle, male Reindeer intended for fattening for venison are generally castrated. In Norway and Sweden it is rare for calves to be operated on, and a bull is generally three or four years of age before it is gelded. Castration, dependent on the time of the year the operation is done, has an effect on the subsequent antler growth (see pages 24–6).

So far as I am aware female Reindeer are not operated on in any form of Reindeer-breeding.

Reindeer from Scandinavia have, during the past seventy years or so, been introduced into a number of new areas, and in the majority of cases have adapted themselves well to their new habitat. South Georgia, in the sub-Antarctic, has about 4,000 head of Reindeer descended from seventeen Norwegian animals introduced shortly before the First World War. In Canada there are thousands at the mouth of the Mackenzie River, and tame herds are increasing in Greenland and have been started in Iceland, the Kerguelen Islands and elsewhere, including Alaska.

In 1949 a plan for establishing a Reindeer herd in Scotland was first proposed by a herd-owner from the Jokkmokk area of Arctic Sweden, Mr Mikel Utsi. In that year the Reindeer Council of the United Kingdom was formed and between 1952 and 1954 about twenty-nine Swedish mountain Reindeer were brought to Scotland as an experiment to see if they could live and breed. The first consignment was released, after quarantine, in an enclosure near Aviemore, Inverness-shire. More Reindeer followed, some of forest type, and more recently a few from southern Norway.

The grazing was extended in 1954 to higher ground in the Glenmore National Forest Park, reaching up to the summits of Cairn Gorm (4,084 feet) and Cairn Lochan (3,983 feet), and the animals were officially permitted to pasture freely like sheep; a few fences in use afterwards were maintained to simplify herding. By 1957 the Department of Agriculture for Scotland recognised that the experimental period was over, and Reindeer breeding took its place among local forms of livestock rearing.

Although the Aviemore herd appears to have settled down well in its new quarters, it hasn't increased in numbers as much as one would have expected – indeed eighteen years after the first introduction the herd had only increased to about a hundred. Whatever the future of the Aviemore herd may be, I cannot see any large scale expansion of the Reindeer project materialising in Scotland – a country which already has enough Red deer (about 180,000) to supply all the venison it needs but doesn't value. As a result, many tons of venison are exported annually to Germany (see page 9).

In its native country the Reindeer has a high reproduction rate and under the best conditions a herd selected for herding, if there is no slaughtering, could well treble itself in three years. A Reindeer breeder can expect about 90 per cent of the females in the herd of from two to ten years of age to calve every year, whilst older females will calve less frequently.

Although the Reindeer of northern Europe is the same species as the Caribou of North America – namely *Rangifer tarandus* – experiments in herding Caribou in bulk have not been successful. Good work, however, has been done in trying out Reindeer/Caribou and Caribou/Reindeer cross breeding. It was found that the resultant cross was a larger, heavier and more self-reliant animal. Caribou are said to be difficult to catch but easily herded when caught. In an effort to introduce Reindeer farming into North America, during the past seventy-five years Reindeer from the west have been introduced into both Alaska and northern Canada.

Reindeer were introduced into Alaska early in the nineties of the last century, and by about 1930 numbered more than 500,000 animals. The success of the experiment was largely due to the fact that private owners were doing a fine job of herd management. Then in 1937 the US government bought all the Reindeer in Alaska not already owned by the natives and turned them over to the Eskimos. But the Eskimo is primarily a hunter, living from day to day without planning ahead. Many thousands of Reindeer were slaughtered and by about 1950 it was doubtful if more than about 25,000 Reindeer remained in Alaska.*

In the Canadian Arctic and Labrador, the Canadian government seems to have avoided the mistake made in Alaska. Reindeer were introduced into the Mackenzie delta region of the North-West Territories in 1935 by two Lapp herdmen – Dan Crowley and Andrew Bahr – after one of the most remarkable animal treks ever known. Setting out on Christmas Day, 1929, these two herders and their assistants undertook to drive 3,400 Reindeer from the Selawik River in Alaska to Kittigazuit, across the Mackenzie delta, in Canada.

The distance Crowley and Bahr had to cover was actually no more than one thousand miles (1,609 kilometres). But it was a thousand miles of unexplored wilderness – of snow-swept tundra and dangerous mountain passes. For months at a time the men were lost and out of touch with civilisation, which supposed that the entire outfit had perished from hunger and privation. Finally, the hardy travellers reached their destination. They had expected to make the trip in eighteen months; instead it actually took them five years and two months!

At Kittigazuit, Crowley and Bahr were able to deliver 2,370 animals – which included 1,500 females – but out of the total stock of animals received it was estimated that only about a fifth were from the original party that had left the Selawik River in 1929. Of the others, some had either strayed away, been returned to home range, or perished *en route* by accident, blizzard or wolves. The other four-fifths of the herd which arrived at their destination were young animals born during the five-year trek.

By 1952 the number of Reindeer in the Mackenzie delta was said to be about 7,000, which allowed an annual surplus of about a thousand head to be killed for food and clothing. The Reindeer have been provided with a reserve covering over

* George Kent in *Reader's Digest,* January 1953.

6,000 square miles (1,554,000 hectares). The winter is spent in the southern half of the range, where the calves are born during April and May. During the short summer the herd has to be moved to the sea coast in order escape the flies and mosquitos which are such a pest at this time of year. In August the animals are counted, marked and any surplus killed.

Not all Reindeer introductions have been successful. In the fall of 1911, the United States government placed forty Reindeer on the Pribilof Islands, Alaska, to provide the native residents with a sustained source of fresh meat. These deer were descendants of the stock of deer brought to Alaska from Siberia by Sheldon Jackson in the period 1892–1902 and placed at Teller from whence some were moved to Unalakleet and finally to the Pribilofs. Four males and twenty-one females were landed on St Paul Island – an island of about 26,500 acres (10,729 hectares) in extent – and three males and twelve females on St George – which lay about forty-one miles south of St Paul and extended to some 22,400 acres (9,069 hectares). Along with each group of deer went an Eskimo herder to instruct the Pribilof islanders in the handling of the Reindeer. The introductions seemed to be an immediate success for in the following spring seventeen calves were born on St Paul Island and eleven on St George.*

By 1922 the St George herd had already reached its ceiling of 222 animals and was soon to subside to a small, stable population numbering about thirty to forty animals. The St Paul herd, on the other hand, grew slowly and steadily until the early 1930s, when it suddenly erupted. By 1938 it had increased to over 2,000 animals – yet twelve years later it had plummeted down to only eight.

Why was there an abrupt rise and then a fall in the size of the St Paul herd? What ecological or perhaps genetic factors were responsible for the fluctuation and differences in pattern of the herds of Reindeer on two islands within a few miles of each other?

As compared to that of St George, the fluctuation of the St Paul herd had been more pronounced, thus throwing into sharper relief the underlying causes and permitting a clearer interpretation of them. Observations on St Paul over the period 1940 to 1950 and examination of the records point to the inescapable conclusion that the lichen flora of the island was the key to the behaviour of the herd. Certain lichens, chiefly the taller, shrublike forms of *Cladonia* and *Cetraria*, only serve as emergency rations for reindeer.

When the St Paul herd was small, numbering in the hundreds only, growth of the food lichens kept pace with the demand. At this point it is perhaps as well to remember that as St Paul Island is only some 26,500 acres (10,729 hectares) in extent, at the peak of the population in 1938 the deer density on the island was as high as 1:13 acres (1:5 hectares), or in fact only 1 deer to every 11 acres (5 hectares) of suitable grazing land. With the disappearance of the lichens the Reindeer were left with inadequate winter food reserves. The year 1938 inaugurated a four-year cycle when midwinter temperatures fell below normal: the winter of 1940 was exceptionally cold and, according to the island records, in 1940 a crust of glaze ice remained on the snow for several weeks. In short, a combination of depleted range and adverse

* V. B. Scheffer (*Scientific Monthly,* vol. LXXIII, No. 6, December 1951).

weather seems to have been responsible for the decline of the herd in the 1940s, to which a further factor also made a small contribution, for during the period 1942–4 the 500 residents of the Pribilof Islands were evacuated and for a short period the islands were occupied by the military, who doubtless killed a number of animals.

In 1908, when whaling became big business, some Reindeer were introduced to South Georgia by Captain C. A. Larsen, a Norwegian, so that there would be a permanent source of fresh meat in the area. The introduction was a success and a recent estimate gave the number of Reindeer on South Georgia as being in the region of 4,000 animals. An interesting point of this introduction was that the deer reversed their breeding seasons to fit the Antipodes in the same manner as the Red and some other species of deer did when introduced to New Zealand.

In 1924, in order to start Reindeer farming in the Kuriles, ten domesticated Reindeer were introduced to the small island of Shinshiru, one of the southern central islands of this group, by the Fisheries Bureau of Tokyo. They increased gradually and by 1940, 224 animals (177 adults and 47 young) were recorded. There have been no records since then. *Cladonia rangiferina*, Reindeer moss, is very abundant on the north and central islands of the Kuriles.

There has always been a demand for deer skin for leather, and by the end of the last century about 100,000 Wapiti skins as well as close on a quarter of a million skins from Mule and White-tailed deer, were being exported annually from North America. About this period some 54,000 Chital skins, together with about 400 tons of antlers, were being imported into London from India, the price of the latter ranging from £1·00 to £1·30 per hundredweight.*

There has always been a demand for Reindeer hides in many parts of the world, and in particular in Germany for the glove trade, for Red deer skins are too coarse. Reindeer hides make excellent parkas, as well as trousers and shoes, whilst calf skins from Alaska have even been used in the European fancy leather trade. Between the wars the market for hides continued, and Reindeer skins were imported from Russia into Britain in consignments of as many as 20,000, largely for the manufacture of ladies' handbags and gloves, and also for re-export to France. However, a high proportion of the skins from the herds in arctic European Russia were of poor quality because of inept tanning, and the importation of skins from Russia seems to have died out by 1932. Many skins were also spoilt by warble infection.

It is of interest to note that some of the best Red deer skins in the world come from New Zealand where the species was introduced during the last century, by virtue of the fact that they are free from warble infection.

At the present time about 300 to 400 Reindeer skins are probably imported into Britain and in some of the big London stores are sold at anything up to £20 or more apiece, as hearthrugs or bedroom rugs. The market price for the wholesaler would be around £10.

In North America an important product of the Caribou is the furred hide which serves as superior quality winter clothing for Arctic peoples. The best hides for this purpose come from animals killed during August and September and, in particular,

* H. Poland, *Fur-bearing Animals* (quoted by R. Lydekker, 1898).

those from calves and yearlings on account of their softer, more flexible hides and shorter, finer fur.

Although modern garments, particularly underwear, are now generally replacing some of the Eskimo outfits, a complete winter Caribou-hide outfit consists of an inner and an outer suit. The number of hides necessary for a complete outfit varies, for much will depend on the sex and age class of the hides used, and the style and completeness of the outfit. A. W. F. Banfield in his paper on *The Barren-Ground Caribou* (1951) suggested that it 'is probable that a total of 25 hides annually would clothe satisfactorily a family of two adults and two young children'. For the various garments 'the average number of hides needed may be calculated as follows: inner parka, 3; outer parka, 4; inner trousers, 2; outer trousers, 2; mitts, stockings and boots, 1; total 12 hides'.

Woollen and horse-hide mitts have generally replaced the Caribou mitts, whilst undergarments, stockings and shirts will now generally be of wool rather than hide.

The hides of Caribou killed in wintertime, owing to the longer hair, are no longer in prime condition for clothing. Such hides are used for making into sleeping robes, four or six hides being sewn together. They are also used for bedding, mats, covers, igloo doors and, in the more remote areas, tents. The modern canvas tent, however, has largely replaced the hide tent, which requires twenty or more hides to complete. Winter hides are often used to insulate winter homes, particularly those with log walls.

Besides skins, the hair has also in the past been imported into Britain from Scandinavia, and used for stuffing upholstery and also as a component in fine woollen material. Even the tails have been used by the natives for shaving brushes.

Reindeer sinew thread is especially good for sewing canoes or repairing boots because it swells, thus making watertight seams. It will not rot or tear leather either. Skin from the head cape is said to produce a non-skid leather which is useful for the soles of shoes intended for walking on ice.

In medieval battles soldiers were equipped with slings made from Elk skin for hurling stones and other missiles. Later, skin taken from the legs of Elk was used for gun sheaths and powder pouches. Elk-skin jackets, being tough and heavy, were at first thought to be proof against bullets, whilst the Elk in Poland was believed, at one time, to have been exterminated because Paul I, Tsar of Russia, ordered his cavalry to be equipped with Elk-skin breeches. Many thousands of Elk skins were used by the people of eastern Siberia as tribute to the Chinese, whilst Russia paid war indemnity to Austria in many hundred wagon-loads of Elk skins.

At one time the tallow from the North American Wapiti – and no doubt many other species as well – was much in demand for making into candles.

The antlers of deer have been put to many uses, ranging from wearing and household utensils to aphrodisiacs. In the former category, antlers of various species of deer are manufactured into buttons, scarf holders, pipes, knife handles, hunting-crop and walking-stick handles. The Lapp craftsmen also fashion them into spoons and cups, whilst in former times prehistoric and Neolithic man fashioned harpoon and hammer heads from deer antlers. Antlers were fashioned into tools for working the earth, whilst the palmated parts of Elk antlers were converted into ladles. During the last century, the Indian of North America would make an instrument out of a large Elk (Wapiti) antler, and using it like an adze, clean off the fat and meat from bison hides. Glue has also been made from deer antlers, whilst at one time it was a source of ammonia.

Many ancient 'remedies' were obtained from the Elk. The left hind foot, if removed from the living deer, was believed to be a cure for epilepsy if part of it was worn about the sufferer's body, ground up in wine and imbibed, or burned and inhaled. The antlers, if taken on the first of September, would do almost as well.

If the antlers were taken at an earlier date, when still in velvet, and sliced and steeped with herbs and spirits, then a good treatment for snake bite was to be obtained. The fat of the Elk was an efficacious ointment, and its heart, when ground or burned, was considered a sure cure for heart troubles. Arthritis, rheumatism and cramp could be cured by wrapping some dried Elk nerves around the affected parts, and if worn continuously, no further attacks would occur.

At the end of the last century the trade in Reindeer antlers was said to be very large and according to Lydekker (1898) Denmark at that period was 'importing about 30,000 from Greenland and 8,000 from Russia annually: they realise from about £13 to £14 per ton'.

There has always been – and still is – a demand in the East for deer antlers in velvet for it is believed to have some aphrodisiac value. The growing antlers of the Sika deer are the most in demand, for they are valued more highly than those of the Wapiti and Maral. Towards the end of the eighties of the last century, a start had already been made in the Far East to breed commercially Sika deer, as well as Maral, to meet this demand and similar concerns also exist in various parts of China.

According to Flerov (1952) the total number of domesticated deer in the Far East in 1928 amounted to approximately 5,500 animals. These deer were maintained in either deer parks into which the animals had been driven, or fenced-in regions of the forest. Several establishments were also in operation on a number of islands. The animals, whilst the antlers were still in velvet, were either shot or snared. In the latter case, the antler could be sawn off and the animal released. However, sawn-off antlers are priced lower than those with the pedicle and frontal bone.

Several subspecies of Red deer are also being bred in captivity for the soft antler industry, the males being killed in the spring and early summer, when the growing antler is in its most valuable condition. Red deer antlers, however, do not have the same value as those from Sika deer. Since the 1830s Red deer have been commercially bred for the antlers on farms in the Altai, the Transbaikal, the Far East and the Sians, and the industry is said to be flourishing. Some of the larger breeding farms are owned by the government.

One of the products manufactured from antler velvet is a tonic elixir called *'Pantocrin'* and the late Arthur de C. Sowerby wrote to me in 1953 saying that whilst in Shanghai in 1946 he had a course of it after being released from a prison camp hospital. 'As a rejuvenator,' he wrote, 'antlers in velvet do seem to have some value, and as far as I was concerned it worked wonders. The stuff was made in Moscow from Sika deer antlers which had been taken there from the Yankowski Brothers' deer farm north of Vladivostok before the Communists captured the latter.' The name *'Pantocrin'* is derived from the Russian word *Panti* which is used to describe immature antlers (in velvet) of the Wapiti or Maral.

Besides the antlers, considerable value is also attached to the testes and the tails of male deer, which are said to possess qualities similar to those of antlers in velvet. In earlier times an extensive market was found in the Far East for extracts of embryos, especially of the male sex. Dried unborn baby deer, as well as certain organs of the male stag, are still bought by the Chinese.

Undoubtedly the most valuable product from any species of deer is musk – a strong-smelling perfume which is obtainable only from the Musk deer. The musk is contained in a bag situated on the belly of the deer. Each bag of musk weighs about 30 grammes (about 1 ounce). Musk is a substance used chiefly in oriental medicaments and to some extent in the perfume industry. In April 1939 musk was used in one of New York's hospitals to treat a case of persistent hiccough. It is a reddish brown substance with a strong odour, thick and oily, and leaves a very small amount of ash when burned.

According to Flerov (1952), 'It is not necessary to kill the animal in order to obtain the musk. To remove the musk from the bag it is only necessary to put a tube into the aperture, when a stream is excreted by slight pressure on the bag. In this way it is possible to develop a new form of industry, Musk deer breeding, similar to the soft antler deer breeding'.

Other materials obtained when Musk deer are killed are used only as by-products. The meat is of low quality, untasty, dry and always musk scented. The hide is of little value.

Musk deer are taken chiefly by driving them into nets placed across the end of a valley or by snares set up in their trails. Hunting with gun and dogs is less productive. The extent of the musk industry is not known, but it has been suggested that the annual toll approaches 100,000 animals. During the seventeenth century the Musk deer were so plentiful that the traveller Tavernier purchased 7,673 musk 'pods' in one journey (Beddard, 1902).

Musk grains removed from the pouches are worth more than £100 per pound, but finally purified musk extracted from the grains can be worth as much as £500 an ounce. So valuable is musk that the temptation to swindle must be very great. Some of the more unscrupulous hunters have, therefore, perfected methods of introducing foreign material into the musk pouch to increase the total amount of 'grain' that can be finally extracted, and also the price. The smell of musk is so strong that anything that comes into contact with it soon becomes as strongly scented as the 'genuine article'. Musk hunting is clearly a profitable livelihood, but it can also be a dangerous one, and many a musk-smelling hunter has been killed by a bandit for the musk pouches he has been carrying.

Several species of deer have been put to harness, but the Reindeer has always been the principal one used for draught purposes. A single Reindeer, as a beast of burden, can carry a load of about 90 lbs (41 kilograms) in saddle-bags whilst on a sledge, which the Lapps call a *pulka*, it can pull a load of about 450 lbs (204 kilograms) weight over smooth surfaces such as snow, and lighter weights over rough country. With suitable rests for feeding, it can travel about 40 miles (64 kilometres) a day. Lapps frequently harness nine or ten Reindeer in single file to their sleds, each animal being tied to the one ahead by the reins. A wild horse can be persuaded between the shafts of a wagon in a month or two, but it takes six months to train a Reindeer to draw a *pulka*.

The *pulka* is fashioned like a boat, about 6 feet (183 cms) long and about 2 feet (61 cms) wide. There are no shafts, and the harness is merely a leather strap which passes between the deer's legs to a wooden collar or rope noose around the deer's neck. The bridle is just a halter. There is only one rein. Reindeer will take a saddle but their backs are not strong enough to support much over 120 lbs (54 kilograms) in weight. It can, however, carry three small children for quite a fair distance whilst a ten-and-a-half-stone (66 kilograms) adult could be forded across a stream or for any other very short distance. For travel over grass and heather, a modified type of sled can be used; for roads not covered by snow, wheeled vehicles have been successfully adapted. In many parts of Siberia Reindeer carry mail and pull buses. For the army they carry messages and haul machineguns.

The European Elk has also been trained to go in harness as a draught animal and being a large, strong animal is capable of travelling long journeys. This deer, however, has never been commercialised to the same extent as the Reindeer.

The famous 66-pointer Red deer head, which the Elector Frederick III of Branden-burg (later King Frederick I of Prussia) killed in 1696, only met its fate because the gamekeeper's daughter, riding a tame Elk, was able to drive the beast within range of the Elector. This head, which was subsequently exchanged by King Frederick with the King of Saxony for a specially tall young recruit for the grenadiers of the Potsdam garrison, was hung in Schloss Moritzburg in Saxony.

On his ranch in Montana, USA, Mr Courtland Du Rand trained a pair of Wapiti to harness, and draw his wagon round the estate. He also trained four others to carry pack saddles.

Red deer have also been trained to harness. During the eighteenth century residents in the vicinity of Newmarket, Suffolk, were treated to the unusual spectacle of George Walpole, Third Earl of Orford, driving around with four Red stags in a phaeton instead of horses. One day, however, whilst driving to Newmarket he met hounds which, quite naturally, caused panic among the stags which immediately bolted, with his lordship clinging on for dear life and hounds in full cry! Fortunately, the earl was able to retain some control over the deer and eventually succeeded in driving them into a barn at the Ram Inn, Newmarket, where someone had the presence of mind to close the door before the hounds could follow him in.

Some four hundred years before the exploits of the Earl of Orford with his stag-drawn phaeton, it is recorded in John Fisher's *History of Berkeley* that following the death in 1327 of King Edward II, Abbot Thokey went, attended by his brethren, solemnly robed and accompanied by a procession, from the City of Gloucester, and claimed the body for burial which, with the observance of all possible respect, he conveyed in his own chariot *drawn by stags* to the Abbey where it was buried with becoming solemnity.

And would the Christmas scene be half so picturesque if Father Christmas used a tractor instead of a team of Reindeer to draw his sledge? I'm sure it wouldn't!

Finally, it should not be forgotten that most species of deer, particularly those bearing the larger antlers, are extremely valuable from a hunting point of view, and vast sums of money are paid by sportsmen to bag a worthwhile trophy. Most deer trophies in Europe are valued in accordance with the number of International points the head would be awarded when assessed by the International formula. Under the formula, there are three medal categories – gold, silver and bronze. A Red deer trophy of gold medal status, if killed in Rumania, Hungary or Yugoslavia could cost a visiting sportsman at least £1,000 to kill. There is undoubtedly big money in big heads, and this state of affairs can only be obtained by good game management and conservation.

3

Antlers

Antlers are outgrowths of true bone which are grown and shed annually. The antlers develop from two permanent stumps of bone generally referred to as pedicles, situated on the skull between the ears. In one genus – *Muntiacus*, the Muntjacs – the pedicles are combined as ridges down either side of the face giving rise to the name 'rib-faced deer', which is frequently applied to this deer. During development which, dependent on the size and age of the deer, takes about sixteen weeks to complete, the antlers are covered with a vascular, sensitive integument coated with hair. This skin is generally referred to as velvet. During the period the antlers are in velvet, the deer is careful to avoid knocking them against any obstacle, for in this state, besides being painful to blows, the growing antlers can so very easily be disfigured. Should a growing antler be knocked, and the velvet skin broken, it will bleed, and if flies are about these insects will soon collect on the damaged antlers to feed off the blood.

If a growing antler is cut off, the stump will bleed profusely and the operation would doubtless cause the deer some discomfort. Once the antler is hard, however, it can be sawn off without any loss of blood or pain to the deer.

Inside the growing antler, as well as on the outside under the velvet, there are numerous blood vessels supplying blood to promote the growth. One of the finer qualities of a trophy is that the antler should be deeply grooved and heavily pearled. These grooves are the channels in which the blood flowed during growth – the deeper the grooves and the rougher the antler, the more abundant has been the blood, and a better quality antler results.

When the antler is nearing completion, a ring of bone referred to as the coronet or burr is formed at its base just above the junction with the pedicle. As soon as antler growth is complete this ring or coronet would appear to constrict the blood vessels, and as soon as that happens the velvet dries up and starts to peel off, leaving the antlers white and hard.

Once the antler is hard and clean of velvet it is no longer sensitive, but whilst the velvet is in process of peeling off it would appear that there is some irritation for the deer will constantly rub its antlers among foliage until the last shreds of velvet have been discarded. Whilst the velvet is being stripped off, the antlers are said to be in 'tatters'. The deer will then carry its antlers for a few months until there is intensive ossification at the base of the main stem or beam below the coronet, which shuts off the internal blood supply thus making the antler necrotic. Subsequently, an absorbent process between the base of the necrotic antler and the living tissue in the socket of the pedicle will cause the antler to fall off, either by its own weight or through contact with some obstacle. The base of a normally shed antler is white without any trace of blood, but if the antler has been knocked off prematurely the base may be stained with blood.

The loosening of an antler, prior to shedding, would appear to be very sudden, for in 1948 two stags were seen fighting in a deer park only about a week or so before shedding, with such fury that had the antlers been loosening one, or both, would undoubtedly have been displaced. On another occasion a Fallow buck, in trying to disengage his antlers from some obstacle, broke one of the pedicles completely off. A few days later the other antler was shed in the normal way, thus proving that prior to casting the antlers must loosen very suddenly and not by degrees. Otherwise the antler would have broken away from the pedicle at the coronet, instead of tearing the pedicle away.

Immediately after the shedding of the antler there is frequently a slight discharge of blood visible on the raw surface of the pedicle, the amount varying from one individual to another. It soon congeals.

Although many females of the hollow-horned ruminants carry horns, these male attributes are not normally possessed by female deer. The genus *Rangifer,* however, is an exception, for the majority of female Reindeer and Caribou carry antlers similar in construction to the males, but very much smaller. Amongst some of the other species of deer, and in particular the White-tailed deer *Odocoileus virginianus* and the Roe *Capreolus capreolus*, there have been rare instances when the females have produced small antlers. About 1870 a doe with antlers was killed in Ayrshire by Mr John B. Fergusson. The antlers were in velvet, one being a simple curved spike about 6 inches (15·24 cms) in length, whilst the other was represented by a short stump. The animal was in good condition and was not barren, for on the day she was shot she was accompanied by a last year's kid and her nipples showed evident signs that she had recently been suckling. Since then several other antlered Roe does have been shot in Britain – some with their small antlers quite hard – and there are numerous instances in Europe. I have several times seen Roe does with well-developed pedicles but no antlers, and on two occasions these does were nursing twin kids.

Antlers depend upon the activity of the testes for their growth, development and shedding. When a female deer starts to assume these male characteristics, it is due to some of the female tissues being replaced by developmental testicular tissue, which secretes the male hormone necessary to promote antler growth. The degree of testicular tissue developed will decide whether or not the antlers will be renewed every year or remain as permanent rudimentary structures. Where there has been much development, the antlers will probably be shed annually, but in the majority of cases the antlers, rudimentary or abnormal in character, will be persistent and permanently covered in velvet.

About 1944 successful experiments were made at the Wildlife Research Center, Delmar, New York, 'in inducing the growth of antlers in two ovariectomised White-tailed deer by the administration of testosterone' (Wislocki, Aub and Waldo, 1947). One of these deer, after three doses of testosterone, given to her during her seventh year, eventually produced a pair of antlers about 8 inches (20·32 cms) in length, which were stripped of velvet during the first week of September. Eventually these antlers were shed some four months later and, as in the male deer, two definite pedicles remained on the forehead. The shed antlers were described as being 'not unlike well-developed ones seen on a yearling buck except for one very definite difference. This peculiarity involves the base of the antlers which have practically no burr or corona as well as relatively low and inconspicuous longitudinal ridges. Furthermore, and unlike normal antlers, the bone at the proximal ends of the shed antlers, instead of being convex, presents a perfectly flat surface as though it had been separated from the pedicle by a straight knife cut.'

In the majority of cases the growth and shedding of the antler is repeated with great regularity each year at about the same period. Most male species of deer, which include Red deer, Roe and Fallow deer, carry their complete antlers about six to eight months before shedding, at which time the new antler growth starts to develop immediately. In some species, however, such as the Reindeer or Caribou, matured males or bulls – as they are generally referred to – shed their antlers shortly after the autumn rut, although the growth of the new antler does not commence until the spring.

In young animals the first-year antlers are always small and simple and in the majority of cases consist of a single spike. In some deer, such as the Brockets and Pudus of South America and the Tufted deer of Asia, the antlers will never improve upon two single spikes, whilst in those of more complex pattern, such as Caribou, it is not uncommon for adult antlers to bear more than forty or fifty points. In those deer in which the antlers are variously branched or palmated, this condition is gradually acquired in several successive annual growths. A full 'head' (antlers) should be attained by the time the deer is adult, and although during the next few years it will tend to increase in size and weight, the time will come when further improvement is impossible and the 'head' will then start to deteriorate or 'go back' from a trophy point of view. Just how long a head will remain in its prime depends very much on the species. For instance, a Red deer head is said to be adult at about seven years of age, and thereafter, provided the feeding is good, it should improve in length and weight for another six or seven years until, when the stag is about fourteen years of age, the antlers will start to go back. A Roe buck, on the other hand, matures much earlier and at three or four years of age will be carrying a fully developed head. By seven or eight years of age, however, most Roe antlers will have started to go back.

With Red deer it has frequently been said that the stag grows an extra point on its antlers for each year of its life, and the deer's age can, therefore, be determined from its antlers. This is completely untrue, for so much depends on the feeding. For

C

instance, in some deer parks where the deer enjoy good feeding it is not unusual for prickets – first-year stags – to grow antlers with forked tops and even small brow points as well. In 1915 there was a pricket in Warnham Park, Sussex, with no fewer than eleven small points whilst from the same park there are several instances of yearlings with six or eight points.

A few species of deer such as Roe and Caribou will grow small antler knobs – generally referred to as buttons – during their first six months, and these will be shed early in the new year so that the animal can produce its first proper yearling head.

Antlers are in themselves a problem, for not only does the annual growth of a fine pair put a severe physical strain on a stag, but the more beautiful the adornment, the less value would they appear to be as weapons of attack against members of their own kind.

The origin and purpose of the deciduous antler has long puzzled zoologists and no one has given an entirely satisfactory explanation. C. Darwin, in *On the Origin of Species,* adopted the view that antlers were sexual weapons acquired by the males for fighting with their fellow males, and assumed that a deer without antlers – i.e. a hummel or bald stag – would be at a disadvantage during the rut or mating season. This hypothesis, however, is not borne out in practice and frequently, in Scotland, a hummel stag is able to hold together a large herd of hinds against antlered opponents. As weapons of defence, however, especially against the carnivorous predator, the antlers, and in particular the more elaborate ones, are undoubtedly efficient. And yet during the winter, at a time when some of the more northern species of deer, such as the Caribou and Reindeer, are easy prey for the wolf because the snow crust makes escape by flight almost impossible, the bulls are without their main weapon of defence – the antlers. On the other hand, the females of this deer retain their antlers until the spring. Elaborate antlers, however, such as those carried by a royal or 12-pointer Red deer stag, are neither efficient offensively nor defensively against another Red deer stag of similar age whose antlers are but two long rapier-like spikes – a true 'switch-horn'.

In most species of deer development of the new antlers commences in the early spring and in many cases before the deer has had time to recover from the rigours of a severe winter. Antlers are bone and to produce, in the matter of about four months, a pair of antlers weighing, in the case of a good Red deer stag, perhaps 20 lbs or more (9 kilograms) is a considerable achievement, particularly when one realises that the antlers alone may weigh over a quarter of the total skeletal weight of the stag. The complete set of cast antlers of a Warnham Park stag were collected annually and weighed, and during the thirteen years of life of this particular animal, the total weight of twelve pairs of antlers, including the final pair, amounted to 140 lbs 10 oz (63 kilograms). During its final years this stag was producing $16\frac{1}{2}$ lbs (7·4 kilograms) of antler bone per annum. Such an annual re-growth, particularly on lime-deficient soil, must be a serious drain on the resources of the organism. Moose antlers, of course, are considerably heavier and a good pair may weigh 60 lbs (27 kilograms) or so, whilst those of the Giant Deer – a deer which has now been extinct several thousand years – weighed half as much again.

Recently someone sent me a pair of Roe buck antlers which had been killed before the velvet had been properly stripped. It was impossible, however, to ascertain the volume of the antlers by weighing in water, for when immersed, they floated because of air entrapped in the numerous venous channels within the antler. These would later disappear as ossification continued internally. Antlers increase in weight for a few weeks after the velvet is ready for stripping.

Mention has already been made of hummels, or nott stags as they are called in south-west England. A hummel is quite distinct from a havier – a castrated male deer – and although without antlers, he is not impotent. Instead of normal pedicles those of the hummel are aborted and covered with skin. No one has discovered how hummels, which seem to occur more commonly in Red deer than any other species, are produced. Some consider that the male calf of a hind which has been served by a hummel will be 'bald' like its father. Others, that a hummel will only result from the union of a hummel with a hind which is herself the progeny of a hummel/hind partnership. Another theory, based on the knowledge that an injury to a stag's genital organs will probably cause a malformed antler, is the assumption that such an injury at birth has brought about this abnormality. There is nothing, however, to substantiate this last-mentioned theory, and the hummel's reproductive capacity would seem to be as normal as that of his antlered brethren.

As a matter of interest and to prove this point I sent the testicles of two rutting stags of approximately similar age, which I shot in October 1961, to the University of Glasgow Department of Veterinary Pathology. One was an 8-pointer and the other a hummel. 'The testicles were very interesting,' wrote Dr Dunn (1.11.61). 'I passed them on to Miss Morgan of the Department of Histology here, and she found, oddly, that the hummel was much more highly fertile and must have shown a much greater degree of libido than the horned stag.'

One thing seems certain, and that is the 'poll' character of the hummel is not as prepotent as the poll in cattle or sheep – otherwise the hummel would be more plentiful in the Highlands than he is. As to the proportion of stags in Scotland which are hummels, this is largely guesswork, for no single forest owner knows exactly how many stags are hummels. However, in order to get some figures to work on, for a number of years I have included on a questionnaire, sent to all deer forest owners in Scotland, a query asking how many hummels had been seen in the forest during the deer stalking season, and how many had been shot.

Replies were received from about 143 estates – which represent about two-thirds of Scotland's deer-stalking ground. From these estates the number of stags killed varied between 4,700 and 5,400, of which about $\frac{3}{4}$ to 1 per cent were hummels. On the area covered by the estates that replied, the total Red deer population is probably about 125,000 animals of which perhaps a third will be stags. Since about 157 live hummels were seen on these estates, it would seem to indicate that the ratio of hummels to antlered stags in the area under review is approximately 1:266. This ratio, however, is probably nearer 1:300 for there is no doubt that so far as the smaller estates are concerned, reports of individual beasts have been duplicated in a number of instances from the same animal – probably a wanderer – having been seen on several estates.

I think one can assume that the 140-odd estates from which reports were received are representative of Scotland as a whole and since they cover about two-thirds of Scotland's deer territory, if one increases the number of hummels seen by a half, it would appear that the approximate hummel population in Scotland is around the 230 to 250 mark – or even slightly less because of duplication of reports.

I have already referred to the fact that a hummel can quite often hold his hinds against an antlered opponent. I have never personally seen a combat between a hummel and a stag, but on one occasion I saw an 8-point stag, on seeing a hummel approaching, just walk away leaving his hinds to the latter. When it comes to a fight, weight must be an important factor, as well as the nature of the beast. Some beasts, like human beings, are born fighters, others are not. It is suggested that hummels fight by standing up on their hind legs – as indeed do hinds – and strike savagely at their adversary with their forelegs. This, of course, is also the manner in which stags scrap when their antlers are in velvet, and I have often wondered if, when an antlered stag sees a hummel approach, it automatically assumes that his antlers have been 'shed' and behaves accordingly. This would account for a stag and hummel boxing in this fashion, or even for the stag walking away from its hinds should it think the hummel was too weighty to take on.

In addition to hummels one also sees half-hummels – stags with a single, normal antler on one side, but a wasted pedicle on the other. In contrast to the hummel or one-antlered stag, one occasionally comes across a beast with three – or more rarely four – antlers all growing from separate pedicles. Such a condition may have been caused by an injury to the pedicle during its formation, which has resulted in one or both of them splitting in two. Some antlers bifurcate above the brow so as to give the effect of two antlers sprouting from the same coronet and pedicle. A true three- or four-antlered head, however, must have three or four *separate* pedicles.

Reference has already been made to the havier (page 23), a castrated stag, which, dependent on the time of the year when castration took place, may or may not have antlers. J. D. Caton in *The Antelope and Deer of America* (1877) goes very fully into the effects of castration on the growth of antlers of Wapiti and White-tailed deer. He found that if the testes were removed from the male deer after the antlers were mature – that is to say, after the velvet had been stripped or was ready to strip – the antlers always dropped off within thirty days afterwards, however distant the time of normal shedding for an ungelded stag might be. In the following summer the antlers would develop again, as in the 'entire' stag, but with several differences. In the first place, if the castrated stag was young, having only a spike antler, the new growth would be a spike of nearly the same length. Secondly, the new growth antlers would never lose their velvet, and in the following spring would not be shed below the coronet as normal. Instead, during the winter the abnormal antlers in velvet might be 'frozen' or perhaps broken off nearly down to the coronet but not below. In the following summer irregular growths would take place on the old antler, covered with persistent velvet. These growths usually took the form of large, irregular knobs or tubercles. As in winter, projections would continually be broken off, and in summer more tubercles would grow. The result was a very irregular velvet-covered antler.

The results of Caton's experiments agreed very closely with those described by Dr Fowler* from experiments carried out on Fallow deer. The latter also found out that when castration was performed at birth, little processes were developed 2 to 4 inches (5 to 10 cms) in length, covered with skin. Messrs Wislocki, Aub and Waldo (1947), who carried out a series of experiments on White-tailed deer, also confirmed that 'deer castrated as fawns do not develop antlers'. Experiments with older bucks revealed that,

> if castration is carried out during the period when the antlers are growing, the velvet is never shed and the antlers are never cast off. If castration is performed at a season when the antlers are denuded of velvet and dead, the antlers are prematurely shed within one or two weeks; but the subsequent year they are renewed and thereafter remain permanently in the velvet continuing to grow by annual increments. This process is modified in so far as in winter the antlers become frost bitten and variably destroyed. In animals which are adequately protected by indoor shelters, or live in milder climates, this denudation of the velvet and destruction of the antlers by freezing are minimal and the castrate antlers become correspondingly large.

Experiments were then made to see what effect the administration of testosterone to castrated White-tailed deer would have. They found that 'administration of testosterone to deer which have never had antlers as a result of castration as fawns induces antler growth.'

'Administration of testosterone to antlered deer, castrated as yearlings or thereafter, results in prompt shedding of the velvet and subsequent shedding of the antlers (tendency to restore normal antler cycle).'

Castration has long been practised by the Lapps upon their domesticated Reindeer. This is generally done when the bulls are three or four years old. Sometimes this is not done by amputation but by crushing the testicles inside the scrotum without complete removal. This method is but a very imperfect one and subsequent antler growth may follow a slightly different pattern to that after amputation.

Castration, or severe damage to the testicles – i.e. by shotgun wound – of a Roe buck causes a malformed head generally referred to as a 'perruque' or 'wighead'. Such a head is produced when a buck's testicles are seriously damaged soon after he has cast his antlers, and the new pair are growing. Growth will continue, but since in the course of time there can be no production of testosterone from the testes, the normal regression of the velvet cannot occur. In such cases the development of the velvet-covered antlers becomes exuberant and a so-called perruque head results. If a buck is castrated when the antlers are fully developed and clean of velvet,

> he will cast his antlers within one week, because the supply of testosterone in his blood, produced by his now active testes, will have been abruptly cut off. But he will immediately start to grow a new pair which, in the absence of the regulating effect of the hormone, will proceed to develop into a perruque, will never be clean of velvet, and will never be cast.†

* *Proc. Zool. Soc.,* 1894.
† M. Woodford, *Shooting Times and County Magazine,* 11th November 1965.

The same authority also mentioned that 'if a Roe buck is castrated when the antlers are fully developed but still in velvet, the velvet will not regress and a certain amount of exuberant growth is to be expected round the coronets'.

The more elaborate antlers of such members of the *Cervidae* as Red deer and Wapiti, Reindeer and Caribou, exhibit a prodigal variety of form and style, no two being exactly alike. This remarkable feature enables individual beasts to be recognised from others in a herd year after year, despite the fact that the antlers are being renewed annually. Provided, however, the stag has not met with an accident affecting antler growth, each year's pair of antlers follows a set style of pattern, and even though the number of individual tines or points may be different, and the weight of the beam advance or decline with age, the same shape of head and other recognisable features will be reproduced throughout practically the whole life of the stag. Antler types are inherited from father to son, and this has been proved by experiments under deer park conditions. What influence the breeding stock of the female has on antler quality is not so well understood.

The 'typical' perfect head of any species of deer should bear the same number of tines or points on each side of its antlers, and although this is generally achieved by those members of the *Cervidae* which normally carry three points or fewer on each side (i.e. Sambar, Chital (Axis deer), Hog deer, Muntjacs, Brockets, Pudus, etc.) and to a lesser extent those bearing four points on each side (the Sika deer), when the number is greater than four a side, there are probably as many non-typical as typical perfect heads. For instance, just as many 12-point Red deer heads have seven points on one antler and five on the other as have six on each. As the number of points increases, so does the number of possible variations, and this is particularly noticeable in the antlers of Caribou and the palmated Moose heads.

Malformed heads occur in all species of deer, and may be caused through heredity, accident or disease. A frequent cause of malformation of the antler is lung worm and animals so affected often have twisted or corkscrew antlers.

Antlers, though white when first stripped of velvet, soon assume a more or less uniform colour ranging from a light yellow to almost black, the tine ends alone generally remaining an ivory-white colour through constant burnishing or polishing among the grass or foliage, etc. Conclusive evidence as to how this colour is achieved is lacking. One theory is that the antlers have attained their colour through the natural objects, such as trees, heather or peat-moss upon which they are frayed. This certainly does deepen the colour tint of the antler, but does not account entirely for the initial staining – otherwise the antlers of deer living in zoological gardens would remain white. It is noticeable, however, that the antler colour of zoological specimens – and to a large extent deer park animals as well – is considerably lighter than those of animals having a free range. The rougher and more deeply pearled antlers are invariably darker in colour than those which have a smooth beam. There is also considerable variation in colour tints between one species of deer and another, and whilst the antlers of Red deer and Wapiti may at times be almost black, the antlers of the Reindeer and Elk never reach quite the same depth of colour. The antlers of that unique deer of China, Père David's deer, are invariably light coloured.

Whilst on the subject of this deer, it is on record that at Woburn Park a stag very occasionally, when given special feeding, has been known to grow two sets of antlers in twelve months. When this occurs, the summer antlers are shed at the usual time, and a small winter pair of simple design are hard by January, only to be shed almost immediately so that the next proper antlers will be complete before the rut in June.

In my opinion the initial tinting of the antler from a white colour, immediately after the velvet is stripped, to one of brown, comes from *within* and may well be due to blood soaking through the bone when ossification is taking place (see page 19).

The colour of the velvet on the growing antler also varies slightly from one species of deer to another. The velvet on the antlers of Roe and Red deer, for instance, is brownish coloured whilst on the Japanese Sika deer it is black. The Formosan Sika deer, on the other hand, has velvet of a red colour as does also the Swamp deer. The colour of the velvet on Fallow deer antlers, however, varies according to the colouring of the deer, being a whitish tint on white or cream coloured bucks and black on the melanistic. White or cream coloured Red deer stags also have a creamy-coloured velvet on the growing antler.

And finally, what happens to all the discarded antlers that the deer all over the world are annually shedding, for it is surprising how seldom one sees them? A number are eaten by the deer themselves in order to benefit by the mineral salts which are contained in the bone. Others are nibbled away by rodents, whilst those that are neglected by both deer and rodent soon get lost in the undergrowth.

4

The Deer of North, Central and South America

Fifteen species and many subspecies of indigenous deer inhabit this vast continent which covers both Nearctic and Neotropical regions. Of these the Moose *Alces alces* of North America and Canada is the largest; the Pudu *Pudu pudu* of South America the smallest, whilst the White-tailed deer *Odocoileus virginianus* has the widest distribution, as its range spreads from Canada in the north down to South America. A number of European and Asiatic deer have also been introduced to a number of areas, and the majority have acclimatised themselves well.

In North America, when anyone speaks about 'deer' it is assumed that they are referring to White-tailed and Mule deer. Otherwise the particular species is generally referred to by name, even if one of them – the Elk – is most misleading. For the name Elk is applied to the 'Red deer' of North America – the Wapiti – whereas the true Elk is the European 'Moose' *Alces alces*. Another deer which is common to both the New and Old Worlds is *Rangifer tarandus,* the Reindeer of Europe, but known in North America as the Caribou. Both the Moose and the Caribou of North America are considerably larger than their European counterparts.

The fifteen species of deer that can be found in North, Central and South America are as follows:

MOOSE	*Alces alces*	4 subspecies	pp. 29–33
CARIBOU	*Rangifer tarandus*	5 subspecies*	pp. 33–9
WAPITI	*Cervus canadensis*	4 subspecies	pp. 39–44
MULE DEER AND			
BLACK-TAILED DEER	*Odocoileus hemionus*	11 subspecies	pp. 44–8
WHITE-TAILED DEER	*Odocoileus virginianus*	38 subspecies	pp. 48–55
BROCKET DEER			pp. 55–60
RED BROCKET	*Mazama americana*	14 subspecies	pp. 56–57
LITTLE RED BROCKET	*Mazama rufina*	2 subspecies	p. 58
BROWN BROCKET	*Mazama gouazoubira*	10 subspecies	p. 58
DWARF BROCKET	*Mazama chunyi*		p. 58

* Includes Reindeer introduced from Siberia.

HUEMUL	*Hippocamelus bisulcus*		pp. 60–2
	Hippocamelus antisensis		pp. 60–2
MARSH DEER	*Blastocerus dichotomus*		p. 62
PAMPAS DEER	*Ozotoceros bezoarticus*	3 subspecies	pp. 62–4
PUDU	*Pudu pudu*		pp. 64–6
	Pudu mephistophiles	2 subspecies	pp. 64–6

MOOSE *Alces alces*   Map p. 30

Four subspecies are recognised in North America, the largest form of which is the Moose from Alaska, *Alces alces gigas,* good specimens of which may stand as high as 6½ feet (200 cms) at the shoulder and weigh up to 1,500 lbs (680 kilograms). Unfortunately, no accurate data is available on the weights of adult Moose killed in Alaska.

In Canada the Moose has a wide distribution occurring in all the mainland provinces except the northern half of the Labrador peninsula. It was introduced to Newfoundland in 1878 but is absent from all the other larger islands situated around Canada's coastline except Cape Breton, which lies east of Nova Scotia. Here there seems to be considerable doubt as to whether the present animals are indigenous stock to the island or from an introduced strain. It is known, however, that in 1928 and 1929 two adults and five calves were introduced and this was followed some twenty years later by a further introduction of about thirty-five Moose from Elk Island National Park, Alberta. The Moose are now said to be increasing on Cape Breton Island.

Its distribution in Canada today is somewhat different to what it was in the middle of the last century. At that time its main concentration was in a broad band stretching from Lake Winnipeg in southern Manitoba, throughout Saskatchewan and the northern half of Alberta to the Great Bear and Great Slave Lakes in the Mackenzie district of North-West Territories. There was also a big concentration of Moose in the provinces of south-east Canada, which included southern Quebec, New Brunswick and Nova Scotia, but in British Columbia the Moose was then virtually absent.

During the present century its range has extended outwards, particularly in a northerly, southerly and westerly direction, at the expense of the more central parts of its former range, and this has resulted in the Moose now being numerous in parts of British Columbia and Yukon, whilst in the area between Lake Winnipeg and the Great Slave Lake of Mackenzie it has virtually disappeared. In western Canada, where the subspecies is *A.a.andersoni*, it is also present in the more central provinces, but not as plentiful as formerly. The range of *A.a.andersoni* extends eastwards as far as Ontario where it is replaced by *A.a.americana*.

In southern Quebec the Moose population has decreased considerably compared with a century ago. Moose are present today in New Brunswick and Nova Scotia as well as on nearby Cape Breton Island where several introductions have taken place. Between 1895 and 1913 twenty Moose were also introduced to Anticosti Island, situated in the Gulf of St Lawrence and, although they increased for a time, by the early thirties they appear to have become virtually extinct. There is a high population

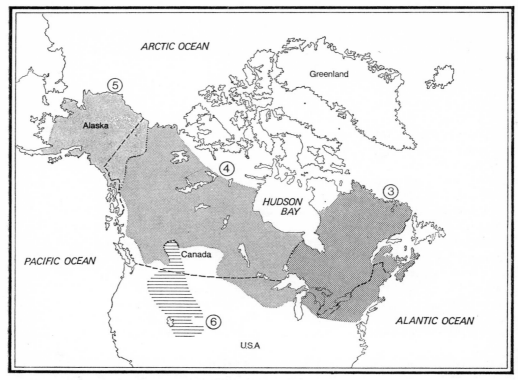

Map. 1. The range of Moose *Alces alces* in NORTH AMERICA

3. *A.a.americana*   Eastern Canada and north-east United States of America
4. *A.a.andersoni*   Western Canada
5. *A.a.gigas*   Alaska and Yukon
6. *A.a.shirasi*   Wyoming, United States of America

of Moose in Newfoundland, but they do not stem from indigenous stock, for there have been several introductions since 1878, the first pair coming from Nova Scotia.

Throughout the whole of Canada a recent estimate (1955) put the Moose population at about 300,000 animals.

In the United States by far the greatest density of Moose is found in Alaska where, in 1963, the population of *A.a.gigas* was estimated at not less than 120,000 animals which was almost double that estimated in 1960. Elsewhere in the United States the Moose is nowhere plentiful and is resident in only about nine States, all of which except two – namely Wyoming and Utah – are situated along the Canadian border. In these two States the subspecies of Moose present is *A.a.shirasi* and this type is also found in Idaho and Montana. Other States include Maine, New Hampshire, Vermont, Michigan (including Isle Royale) and Minnesota, the type in the first three being *A.a.americana* and in the last two *A.a.andersoni*. In all these States the total Moose population is probably not much more than about a tenth of the population in Alaska. Straying animals can also be expected in some of the adjacent

States such as Colorado, Massachusetts, North Dakota, Oregon, Washington and Wisconsin.

Comparing the present-day distribution of Moose in Alaska with a century ago, it would appear that whereas the Moose was formerly concentrated in the interior, away from the coast, the position today is rather the reverse, and we find the species present in many coastal regions where, fifty to sixty years ago, it was unheard of, whilst many of its former haunts are now deserted. In 1948 a bull Moose was killed at Cape Prince of Wales on Seward Peninsula – the most westerly record (168·05 W) for Moose in North America. In general it can be said that forest fires have improved the Moose range in Alaska through the replacement of the spruce forests by broad-leafed trees. In some places, therefore, Moose have increased in the interior as well as dispersing to the coastal regions.

The Moose, with its humped shoulders and heavy, pendulous muzzle, is an un-gainly looking animal, and of all the various species of deer is probably the ugliest. Nevertheless, an adult bull with broad, palmated antlers extending, perhaps, 6 feet (183 cms) in spread can look extremely impressive, especially when seen in its native setting of a Canadian backwood. From the throat there hangs a growth of skin and hair which is called the 'bell'. Generally, the cow's bell is smaller. No one has yet given any satisfactory explanation for this bell, which may vary in length from but a few inches to about 20 inches (50·8 cms). Indeed Thompson Seton (1910) records a bell *38 inches long* (96·5 cms) exclusive of hair which was found on a cow Moose shot in 1903 by an Indian in eastern Manitoba. The naked patch on the muzzle between the nostrils, triangular in shape, is extremely small, while other distinguishing features are the large ears, short neck, long legs, short tail and, of course, the large palmated antlers of the males, or bulls as they are generally called. The females are called cows and the young, calves.

Shoulder heights vary according to locality and subspecies, and whilst the Alaskan Moose of the Kenai peninsula *Alces alces gigas* may measure up to 90 inches (229 cms) at this point, the shoulder height of the eastern type, *A.a.americana,* will measure about two feet less (168 cms). Weights also vary considerably from around 900 lbs (408 kilos) to almost double this figure for exceptionally large bulls from Alaska. Females are about 25 per cent smaller.

The colour of the upper parts of the adult animal is blackish brown to black, with the belly and lower limits of a more brownish shade. The new-born calf, unlike most young deer, is unspotted at birth, the coat being a uniform light-bay colour.

The calf, often a twin but very rarely a triplet, is born in late May or early June, and not infrequently, if available, an island is selected for its birthplace. After the first week or so, which is spent close to its place of birth, the calf will follow its mother for about a year. But during the next spring, when the time of birth of the new calf approaches, the cow will drive its yearling calf away to fend for itself. Twin calves are often reared successfully but on the rare occasions when triplets are born, one of the three is invariably weaker than the other two and will probably succumb, being crowded out at milking time.

During the summer the cows and calves keep mainly to the marshes and swamps of the lowland, whilst the bulls, particularly if flies and mosquitos are proving troublesome, will seek higher altitudes often well above the timber line, where the breezes and cooler temperatures will help to keep these winged tormentors away.

Moose have amazing stamina and will swim considerable distances with comparatively little effort. There are numerous records of Moose having swum distances of eight or nine miles (13 to 14 kilometres), or even more, when crossing bays and lakes. There are tales that Moose have been seen swimming across Lake Superior between Whitefish Point, Michigan, and the Ontario shore – a distance of about sixteen miles (26 kilometres). Occasionally the swim ends in tragedy and the Moose is drowned, whilst attempts to cross a frozen stretch of water have often ended in similar fashion when the ice has given way. Sometimes, when a calf has been swimming with its mother and becomes exhausted, it has been seen to rest its neck on the cow's withers or throw a front leg over her neck. The mother then tows the calf alongside her shoulder.

Water is definitely one of the elements in which a Moose is very much at home. When feeding on submerged aquatic vegetation Peterson (1955) states that,

> they occasionally dive for plants in water over 18 feet (549 cms) deep. They were frequently seen to submerge so completely that not a ripple remained in the water near where they went down. In the majority of cases the rump would float to the top and break water before the animal raised its head. Occasionally animals were seen to make at least a 180-degree turn while completely submerged, and at other times they would seem to roll to one side while attempting to stay under.
>
> The average length of submergence was slightly under 30 seconds. The greatest time actually checked was 50 seconds, although some appeared to remain under slightly longer.

Despite this preference for aquatic vegetation such as pond weeds and lily roots, Moose are also browsers and amongst the trees and bushes of their choice are the following: willow, cottonwood, cherry, mountain ash, aspen, white birch, etc. It is nothing at all for a Moose to reach 8 or 9 feet (244 or 274 cms) from the ground to tear down foliage. By standing on its hind feet, a Moose can go still higher, and reach foliage growing some 12 feet (366 cms) above the ground. And if this isn't high enough, by running his chin up and along saplings, thus forcing them lower, he can strip off the leaves that were growing even 20 feet (610 cms) or more above the ground. As often as not the Moose will 'ride down' the sapling between its forelegs, and not infrequently trees up to 3 inches (7·6 cms) in diameter will snap under its weight. Many shrubs are also taken and these include honeysuckle, dogwood, blueberry and hazel, etc.

During the winter many of the Moose's favourite foods are either withered or under snow. The Moose then eats the buds and twigs of the browse species, and in particular balsam fir in some areas supplies about a quarter of its winter diet. Willow is an important winter food in many localities as is also white birch and quaking aspen. During the winter and spring some bark, particularly from the aspen, is also taken, the Moose ripping it off the standing tree with its lower incisors.

Antlers are shed during the five months from November to March, and in particular during the middle months of this period, the older animals usually being the first to lose them. The growth of the new antler does not commence until the spring, the older animals being the first to show development. Once started, the growth of the antler continues at a remarkable rate, and by the latter part of August the big bulls will be rubbing their antlers against shrubs and trees to remove the velvet.

Within a month of the antlers being cleaned of velvet the rut starts, and this period of real activity in the Moose's annual life cycle lasts about a month – from mid-September until mid-October. At this season, when a bull is following a cow, it will often utter a succession of low grunts at intervals of a few seconds. When in season, the cow will also make her presence known to any bull in the vicinity by making a few low, vibrant calls. At all other times of the year Moose are normally silent, but a young calf will sometimes utter a high-pitched cry which is almost human in quality, perhaps when it finds itself struggling to keep pace with its mother.

During the rut the bulls will frequently fight with each other for the favours of a cow, and in the course of such combats the clash of antlers – particularly on a still day – can be heard over a wide distance.

During the rutting period the matured bulls will often be observed to paw out small depressions or wallows, and after urinating in them several times, will roll in the depressions presumably to cover their bodies with mud. Cows have also been observed to lie down and roll in these wallows.

The wolf is probably the most important natural predator of the Moose. Bears and coyotes also kill a certain number of calves, but predation on their account does not seem to be particularly serious.

CARIBOU *Rangifer tarandus*   Map p. 35

Caribou or Reindeer were members of the late Pleistocene fauna of North America, and at the present time two types – the Barren-ground Caribou and the Woodland Caribou – are recognised on this continent, which includes the United States, Canada and adjacent islands. Greenland has also been included.

The word *'Caribou'* is a native American word – the Indian name of the animal, who also formerly described it as *Maccaribo*.

The Barren-ground Caribou – which Banfield (1961) prefers to call Tundra Reindeer – are distributed throughout northern Canada from Labrador in the east to Unimak Island, Alaska, in the west. Included in this range are the Canadian islands of Ellesmere and Baffin, as well as many of the smaller islands. The Barren-ground Caribou also occurs on Greenland.

The typical Barren-ground Caribou of the mainland is known as *Rangifer tarandus groenlandicus,* the type specimen of which, as its name suggests, came from the south-west coast of Greenland. In addition to its occurrence in western Greenland and on the mainland between Hudson Bay and the Mackenzie River Valley, this type of Caribou is also found on Baffin Island and on one or two other smaller islands at the mouth of the Hudson Bay. Despite its huge range, there has, during the past decade, been a rapid decline in the numbers of the Barren-ground Caribou, particularly in northern Mackenzie and northern Keewatin districts, and throughout its range it is doubtful if its population exceeds a quarter of a million animals. It still occurs, however, in some numbers in the central part of its range and locally in the northern Keewatin district. Intergradation between the Barren-ground and Woodland type Caribou (*R.t.caribou*) occurs in the region between the Anderson River and the Mackenzie delta.

Until about 1900 another type of Barren-ground Caribou *R.t.eogroenlandicus* was recognised for eastern Greenland, but this form now appears to be extinct. In north-west Greenland, however, another extant race of Barren-ground Caribou occurs – namely Peary Caribou *R.t.pearyi*. The type locality of this Caribou is the east coast of Ellesmere Island. Peary Caribou is also found on a number of the Arctic Ocean islands around Ellesmere, which include Melville Island, Prince Patrick Island, Banks Island, Prince of Wales Island, Ellef Rignes and one or two others. The Peary Caribou seems to have been less affected by human interference than any other subspecies because its distribution is largely north of recent Eskimo habitation. However, their numbers are not large and on Ellesmere Island alone its total population is probably only about 500. Melville Island probably has the greatest number of Peary Caribou, about 3,000. Further to the west on the Alaskan peninsula, another subspecies of Barren-ground Caribou, known as Grant's Caribou *R.t.granti,* occurs.

These groups have gradually amalgamated and Banfield (1961) suggests that the 'Caribou population in Alaska and Yukon Territory indicate a broad belt of intergradation between the Woodland Caribou, *caribou,* and the Tundra Reindeer, *groenlandicus*'.

Before leaving this area it should be noted that domestic Reindeer from Siberia *R.t.tarandus* were introduced to Alaska about 1890 whilst about 1935 domestic Reindeer were driven from this state into the Mackenzie delta of North-West Territories in Canada. A full description of these introductions is given in Chapter 2 (page 11). From time to time these domestic Reindeer have crossed with the native Caribou. In 1969 the population of Caribou in Alaska was estimated to be about 600,000.

At one time the range of the Woodland Caribou *R.t.caribou* stretched from Newfoundland in the east to British Columbia and Queen Charlotte Islands in the west. Included in this range were all the southern provinces of Canada as well as some of the northern States of the United States of America such as Maine, New Hampshire, Vermont, Michigan, Wisconsin, Minnesota, North Dakota, Montana, Idaho and Washington State.

The present distribution of the Woodland Caribou is much reduced, the southern limits of their range having been pushed northward with the result that excluding Alaska, only about 115 animals still remain in the United States of America, about 100 of which are in northern Idaho with the remainder in Nevada and Washington State. In Alaska, the Woodland Caribou is extinct on the Kenai Peninsula but about 150 animals are reported from the Copper River area in the south-eastern part of this state.

In Canada the species is present in all provinces except Nova Scotia and New Brunswick, in both of which it became extinct during the early part of the present century. It is most plentiful in the forests of Ontario where, in 1960, the population was estimated to be about 10,000. A somewhat similar number frequented the

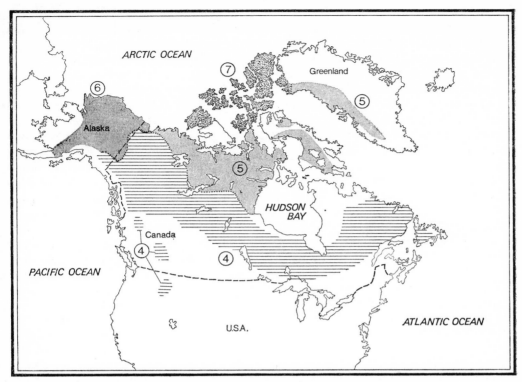

Map 2. The range of Reindeer/Caribou *Rangifer tarandus* in NORTH AMERICA

4. *R.t.caribou*   Canada and South-east Alaska
5. *R.t.groenlandicus*   Greenland and Canada
6. *R.t.granti*   Alaska peninsula
7. *R.t.pearyi*   North-west Greenland and adjacent islands

Two other subspecies, *R.t.dawsoni* and *R.t.eogroenlandicus* are now extinct. *R.t.tarandus* have been introduced

Ungava-Labrador peninsula, whilst a comparable population exists in both New-foundland and British Columbia – namely 5,000 deer in each province. Woodland Caribou are probably scarcest in Alberta and Yukon for in neither province does their population much exceed 1,000. Altogether, Banfield (1961) suggests that the total Woodland Caribou population in North America may be about 43,000 animals.

Until about 1935 there was a diminutive form of Caribou *R.t.dawsoni* present on Queen Charlotte Islands but it is now extinct.

The Caribou is a rather ungainly looking animal with a thick muzzle, maned neck and broad, flat hooves that are concave underneath and designed for travelling over snow and boggy terrain. In summer the body colour of the bulls is brown, with the chest and legs darker. The belly, rump, tail and a ring above each hoof are white, whilst the neck is a palish-grey shade, which in winter turns white. In winter, the hair on the coat lengthen and becomes denser, whilst the colour of the back becomes grizzled with hair tips breaking off. Albinos are rare, but some of the Arctic island forms are almost white in colour. The ears and tail are short and the muzzle well furred, which protects it from frost bite.

A full grown Caribou bull will vary in height at the shoulder from about 42 inches (107 cms) to just over 50 inches (127 cms), according to subspecies, whilst the weight will also vary accordingly from about 200 lbs (91 kilograms) to about 600 lbs (272 kilograms) complete. The heavier specimen is, therefore, a much larger animal than its north European relative the Reindeer. There is, of course, much individual difference between the animals of the same subspecies, some beasts attaining a larger size than others at the same age. On average, however, it would appear that the Woodland Caribou of north British Columbia – which some authorities refer to as the Mountain Caribou – attain the largest size both as regards antlers and body weight. Seasonal variations are also great, an old bull in September weighing much heavier than the same animal would have done in spring or winter. The cows are considerably smaller.

Caribou are probably the most amphibious of deer, and will readily take to water in order to cross lakes and rivers, or escape from predators. Even a young calf will not be daunted when faced with water to cross, but its progress when swimming will obviously not be as fast as the adult deer, which can maintain a speed of about four miles (6·5 kilometres) an hour.

When travelling over land one of the most singular sounds made by the Caribou and Reindeer is the clicking of its tread – a sound which from an individual animal on a still day may be heard at a distance of over thirty yards (27 metres). When a large herd of Caribou is moving along, the volume of noise made by the countless hooves clicking is considerable. The only other deer which has somewhat similar hooves to the Caribou is the Père David's deer of China *Elaphurus davidianus* and when on the move this animal also makes the same – but less audible – clicking noise.

The Caribou or Reindeer, *Rangifer tarandus,* is the only species of deer in which both sexes normally carry antlers, although those on the females, or cows as they are generally called, are insignificant when compared to some of the fine trophies produced by the bulls. The Barren-ground Caribou produces the finest antlers and in particular some of the best trophies have come from Alaska where an outstanding head, bearing no fewer than forty-four or more points, may have an antler length of some 58 inches (147 cms). The world record Caribou head, however, with an antler length of $61\frac{1}{8}$ inches (155·3 cms), inside spread of $58\frac{1}{4}$ inches (147·9 cms) and bearing no fewer than fifty-two points, came from Nain in Labrador. It was killed by Zack Elbo in 1931. British Columbia has also produced some fine trophies.

A feature of a good trophy is the wide brow shovel point, and whilst this is normally present on one side only, occasionally there will be a double shovel. It has frequently been stated that the animal uses this brow shovel point to scrape the snow away during the winter, so as to expose the lichen which is its staple diet. There is no foundation for this suggestion, however, for by mid-winter the older Caribou bulls will have cast their antlers. Moreover, even if the antlers were retained throughout the winter, this brow shovel does not extend beyond the deer's nose, and as it is set so nearly parallel to the animal's face, it would be a most awkward weapon to use for this purpose. The truth is that they scrape away the snow with their fore-feet, as do other deer.

There is a marked variation in the dates of shedding the antlers, according to sex, age and physiological condition of the individual. This has resulted in various conflicting statements in the literature. Generally speaking it can be said that the older the bull, the earlier will be the shedding of the antlers, and within a month of the termination of the rut in October the oldest bulls will have started to shed their antlers. The young bulls, however, retain their antlers until late in April, whilst the antlers of the cows will not be shed until about the time of calving in late May and early June. Old cows are likely to drop their antlers a little earlier than the younger ones, just as old bulls shed theirs several months before the young bulls, although in the latter case the difference is much greater. Generally speaking, it can be said that the period of growth and shedding of the antlers of the cows is about six months out of phase with that of the adult bulls.

It has been suggested that the purpose of late shedding of the antlers of the female is for the protection of the young, but this can hardly be so, for although some of the younger cows may still retain their antlers when the calf is born, the majority will have shed them. Furthermore, as a protection against predators, the hooves are far more formidable weapons than the insignificant antlers of the cows. A few cows never develop antlers. The wolf is the principal predator.

As one would expect, the season at which the new antlers start to grow also varies according to sex and age. The new growth of the old bulls which have shed their antlers in early winter will not commence until about March or April. Thereafter, however, development is rapid and continuous, and by September the velvet on the antlers of the older bulls will be ready for cleaning. The younger bulls and the cows will lose their velvet towards the end of September or early October.

During the summer, and in particular during the early autumn, the bulls have been quietly feeding, away from the cows, and accumulating a considerable amount of fat in preparation for the exhausting activity of the rutting season. During September the necks of the old bulls start to enlarge and the white hairs around the throat and chest develop into a mane which contrasts splendidly with the deep brown colour of the body and so transform them into truly magnificent specimens. By this time the bulls are starting to leave their summer haunts and seek out the bands of cows which have also been putting on weight since the birth of their calves. Naturally, it is the barren cows that will be in the fattest condition.

By the end of September the rut will have commenced, and by mid-October will have reached its peak. As with the Red deer, the bulls are continuously on the move during the rut, rounding up their herd of cows or meeting challengers. In consequence there is little time for feeding and their reserve fat is soon gone. Thus, when the rut is over, the bulls are not in the best condition to face bitter winter. Somehow they are able to survive for it will not be until the spring that they will have much opportunity to regain their lost condition.

Caribou and Reindeer are usually silent, and during the rut the bulls have no special challenge call. When surprised at close range, however, or annoyed by insects, both sexes will give a loud snort. When in large groups, particularly the cows, some grunt-like noises can be heard.

Whilst a few calves will appear in late May, the majority are born in early June,

D

and unlike most species of young deer, but similar, however, to young Moose, they are not spotted at birth.

Within about two months from birth small bony knobs may be felt under the skin covering the frontal bone of the young calf, and by September these will have developed into small spike antlers in velvet. By late winter these spikes will be clear of velvet and will not be shed until early summer.

During the second season there is a considerable growth, and in the field, at a distance, it is often difficult to distinguish the antlers of a yearling bull from those of an adult cow. By the third season the antlers are generally adult in pattern.

This deer is a gregarious animal, and is usually met in small herds. The herd is a social group, consisting of different ages and sexes. However, except during the rutting period, the mature bulls are inclined to keep together in small bands of their own, and during the migration will generally be found on the outskirts of the herd.

The Woodland or Mountain Caribou does not congregate into such immense herds nor undertake such long migrations as the Barren-ground Caribou. The former does, of course, move periodically from one grazing ground to another but the area covered is nothing like so extensive as that of the Barren-ground Caribou, which may extend up to 800 miles (1,280 kilometres) in length between the summer and winter ranges.

The Barren-ground Caribou undertakes three migrational journeys each year. During April and May, when the spring migration takes place, there is a general movement of large herds of animals from their winter ranges near the woods towards the tundra summer range. This will continue during the summer months, until by July it will have exhausted itself. By the end of this month there appears to be a general retracing movement until by late August the herds will have collected on the southern limits of the tundra. The herds are then complete, with the cows and bulls in close proximity. This comparatively short retracing movement is generally referred to as the midsummer migration.

However, this summer movement of the Caribou herds does not end here. During September the Caribou start to retrace some of their spring migration route but this retreat ends with the onset of the rut in October, following which, in late October or November, the autumn migration towards the wooded area commences. Weather, however, affects the tempo of migration, for the Caribou will seldom leave the tundra until the arrival of the first winter storm. The winter ranges are generally reached in December but if the weather has been open, their arrival there may be delayed until January. Here the Caribou remain until April and May, when once more they will set out on the spring migration. If the winter has been mild they will often remain near the tree line, but if the weather is severe, the herds will migrate deeper into the woods.

One of the suggestions for the Caribou's migratory habit is that these animals move south in winter for the shelter of the forest, returning northward in the spring to spend the summer on the tundra. Whilst this might be true for some of the Barren-ground Caribou, it cannot apply to some of the Woodland or Mountain types of Alaska and Yukon where the summer and winter ranges are substantially alike. Another theory is that they leave the timber line during the summer months to escape the hordes of flies and mosquitos which torment them at this time of year. This, again, may in some part influence the movement of the Barren-ground Caribou whose spring migration takes place before the start of the fly season, which doesn't reach plague proportions on the tundra until July. However, as mentioned above, the winter and summer ranges of many of the Woodland Caribou are so similar as to make little difference from a fly infestation point of view. Food requirements seem to be the main cause of these migrations, for only by movement can all members in a large herd of deer obtain fresh grazing.

Besides the flies and mosquitos, which at times make the Caribou rush off frantically in search of snowfields on which to find relief from their tormentors, the warble fly is a most persistent parasite. This fly, which is on the wing in July and August, deposits its eggs on the Caribou hair near its base. When the eggs are hatched, the larvae bore through the hide and migrate to the back muscles where they develop. In this manner a single Caribou may become the host to a hundred of these grubs. In due course, during the following June, the grub squirms out and falls to the ground, leaving a hole in the hide. On the ground the grub remains for a short time in a pupal state from which the adult fly will eventually emerge. These punctures cause great damage to the hides. The nasal bot fly is another parasite which attacks the Caribou.

All Caribou, particularly during the rutting season, are curious of strange objects, and it is often possible for a man, especially when accompanied by a horse, to approach a herd of Caribou to within about forty yards (36 metres), even though the terrain be perfectly flat without any semblance of cover. This curiosity has been the downfall of many a fine antlered bull at the hands of a hunter.

Although lichens form the staple diet of the Caribou, the following are also eaten with relish: mushrooms, willows, mosses, sedges, grasses, bilberry and birch, etc.

WAPITI *Cervus canadensis*   Map p. 41

Wapiti – the Red deer of North America – is the second largest deer on the American continent, with good bulls weighing up to 1,000 lbs (454 kilograms) live weight and standing about 5 feet (152 cms) high at the shoulder. In North America, however, this fine deer is generally referred to as Elk, which is really the proper name for the European Elk or Moose *Alces alces alces*.

Six subspecies of Wapiti are recognised in North America, but two of these, the typical form *C.c.canadensis* which formerly frequented eastern America, and Merriam's Wapiti *C.c.merriami* of Arizona and north Mexico, are now extinct. The four types which are still extant are Roosevelt's Wapiti *C.c.roosevelti* – also called Olympic Elk – of western North America; the Rocky Mountain Wapiti *C.c.nelsoni*; the Wapiti of Saskatchewan, *C.c.manitobensis*; and the Dwarf or Tule Wapiti of California *C.c.nannodes* which, as its name suggests, is the smallest member of the North American Wapiti.

In former times the Wapiti was one of the most widely distributed of the deer of North America, with a range stretching from the Pacific Ocean in the west to almost the Atlantic in the east, and from about what is now Mexico and Georgia in the south to northern Alberta in Canada. In the east no records exist to show that it ever actually reached the Atlantic Ocean, but some of the early writers have expressed the opinion that at some early date the Wapiti probably did occupy some of the Atlantic coastal areas. What is certain, however, is that during the sixteenth and seventeenth centuries this fine deer was extremely abundant in North America, and although no one knows what their total population was at that period, it has been suggested it may have been 10,000,000 head.

During the latter part of the last century a great slaughter of Wapiti took place: first by hide hunters to make money, and then at the close of the century by 'tusk hunters' who killed the bulls just for the sake of their canine teeth, for which there was a profitable market among members of the Elk's Lodge. Eventually this wanton slaughter was checked, but not before the Wapiti had been exterminated from about 90 per cent of its former ranges.

As a result, by the beginning of the present century, all the indigenous Wapiti in eastern United States had disappeared, and indeed the only localities, south of the Canadian border where sizeable herds of Wapiti still existed, were in the Yellowstone National Park, Wyoming, and the Olympic peninsula of western Washington – the former area being occupied by the Rocky Mountain Wapiti and the latter by the Roosevelt or Olympic Wapiti. A few Wapiti also survived in Montana, Idaho and north Colorado which bordered Wyoming, but nowhere were they plentiful. In Canada the chief refuge of the Wapiti at the beginning of this century was in Manitoba, Saskatchewan and Alberta.

Now, as a result of introductions during the present century, many of the former haunts of the extinct *C.c.canadensis* have been repopulated by the Rocky Mountain form *C.c.nelsoni,* and by 1955 the Wapiti was present in over twenty states of the United States, with the biggest populations being in Colorado, Idaho, Montana, Oregon and Wyoming. In 1941 eighteen Wapiti from the Wichita National Wildlife Refuge in Oklahoma were liberated in northern Coahuila, Mexico, but the introduction failed and by 1943 all the deer seem to have died or been killed. In 1952 and again in 1955 thirty animals on each occasion from the Yellowstone National Park were liberated in Coahuila, but whether the species has succeeded in establishing itself in the wild is not known.

The range of Roosevelt's Wapiti is confined to the humid forest belt along the Pacific coast stretching from Vancouver Island (Canada) in the north, through the coastal regions of Washington and Oregon to California in the south. It also occurs in Afognak Island, off the Alaskan coast, where it has been introduced.

The only other Wapiti that exists in the United States is the 'Tule Elk', also called the 'Valley or Dwarf Elk', which prior to 1860 was quite common in the central parts of California. This Wapiti, which appears to have the greatest tolerance for desert conditions, is now restricted to Owens Valley and a fenced preserve at Tupman, near Bakersfield in California.

During 1969 over 89,000 Wapiti were killed in the United States of America (*Wild Life Leaflet* 492, September 1970). This would suggest that the total population of Wapiti in the United States must be in the region of at least half a million animals.

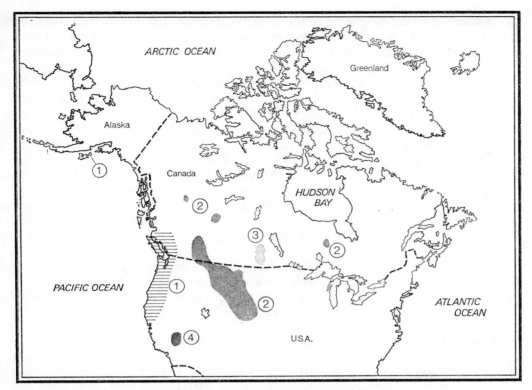

Map 3. The range of Wapiti *Cervus canadensis* in NORTH AMERICA

1. *Cervus canadensis roosevelti* Western North America
                                   (also introduced to Afognak Island, off Alaska)
2. *C.c.nelsoni*   Western North America, except coast
                                   (including a number of introductions as shown by smaller
                                   shaded areas)
3. *C.c. manitobensis*   Saskatchewan and south-west Manitoba
4. *C.c.nannodes* (Tule Elk)   California

Wapiti from North America have been introduced to South Island, New Zealand,
where they thrive

NOTE

Two other wapiti *C.c.canadensis* and *C.c.merriami* are now extinct (page 145)

In Canada three subspecies of Wapiti still survive – the fourth member, the
Eastern Wapiti *C.c.canadensis*, which formerly ranged from the southern region of
Quebec and Ontario into the adjacent parts of the United States, having long been
extinct.

In the extreme west, the presence of Roosevelt's Wapiti on Vancouver Island has
already been mentioned. In the Rocky Mountain region of south-western Alberta
and south-eastern British Colombia *C.c.nelsoni* is tolerably abundant in certain
localities such as in the national parks. Formerly its range extended almost to Lake

Athabaska but by the beginning of the present century it had disappeared from this area. In 1948–9 the Federal Government reintroduced the Wapiti to Lake Claire district in northern Alberta, and two years later others were reintroduced to Braeburn Lake in southern Yukon territory. Wapiti have also been reintroduced to Ontario.

Well to the east of the Rockies, in south Saskatchewan and south-west Manitoba *C.c.manitobensis* finds refuge in the region of three game reserves – the Moose Mountain Reserve, the Prince Albert National Park and the Porcupine Reserve.

Reference has already been made to the size of the Wapiti (page 39). In colour this deer somewhat resembles a Red deer, only in summer pelage it is perhaps not quite so red. At this time of the year the general colour pattern is light bay rather than deep red with the legs and head remaining dark, as in winter coat, only the hair is less rough. In winter the pelage assumes a somewhat darker shade with the colour on the lower part of the body varying from a light to a very dark grey in some animals. A typical feature of Wapiti colouring is the light coloured rump patch which is more developed in this animal than in the Red deer. In autumn the bulls develop a dark mane.

The calves, the majority of which are born in June, are spotted at birth and they, too, have a very pronounced yellowish-brown rump patch. Down the neck and back there are two rows of spots, one on either side of the median line, and the rest of the body is also well spotted. By July, as the hair lengthens, the spots will gradually disappear.

A typical pair of antlers of an adult Wapiti bull will bear six points on each side, with the three lower points – brow, bay and tray – sprouting from the main beam in similar fashion to those on the Red deer antlers, but the two succeeding tines pointing upwards in the same place as the beam, rather than forming a cup as in the latter beast. Occasionally, however, Wapiti antlers will terminate in a good cup, similar to a Red deer, and this is very apparent in areas where Red and Wapiti have been allowed to intermingle, such as in New Zealand (see page 146).

The first antlers begin to grow when the young bull is about eleven months old, but individual animals have been seen with prominent knobs as early as February. March is the month when the majority of antlers will be cast but the oldest bulls will probably have discarded theirs towards the end of the preceding month. The old bulls are generally the first to complete their antler growth, and by the end of August most of the bulls in this age group will have been in hard antler, free of velvet, for a week or two. As mentioned previously, the typical adult bull's antlers should have six points, but heads bearing as many as nineteen points have been recorded, whilst freak heads with irregular tine formations are not uncommon. Cows with small antlers have also been recorded, but invariably the velvet has been retained.

The Wapiti has a wide range of vocal sounds. When alarmed all animals of one year old and above, irrespective of sex, make a kind of hoarse bark, and this may be uttered at any time of the year. Calves, when alarmed, will utter a prolonged scream. At other times, when calling its mother, the calf will give a kind of low bleat, and this will be answered by the cow giving a somewhat similar, though deeper, call. The most impressive sound of all, however, is the bugle which the bulls utter during the rutting season. The bulls will start to bugle about the last week in August and will continue until the end of October, by which time the rut will have terminated. Intermittent bugling may, however, still be heard during early November. Spike bulls will not bugle. Cows will also give a kind of bugle, particularly during the months of May and June. Cow Wapiti have also been heard bugling in July and August, but this is not very common.

The rut starts in September and reaches its height about the end of the month. The Wapiti, similar to the Red deer, is a polygamous animal and during the period of the rut the bulls attempt to round up as many cows as they can hold against local opposition. Needless to say there are frequent battles amongst the males, a few of which end with fatal results to one of the contenders.

Wapiti, like some other species of deer and in particular the Red deer, make mud wallows which are frequently visited by the bulls during the rutting season. The purpose of these wallows seems to be to provide a soothing influence on the bulls who get very worked up at this season. During the summer other wallows are used by deer of both sexes but these are wetter than the rutting mud wallows of the bulls.

Wapiti are strong swimmers and will not hesitate to cross lakes up to a mile (1·6 kilometres) in width.

In some parts of its range, and in particular in the more mountainous districts such as the Rocky Mountains, the Wapiti can be considered as a migratory animal. This, of course, is quite understandable for the snows of winter will soon make its summer range not only unattractive, but quite unlivable. In many areas the Wapiti, when journeying from summer to winter territory, follow well-defined migration routes.

In normal seasons the migration to their wintering grounds does not take place until after the rutting season, the date varying in accordance with the prevailing weather conditions. Should there be a heavy snowfall in October affecting the availability of their forage, then the Wapiti will start to move to lower altitudes. In normal winters, however, it will be November before there is any weight of snow, whilst in a very open winter many of the Wapiti will remain in the mountains until a much later date.

In the spring there is a migration in the reverse way, but the urge to reach the mountains is strong and quite a few animals will have returned before the snows have disappeared and before the vegetation has reached the abundance of the valley below.

Wapiti prefer grass ranges and grass, when available, may be said to be their staple food. Browse, however, particularly in winter ranges, is most important, for it is available when deep snow deprives the Wapiti of access to grass. Many browse species, however, are also highly palatable, and these include fir, Rocky Mountain maple, alder, birch, dogwood, galax, juniper, myrtle, pine, aspen or cottonwood, Douglas fir and wild rose, etc. The size of the animal is a considerable advantage in areas where the Wapiti has to share its range with Mule deer, for it is able to browse off foliage beyond the reach of the latter deer. In areas of high Wapiti density, the deer will often peel the bark from trees, and in this respect the willows and aspens are particularly favoured.

Although Wapiti are good swimmers, a fair number are drowned, particularly when attempting to cross partly frozen lakes or rivers. Death by accident or predators, however, is negligible, and in some areas, but for the fact that a fair number are being killed annually by hunters or game wardens, the number of Wapiti would quickly exceed range capacity and this particularly applies in those areas which it shares with other species such as Mule deer and sheep. Probably most deaths from natural causes occur in the spring when the first flush of soft, green grass eaten to excess causes severe diarrhoea which proves fatal to many animals, especially the older ones.

MULE DEER or BLACK-TAILED DEER *Odocoileus hemionus*   Map p. 45

Mule deer, which are called Black-tailed deer in north-west Pacific coastal areas, are found over a vast expanse of western North America and in a variety of habitats, from the high mountains to the plains and deserts. Their range is confined almost entirely to the western half of the United States, extending northwards from about central Mexico to Southern Alaska and the Great Slave Lake of North-West Territories in Canada. In this vast area no fewer than eleven subspecies are recognised, of which the typical deer *Odocoileus h.hemionus* has the greatest range in both Canada and the United States.

In Canada *O.h.hemionus* extends westwards from about the south-western shores of Lake Winnipeg in Manitoba, through southern Saskatchewan and Alberta to British Columbia where, towards the coast, it is replaced by *O.h.sitkensis* – more generally known as the Black-tailed deer or Sitka deer. This latter deer also occurs in the adjacent mainland and islands of southern Alaska, as well as on Queen Charlotte Islands.

A third subspecies *O.h.columbianus*, sometimes referred to as the Coast deer, occurs in south-west British Columbia, including Vancouver Island, and this race extends southwards along the coast through Washington, Oregon into north-west California.

East of this coastal race, and distributed in about seventeen states eastwards as far as Minnesota in the United States, is found once again the typical Mule deer *O.h.hemionus*. To the south, the typical race is replaced by *O.h.crooki* in northern Texas, New Mexico and Arizona and by *O.h.inyoensis* and *O.h.californicus* in eastern California.

The Mule deer of California have been divided into four subspecies, with *O.h. columbianus* in the north, *O.h.californicus* and *O.h.inyoensis* in the more central parts and *O.h.fuliginatus* in the extreme south, the last named extending its range southwards into Baja California where it is replaced by *O.h.peninsulae*. East and west of Baja California are situated two islands, Tiburón Island in the Gulf of California and Cerros Island in the Pacific Ocean, and each has its own subspecies of Mule deer, *O.h.sheldoni* on the former and *O.h.cerrosensis* on the latter.

East of the Gulf of California in Sonora, Mexico, a subspecies of Mule deer known as *O.h.eremicus* – the Desert Mule deer or Burro deer – occurs, but this type is replaced in north-east Sonora by *O.h.crooki* – a race whose range spreads eastwards

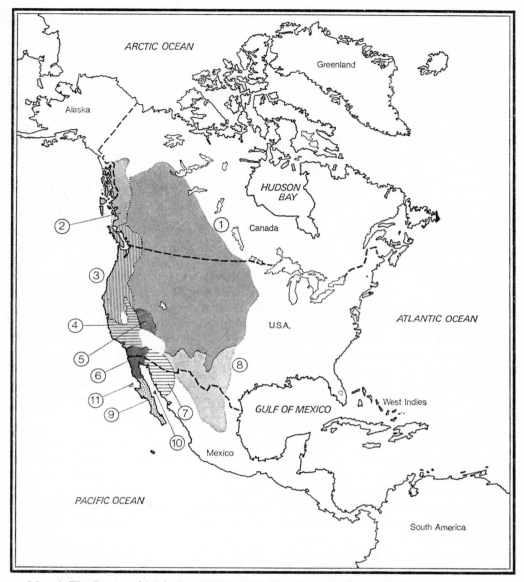

Map 4. The Range of Mule deer/Black-tailed deer *Odocoileus hemionus* in NORTH AMERICA

1. *Odocoileus hemionus hemionus* West and central North America
2. *O.h.sitkensis* Coastal area and islands off British Columbia
3. *O.h.columbianus* British Columbia to northern California
4. *O.h.californicus* Mid California
5. *O.h.inyoensis* California
6. *O.h.fuliginatus* California
7. *O.h.eremicus* North-west Mexico and Arizona
8. *O.h.crooki* North Mexico
9. *O.h.peninsulae* Baja California
10. *O.h.sheldoni* Tiburón Island
11. *O.h.cerrosensis* Cerros Island, Baja California

Based on Hall & Kelson (*The Mammals of North America*)

into western Texas and southwards as far as Zacatecas in central Mexico, which marks the extent of the Mule deer's range in the south. Where the territories of two different subspecies adjoin or overlap, it is obvious that intergradation occurs and this is evident in some of the deer from California.

The typical Mule deer *O.h.hemionus* is a medium-sized deer, a good average buck standing about 40 inches (101·6 cms) high at the shoulder and weighing about 250 to 300 lbs (114 to 136 kilograms) live weight. Exceptional beasts may weigh up to 400 lbs (181 kilograms) whilst the bucks of the coastal Black-tailed deer average about 160–190 lbs (73 to 86 kilograms).

The smallest race is that found in lower Baja California, *O.h.peninsulae*, whilst the two insular types, *O.h.sheldoni* and *O.h.cerrosensis* from the islands of Tiburón and Cerros respectively, are not much bigger. Generally speaking the races of *Odocoileus hemionus* conform to Bergman's Law in that the individual races inhabiting the colder localities are larger than those of races inhabiting the warmer regions, a possible exception being *O.h.sitkensis*.

The Mule deer is fairly uniform in colour throughout its range, and distinctions between several of the named subspecies are not well defined. The colouration of this deer has a number of slight variations, but all are in shades of red, grey and brown, and they are mainly seasonal.

Generally speaking the winter coat of a Mule deer is a warm, brownish-grey colour, thickly peppered with black tips and rings on individual hairs. The inside of the legs, belly and caudal patch are white. The face and throat are also whitish, with a black patch on the forehead and a black bar round the chin. The tail of the typical Mule deer is white and rounded with a black tip but in the case of the Black-tailed deer, the black extends up the outer surface of the tail.

In summer the coat is rusty red or tan, the change taking place about May and this is retained until about August when the winter pelage is assumed. The Mule deer of lower Baja California, *O.h.peninsulae*, is the lightest in colour. The fawns, the majority of which are born in June, are spotted at birth, but by the time the fawn is about four months old these spots are but faintly indicated.

Mule deer undergo two moults each year, one in the autumn and the other in the spring. Though the actual times of these moults varies with the geographical location of the deer, it can be said that the autumn moult takes place in August and September, and normally the bucks acquire the winter pelage several weeks earlier than the does with fawns. The spring moult takes place in May and June, and of the females, the barren does are the first to acquire their summer pelage.

The antlers of an adult buck are widespread and are sometimes described as being 'dichotomous' – that is to say the tines are an arrangement of even forks instead of a main branch with simple tines sprouting from it. A typical pair of Mule deer antlers will consist of short, upright brows and double forks or bifurcations on each side, making it a 10-pointer. Black-tailed deer antlers will often bear only eight points, the third main tine being omitted. In abnormal antlers, however, the number of points may be doubled or trebled, and some exceptional trophies have been recorded with over forty points. The best trophies probably come from Wyoming and Colorado.

In some heads, particularly those of immature animals and some adult Black-tailed *O.h.sitkensis,* it is sometimes difficult to distinguish antlers of Mule deer from White-tailed deer, but generally speaking the basal snag on the former is shorter than on the White-tailed deer. Moreover this basal snag on the White-tailed deer antler develops in the second-year head, whilst in the case of the Mule deer, the basal snag is never present on the 2-point antler of an *immature* buck.

The antlers are shed between January and March, the older bucks shedding first. Antler replacement does not become visible immediately and it will generally be March or April, dependent on when shedding occurred, that the new growth gets under way. The antlers of the older bucks should be hard and clean of velvet by the end of August and early September.

Buck fawns grow 'buttons' or small antler stumps when about three months old, and in exceptional cases these buttons may develop into small spikes about half an inch (1·27 cms) in length. True antler growth, however, for the yearling buck generally commences at about 9–10 months of age, the first head normally consisting of two points on each side. Normally the antler increases in size with age up to about seven years and after remaining constant for a year or two, the trophy will then start to 'go back'. Very occasionally bucks without antlers have been reported, and still more rarely, does with small antlers.

The rut takes place between late September and about mid-November, the deer in the southern part of their range rutting rather earlier than in the north. The fawns, as already mentioned, are born principally in June, though there are records of April and late July births. Twins are common, and on occasions, triplets may be born.

Direct vocal communication between deer takes place in a number of ways. During the rut, bucks will utter repeated low, short, strained bleats, which are increased to a grunting bellow or bark when an aggressor approaches. The does will also bark at any season of the year, and during the rutting season both sexes will bellow. A fawn or its mother when separated will often be heard to bleat.

Although at times a buck will fight fiercely for the possession of his does, the majority of Mule deer conflicts are 'battles of bluff' and at the moment when an earnest battle seems inevitable, one or other of the contestants will turn away. During the rut the search for a mate seems mutual between the sexes, and both bucks and does will range widely in search of a partner. When the breeding season is over, the bucks have lost a lot of condition and look thin.

In mountainous areas the Mule deer is a migratory animal, for it likes to spend the short summer months high up on the mountains where it can graze the rich grasses and low herbage. Indeed, in suitable localities it is not uncommon during the summer to see Mule deer as high as seven or eight thousand feet (about 2,300 metres) above sea level – generally on a slope facing south-east or south-west where it can enjoy the early morning or evening sunshine. Southern-facing slopes are also much favoured, for the same reason, during the winter, which is spent in the valleys where food is still available and snow not too deep. However, life is never easy for the deer in winter time.

Among the predators of the Mule deer the cougar or mountain lion is probably the most important but, during the fawning season, fawns are frequently picked up by bears and bobcats. Coyotes hunt deer at times, and being numerous in many parts of the Mule deer's range, probably account for more deer than the comparatively rare cougar. Under ordinary circumstances, most of the deer casualties accounted for by coyotes are diseased, wounded or young animals. Wolverines will also occasionally take a deer when handicapped by deep snow, and the golden eagle may, at times, account for the odd fawn.

Ticks are a great nuisance to Mule deer in the summer, and dozens of them will burrow into the skin of a deer in order to feast off its blood. During 1924–5 there was a serious epidemic in California of foot and mouth disease which, it was alleged, caused the death of many thousands of Mule deer. In addition, at least a further 22,000 were slaughtered in an effort to check the disease.

As far as foot and mouth disease is concerned, although all deer and other free-living ruminants are susceptible to the disease which occasionally appears enzootically, there are very few instances where deer of any species have actually contracted it, and none in Great Britain. The point about its incidence in animals is that it affects principally cloven-footed creatures and the symptoms of lesions on the foot and in the mouth are common to all those animals so affected. There is always the risk, however, of mechanical transference of the foot and mouth disease virus on the feet whether it be on the cloven feet of cattle and deer or on the feet of solipeds such as horses, and undoubtedly the majority of deer slaughtered in California were potential carriers rather than affected beasts.

No one knows what the total Mule deer population is in North America, but it must be over three million in the United States alone, where the annual cull by licensed hunters in 1969 was close on 600,000.

WHITE-TAILED DEER *Odocoileus virginianus*   Maps pp. 50, 53

This deer has a very wide distribution in North America for it is resident in practically every state in the United States except Alaska, and possibly Utah, although wanderers may occur in the extreme north.

Northwards the range of the White-tailed deer extends into southern Canada, being present in the southern part of all the adjacent provinces and also Nova Scotia. It is absent from Labrador, North-West Territories, Yukon and Newfoundland.

To the south, the range of the White-tailed deer extends through Mexico and Central America into the northern half of South America. Throughout its entire range from southern Canada to northern South America, no fewer than thirty-eight different subspecies are recognised. Since the range of many of these subspecies overlap, intergradation has occurred widely. Moreover, the situation has been further confused by the widespread transplanting of various races of White-tailed deer into the geographic ranges belonging to others. However, it can be generally said that the larger forms of *Odocoileus virginianus* are found in the north and the smaller in the south. Thus the maximum size is attained by the three races which extend westwards from the Atlantic coast across southern Canada and northern United States to eastern Oregon. These are: *O.v.borealis* in the east up to Manitoba and Minnesota;

then *O.v.dacotensis* to about the Rockies, which conveniently separate that race from *O.v.ochrourus* which is found to the west of this mountain chain. However, the range of *O.v.ochrourus* does not quite reach the Pacific coast, for in the coastal region of south-west Washington and north-west Oregon the Columbian White-tailed deer *O.v.leucurus* occurs sparingly, and in particular on Puget Island.

The principal habitat of the typical White-tailed deer or Virginian White-tailed deer, *O.v.virginianus* is, as its name would suggest, Virginia and west Virginia, ranging south to central Georgia, southern Alabama and Mississippi, intergrading in the north with *O.v.borealis,* in the west with *O.v.macrourus* and in the south with *O.v. osceola* in southern Alabama and *O.v.seminolus* in northern Florida. Dotted along the eastern coast a further four races have been designated to the islands of Bulls (*O.v.taurinsulae*), Hunting (*O.v.venatorius*), Hilton Head (*O.v.hiltonensis*) and Blackbeard (*O.v.nigribarbis*).

Another insular form *O.v.clavium* occurs in the southern group of Florida Keys, but because of human occupation and some disastrous hurricanes only about 500 are now left. A sixth insular form, *O.v.rothschildi*, is found on Coiba Island which lies off the west coast of Panama.

Whilst sea, marsh-land and open channels may have been successful in segregating these insular forms, intergradation of most of the other races has occurred widely, the extent of overlapping being dependent on the intervening country. For instance, in the southern part of the range of *O.v.texanus* which comes between *O.v.macrourus* in Mississippi and *O.v.couesi* which inhabits Arizona and the Mexican coastal regions of the Gulf of California, there is a mountainous area inhabited by a race known as the Carmen Mountain White-tailed deer *O.v.carminis*. Apparently the ranges of these two subspecies do not overlap. Along the coast of south-east Texas to near the border (Pearl River) of Louisiana is found the Avery Island White-tailed deer *O.v.mcilhennyi*, which intergrades on the west with *O.v.texanus* and on the east with *O.v.osceola*.

Further south, in Mexico, no fewer than ten subspecies are recognised, namely *O.v.veraecrucis* (Veracruz area); *O.v.miquihuanensis, O.v.mexicanus, O.v.toltecus* and *O.v.oaxacensis* in the more central parts; *O.v.sinaloae* and *O.v.acapulcensis* along the Pacific coastal regions; whilst in the south-east corner there is *O.v.yucatanensis* in Yucatán, *O.v.thomasi* and *O.v.nelsoni* in Chiapas, the latter race extending its range eastwards into Guatemala in Central America where a further three races are recognised – namely *O.v.truei* in eastern Nicaragua and *O.v.chiriquensis* in Panama, with *O.v.rothschildi*, as already mentioned, on the adjacent island of Coiba.

The White-tailed deer in South America – generally referred to as Venado – was previously considered a separate species *Odocoileus cariacou* but is now included in *Odocoileus virginianus*. In Brazil the White-tailed deer is referred to by a number of names such as *cariacus, cariacú, amapa* or *veado galheiro*. It is also referred to as the Savannah deer, especially in the Guianas. Its range does not extend to south of about latitude 23°S and it is entirely absent from Argentina, Paraguay, Uruguay and southern Brazil. On the mainland six races have been recognised, whilst on two of the islands off the north coast of Venezuela two other insular types occur, namely *O.v.margaritae* on Margarita Island and *O.v.curassavicus* on Curaçao Island. Dr

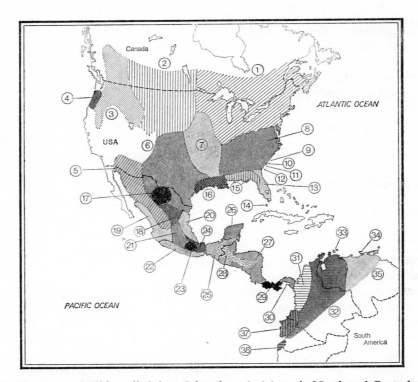

Map 5. The range of White-tailed deer *Odocoileus virginianus* in North and Central America –
(see also p. 53)

(see also p. 53)

1. *Odocoileus virginianus borealis*   South-east Canada and north-east U S A
2. *O.v.dacotensis*   Alberta to north Dakota
3. *O.v.ochrourus*   North-west U S A and Canada
4. *O.v.leucurus*   Oregon and west coast
5. *O.v.couesi*   Arizona
6. *O.v.texanus*   Texas and adjoining States
7. *O.v.macrourus*   Kansas and adjoining States
8. *O.v.virginianus*   Virginia and adjoining States
9. *O.v.taurinsulae*   Bulls Island
10. *O.v.venatorius*   Hunting Island
11. *O.v.hiltonensis*   Hilton Head Island
12. *O.v.nigribarbis*   Blackbeard Island
13. *O.v.seminolus*   Florida
14. *O.v.clavium*   Florida Keys
15. *O.v.osceola*   North-west Florida
16. *O.v.mcilhennyi*   Louisiana
17. *O.v.carminis*   North Mexico
18. *O.v.miquihuanensis*   Central Mexico
19. *O.v.sinaloae*   Mid-west Mexico
20. *O.v.veraecrucis*   East Mexico
21. *O.v.mexicanus*   Central Mexico
22. *O.v.acapulcensis*   South-east Mexico
23. *O.v.oaxancensis*   South Mexico
24. *O.v.toltecus*   South Mexico

(continued opposite)

Hummelinck (*in litt.* 1954) considers that the latter race may also occur 'on the Peninsula of La Goajira in northern Colombia where it is more numerous than on the island'.

On the mainland, the distribution of the six races is approximately as follows: *O.v.cariacou* occurs in north Brazil and French Guiana, and its range probably extends into Dutch Guiana where it may intergrade with *O.v.gymnotis.* The typical locality of this race is stated to be the Savanna area of the lower Orinoco of eastern Venezuela. In western Venezuela *O.v.gymnotis* is replaced by *O.v.goudotii,* which extends its range to the Andes of Colombia. Two other races occur in Colombia – *O.v.tropicalis* which is confined to western parts, and *O.v.ustus* in the extreme south near the border with Ecuador, which is the typical haunt of this last-mentioned race. *O.v.peruvianus* also occurs in southern Ecuador, extending its range south throughout the coastal area to southern Peru. It occurs in all the green valleys running up from the sea, and in the sierras of the western Andes up to an altitude of about 9,800 feet (2,985 metres).

White-tailed deer were introduced to Cuba about 1850, but are not as plentiful as formerly.

The White-tailed deer has a longish white tail from which its name is derived. When alarmed, the tail is raised erect and as the deer bounds away it appears to be waved from side to side as a sign of danger to other deer. Sometimes – and particularly in the past – this deer was often referred to as the Virginian deer, after its name *Odocoileus virginianus.* However, this name should only be used when referring to the typical deer of the eastern states, *O.v.virginianus,* and to be more correct it should be Virginia White-tailed deer. Other names have been Longtailed-deer, Bannertail and American Fallow deer.

As already mentioned, the northern races of White-tail run the largest, and a good buck *O.v.dacotensis* from northern Dakota will stand about 40 inches (102 cms)

25.	*O.v.thomasi*	South-east Mexico
26.	*O.v.yucatanensis*	Honduras
27.	*O.v.truei*	Nicaragua and adjacent States
28.	*O.v.nelsoni*	South Mexico and Guatemala
29.	*O.v.chiriquensis*	Panama
30.	*O.v.rothschildi*	Coiba Island
31.	*O.v.tropicalis*	West Colombia
32.	*O.v.guodotii*	Colombia and western Venezuela
33.	*O.v.curassavicus*	Curaçao Island
34.	*O.v.margaritae*	Margarita Island
35.	*O.v.gymnotis*	Venezuela and the Guianas
36.	*O.v.cariacou*	French Guiana and northern Brazil
37.	*O.v.ustus*	Ecuador (Andes)
38.	*O.v.peruvianus*	Peru and marginally

White-tailed deer have been introduced to New Zealand (South Island) and to a number of other areas outside their normal habitat. See also Map 6, page 53

Part based on map 491 E. Raymond Hall and K. R. Kelson (*The Mammals of North America*, Vol. II)

at the shoulder, and may weigh just over 300 lbs (136 kilograms) with exceptional animals reaching 400 lbs (181 kilograms). At the other end of the scale, some of the Central American races are hardly as big as the European Roe deer and may weigh only about 40 lbs (18 kilograms). The largest of the South American races is *O.v. cariacou* of Brazil, which stands about 32 inches (81 cms) high at the shoulder. Of the two insular forms in South America, the deer of Margarita Island, Venezuela, *O.v.margaritae*, is the smallest, the average shoulder height being about 24 inches (61 cms).

In summer the general colour of most subspecies is one of reddish brown with a whitish patch on the throat and white inside the ear. The belly and inside the thighs are white as is also the underside of the tail. In winter the red coat is replaced by a more sombre one of grey to greyish brown. Colour variation between subspecies is only slight. Fawns are spotted at birth.

Although some of the races of White-tailed deer are similar in size to some Mule deer or Black-tailed deer, there are a number of features which should help to differentiate between the two species. The metatarsal gland below the hock on the outside trailing edge of the hind leg on the White-tailed deer is much shorter in length, extending to only about one inch (2·54 cms) as compared to about 3 inches (7·62 cms) on the Black-tailed deer, and 5 inches (12·7 cms) on the Mule deer. The tail is also longer, and lighter coloured, whilst the antlers of a *typical* adult White-tailed buck should never be confused with those of the Mule deer. In typical adult antlers of White-tail the tines do not bifurcate as in the Mule deer and the beams tend to curve forward and turn inwards more than in the case of the other deer. As mentioned on page 47, however, some antlers of the Black-tailed deer *O.h.sitkensis* are difficult to distinguish from those of the White-tailed type.

Most White-tailed bucks in North America shed their antlers during January and February and as is the case with other species of deer, the first 'shedders' are the older bucks. Some bucks with shed antlers have been recorded in Pennsylvania as early as late November or early December, whilst immature or animals in ill-health may not shed the antlers until late March or even early April. In South America, however, the antlers are shed irregularly and at almost any season of the year one may see a buck in velvet. It is difficult to generalise with a species that covers such a tremendous territory. Female deer with antlers, although rare, have been recorded.

The new antlers of North American White-tailed deer start to grow in April or May, becoming hard by September when the velvet is shed. It has been shown that the size of the antler is dependent upon the age of the individual deer, the quantity and quality of the forage available and hereditary background. Until a buck is mature, there should be an increase in the number of points in both antlers with an increase in age.

As to the number of points grown on the antlers of White-tailed deer, this varies enormously, and whilst the most usual number will be about seven or eight, some abnormal antlers may bear as many as seventeen points or more. The majority of South American specimens bear few points.

The rutting season, which in North America takes place from October to early

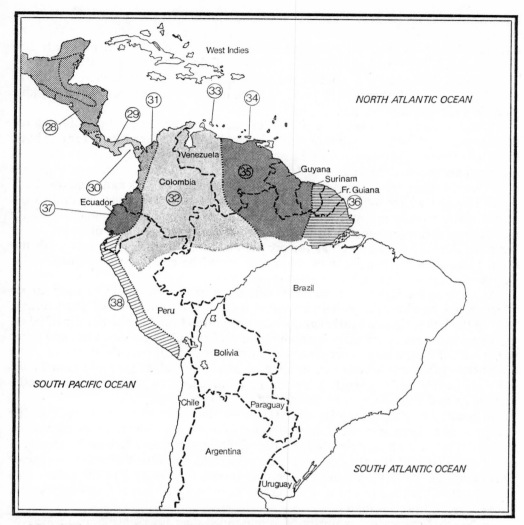

Map 6. The range of White-tailed deer *Odocoileus virginianus* in SOUTH AMERICA

28.	*O.v.nelsoni*	South Mexico and Guatemala
29.	*O.v.chiriquensis*	Panama
30.	*O.v.rothschildi*	Coiba Island
31.	*O.v.tropicalis*	West Colombia
32.	*O.v.guodotii*	Colombia and west Venezuela
33.	*O.v.curassavicus*	Curaçao Island
34.	*O.v.margaritae*	Margareta Island
35.	*O.v.gymnotis*	Venezuela and the Guianas
36.	*O.v.cariacou*	French Guiana and northern Brazil
37.	*O.v.ustus*	Ecuador (Andes)
38.	*O.v.peruvianus*	Peru and marginally

E

December, reaches its height during November. Unlike the Wapiti or Caribou the White-tailed buck does not collect a large harem together, but generally runs with an individual doe for a day or two before moving off in search of a fresh mate. In this way, an adult buck will mate with a number of does during the rutting season.

In South America the season of the rut varies according to locality, and fawns have been seen at all times of the year. In Peru, however, most rutting seems to take place in February and March.

At this season, fights between rival bucks are everyday events but it is rare for these contests to end in serious injury to either and it is quite exceptional for one buck to be killed by another. Sometimes, however, an enraged buck may savage a doe, and although instances of this nature seldom occur in the wild state, as the doe is able to elude her pursuers, there have been numerous such cases in parks and enclosures.

During the winter months the deer of both sexes will mix together, and in the north, where winters are more severe, seasonal movements from summer to winter ranges are more pronounced. In such winter ranges yarding areas of heavy cover serve the deer for food as well as for protection from storms. These deer yards are often cedar swamps, but in some areas they could be conifer swamps with cedar varying in amount from none to solid stands.

As soon as the snows start to disappear, the deer move to their summer ranges which could be almost anywhere provided there is an abundance of good forage. During the late spring and early summer deer are often found in the vicinity of lakes, ponds and streams where there is an abundance of succulent grasses, lilies and other water plants. As the season progresses and these foods disappear the deer will move elsewhere – often into woods surrounding an area where algae grows in abundance. When these dry up in August, there will be a movement to areas that produce the early mast and fruit, such as chestnuts, etc.

In South America, during the dry season on the coast, the deer remain in the valleys so as to keep near water, as well as to make regular visits to crops planted by Indians. They are also extremely fond of a fruit from a tree which in Venezuela is called *moquillo,* and also the pods of the corocaro tree. Towards the end of December or January, as the rains commence, the deer retreat further up into the valleys and eat the natural grasses until the dry season returns about May, when they descend, once more, to lower altitudes.

In North America the majority of White-tailed deer fawns are born in May or early June, twins being common and even triplets on occasions. One or two cases of quadruplet embryos within a doe have been recorded but whether the doe would have been able to successfully rear all four after birth is extremely doubtful.

During their first few days the fawns are helpless in flight, and so rely on hiding for protection against predators. It has often been stated with some justification that fawns during their first few days of life have no scent. To prove this, tests have been made with a dog passing close by the known location of a very young fawn, and the dog has not paid the slightest attention to the little deer. Whether or not this proves the point, it does seem probable that young deer of all species are scentless.

However, this scentless period is of short duration for sporting hounds have little difficulty in winding or picking up the trail of older animals. Indeed, deer have what appears to be a natural instinct to leave an individual odor in their tracks. This is accomplished by urinating down the inside of their hind legs so that the fluid saturates the hairs of the tarsal gland. This habit appears within a week or ten days after birth, and it is interesting to watch a small fawn try to hold its heels together, move its legs so as to rub these glands together, and still keep its balance. . . . On numerous occasions one of the authors has watched a doe track her fawn to its bed. This ability may result from the habit of scenting its legs with urine together with the secretion from the tarsal glands (Severinghaus and Cheatum, 1956).

Normally silent, the deer occasionally snorts or whistles when alarmed, and will shriek out when injured or captured.

As to the White-tailed deer population of the United States, no one really knows, but from the limited population figures that are published by states that make an annual census it must be over 8,000,000 deer. No figures are available for Canada, Mexico or Central America. In addition to hunters, who kill over a million deer per annum, many thousands of deer will also be taken by natural predators which are the same as for the Mule deer (page 47). However, about 100 hunters per annum fail to return home after hunting, having been mistaken for a deer by a fellow hunter!

Mosquitos, ticks and deer flies are among the foes of White-tailed deer and at times the deer avoid their attention by sinking themselves in mud and water. The nasal bot fly often causes great discomfort to a deer, and many a beast has been killed by hunters with its nasal passages crammed full of larvae.

If the present White-tailed deer population in the United States is in the region of 8,000,000 this is but a fifth of the number Ernest Thompson Seton (1910) estimated it was in 1818 – about 40,000,000 deer. During this period a great slaughter was taking place and as a result, by the end of the last century the stock of deer had reached a very low ebb, and in some states were virtually exterminated.

During the early years of the present century, however, a number of refuges were established, and the deer re-introduced to areas where the species no longer existed. In areas where hunting was permitted, a 'Buck law' was introduced which permitted the killing of male deer only. This resulted in a rapid increase in deer stocks, and indeed in some areas the deer became too abundant, which resulted in depleted ranges, starving animals and survivors of poor quality. It was not long before some of the State Game Commissions saw the folly of the 'buck law' and gave authority to open the hunting season on does and fawns. Despite this, and the increased hunting pressure of today, deer stocks in North America continue to increase, and apart from one or two races such as the Keys deer *O.v.clavium* of the Florida Keys, the species is in no danger whatsoever.

BROCKET DEER *Mazama*   Map p. 56

The Brocket deer, whose range extends from Mexico in the north to Argentina in South America has a wide distribution in the latter country, occurring in every republic except Chile and Uruguay. In South America four species and some twenty subspecies are found, with a further race in the West Indies.

In Mexico, two species of Brocket are recognised, the Red Brocket *Mazama*

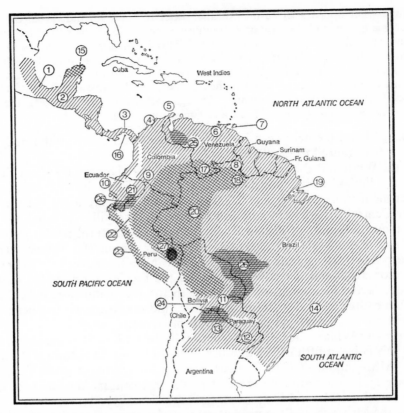

Map 7. The range* of Brocket deer *Mazama* in CENTRAL and SOUTH AMERICA

RED BROCKET. *Mazama americana*

1.	*Mazama americana temama*	Mexico
2.	*M.a.cerasina*	Guatemala to Costa Rica
3.	*M.a.reperticia*	Panama to South America
4.	*M.a.zetta*	North Colombia
5.	*M.a.carrikeri*	North Colombia
6.	*M.a.sheila*	North Venezuela
7.	*M.a.trinitatis*	Trinidad Island
8.	*M.a.americana*	North-east of South America
9.	*M.a.zamora*	South-east Colombia to north-east Peru
10.	*M.a.gualea*	West Ecuador
11.	*M.a.sarae*	Bolivia and north-west Argentina
12.	*M.a.rufa*	Paraguay and Argentina
13.	*M.a.rosii*	North Argentina
14.	*M.a.jucunda*	Brazil

(continued opposite)

*The exact range of the various species and subspecies of the genus *Mazama* has never been fully studied and this map is only an indication of the general range of the four species: *Mazama americana* (Red Brocket); *Mazama rufina* (Little Red Brocket); *Mazama gouazoubira* (Brown Brocket) and *Mazama chunyi* (Dwarf Brocket). Overlapping occurs in many areas.

americana temama, which inhabits the virgin rain forest of the south-east, and the Brown Brocket *Mazama gouazoubira pandora* which is found mostly in Yucatán. It is not known if the range of this latter Brocket extends as far south as British Honduras or Guatemala but the range of *M.a.temama* does reach British Honduras.

Two other races of the Red Brocket also occur in Central America, *M.a.cerasina,* which has a widespread distribution in all republics except Panama where it is replaced by *M.a.reperticia.* An insular form of the Brown Brocket, *M.g.permira,* occurs on the Isla San José which lies off the coast of Panama.

The Red Brocket, *Mazama americana,* which over its entire range is divided into fourteen subspecies, is represented by ten in South America with a further race on Trinidad Island in the West Indies. It has the widest distribution of the four Brocket species in South America, followed closely by the Brown Brocket *Mazama gouazoubira,* of which eight of its ten subspecies occur. In addition, both races of the Little Red Brocket *Mazama rufina* and the Dwarf Brocket *Mazama chunyi* are represented.

The approximate distribution of the various species and races of Brockets in South America is as follows:

RED BROCKET *Mazama americana*

M.a.americana Brazil (N); Guianas; Venezuela (SE)
M.a.rufa Argentina (N); Brazil (SW); Paraguay
M.a.jucunda Brazil (SE)
M.a.zetta Colombia (N)
M.a.sheila Venezuela (N)
M.a.gualea Ecuador (W)
M.a.zamora Colombia (S); Ecuador (E); Peru (NE)
M.a.rosii Argentina (N)
M.a.sarae Argentina (NW); Bolivia (S)
M.a.carrikeri Colombia (N)

BROWN BROCKET. *Mazama gouazoubira*

15. *M.gouazoubira pandora*	Yucatán, Mexico
16. *M.g.permira*	Isla San José
17. *M.g.citus*	Venezuela
18. *M.g.nemorivaga*	South-east Venezuela and the Guianas
19 *M.g.mexianae*	Mexiana Island
20. *M.g.superciliaris*	Brazil
21. *M.g.murelia*	South-west Colombia and Ecuador
22. *M.g.tschudii*	Peru
23. *M.g.whitelyi*	Peru
24. *M.g.gouazoubira*	Paraguay and North Argentina

LITTLE RED BROCKET. *Mazama rufina*

25. *M.rufina bricenii*	North Venezuela
26. *M.r.rufina*	Ecuador, South-east Brazil and adjacent republics

DWARF BROCKET. *Mazama chunyi*

27. *M.chunyi*	Andes of north Bolivia and south Peru

LITTLE RED BROCKET *Mazama rufina*

> *M.r.rufina* Argentina (NE); Bolivia; Brazil (S); Ecuador; Paraguay; Peru
> *M.r.bricenii* Venezuela (N)

BROWN BROCKET *Mazama gouazoubira*

> *M.g.gouazoubira* Argentina (N); Paraguay
> *M.g.nemorivaga* Brazil (NE); Guianas; Venezuela (SE)
> *M.g.superciliaris* Brazil
> *M.g.tschudii* Peru
> *M.g.whitelyi* Peru (S)
> *M.g.mexianae* Mexiana Isle, Brazil
> *M.g.citus* Venezuela
> *M.g.murelia* Colombia (SW); Ecuador (E)

DWARF BROCKET *Mazama chunyi*

> *M.chunyi* Bolivia (N); Peru (S)

Only one Brocket occurs in the West Indies – *M.a.trinitatis* on Trinidad Island.

Except for their colour the Red and Brown Brockets are very similar both in size and habit. Leopold (1959) is of the opinion, however, that 'the two types are genetically distinct'. The general body colour of the Red Brocket is, as its name would suggest, redder than the Brown Brocket of the Yucatán peninsula. The neck is greyish whilst the underparts are white. The tail, about 5 inches (13 cms) in length, is brown dorsally, with white underneath. According to Leopold (1959) the females are virtually as large as the males, and he gives the live weight of a yearling from Vera Cruz as being 17 kilograms (about 37½ lbs.)

The colour of the Little Red Brocket seems to vary from one locality to another, being described as 'dark coloured, occasionally toast brown in colour, and some beasts a deep chestnut colour'. The head and lower limbs are always much darker and in some animals almost black.

It is certain that intergradation occurs in all the limit zones between two races which are adjacent. The fawns are spotted at birth. Twins probably occur more frequently with the Brown than with the Red Brocket.

The general colour of the head and body of the Dwarf Brocket *Mazama chunyi* is described by P. Hershkovitz (1959) who named the species, as being 'cinnamon brown to rufous brown, shoulders and outer side of limbs more uniformly brown than back . . . throat, chest, inner sides of fore and hind legs buff to ochraceous-tawny; belly white; tail short . . . sharply defined white beneath'.

The same authority suggests that

> Peruvian specimens from San Juan (1,500 meters) and Tío (2,000 meters) are darker, more reddish brown on dorsal surface, more reddish on underparts, and with pelage

harsher than the type. . . . Available material suggests that the difference in color between the pale holo-type of the temperate zone of the Andes in Bolivia and the darker individuals of the sub-tropical zone of the same slope of the Andes in Peru, is clinal.

Compared with the other Brockets, the Dwarf Brocket is distinguished from the much larger Red Brocket 'by absence of whorl or reversed direction of hair growth on nape, absence of supraorbital streak or circumorbital band, and by the much shorter tail'. It is much smaller than the Brown Brocket, darker in colour and has much shorter tail. The Little Red Brocket differs from the Dwarf Brocket 'by its deeper red or reddish-black body colour, contrastingly darker metapodials, and the extremely large preorbital gland . . .'.

In Peru the Dwarf Brocket is found in Cusco and Puno in the south-east, where destruction of habitat is a serious threat to its survival.

The Brocket bucks have simple spike antlers which, in the Red and Brown species, are seldom more than about 4 to 5 inches (about 10 to 13 cms) in length. The antlers of the Little Red Brocket are shorter, seldom exceeding 3 inches (7·6 cms) in length. In the antlers of very old animals there is sometimes evidence of slight bifurcation, but such examples must be considered very rare.

There does not appear to be any fixed season for the shedding and development of the antlers and this irregularity has caused some observers to suggest that these deer never shed their antlers.

The largest species in South America is the Red Brocket *M.americana* and some of the races, such as *M.a.rosii* and *M.a.rufa*, will reach about 28 inches (71 cms) in height at the shoulder. It is still fairly abundant in many parts of its range, but it is subject to intensive commercial hunting for its hide as well as for food.

Next in size is the Brown Brocket *M.gouazoubira* and whilst some races stand about two feet (61 cms) high at the shoulder, the height of *Mazama gouazoubira nemorivaga* is only 14 or 15 inches (35 to 38 cms). There is not much difference, therefore, in the size of *M.g.nemorivaga* and either the Little Red Brocket *M.rufina*, or the Dwarf Brocket *M.chunyi*.

The Brocket is an animal which lives in dense thickets on the mountain, generally wandering around singly or in pairs, and only emerging from the thickets on the approach of nightfall or in the early morning, to seek the cultivated fields and farms, where it causes great damage.

It is an expert swimmer, and it is not unusual to see it crossing rivers of 300 metres (328 yards) in width.

Not much is known about the habits of the Little Red Brocket *M.rufina* which has a rather limited range. It is, however, an animal that prefers to live in mountainous terrain, and in Ecuador is found up to an altitude of about 12,500 feet (3,800 metres) above sea level. The Red Brocket, on the other hand, keeps more to dense thickets which is in contrast to the Brown Brocket which prefers more open terrain.

All Brockets, of course, are small enough to have many natural predators, which include the puma, jaguar and ocelot, as well as some of the larger birds of prey such as the Crested eagle. Near the villages the domestic dog is probably their worst enemy. The deer is also extensively hunted by the natives but so adept are they at dodging away, relatively few are killed. Although Brockets frequent dense cover during the day, they emerge into the open at night to feed. Little is known of their food preferences, but where cultivated crops are at hand, they are fond of melons, beans, chilli and corn. In the forest a variety of wild fruits is generally available throughout the year and no doubt these figure very largely in their diet.

HUEMUL *Hippocamelus*   Map p. 61

A deer which is found only in South America is the Huemul or Guamal of the Andes, of which two species are recognised – *Hippocamelus bisulcus* in the Andes of Chile and western Argentina, and *Hippocamelus antisensis* of Ecuador, Peru, Bolivia and extreme north-west Argentina. These two species are separated by a wide gap represented by that part of Chile north of the Colchagua province, and by the provinces of Mendoza and San Juan in Argentina. Intergradation is, therefore, impossible.

The Huemul, standing about 3 feet (91 cms) high at the shoulder, is of a relatively robust build with large mule-like ears, short tail and, in the case of adult males, simple forked antlers of about 11 inches (28 cms) in length. Very occasionally a pair of antlers will bear more than four points, but such heads are abnormal.

In colour the Huemul of the southern Andes, *H.bisulcus,* is dark brown, which turns somewhat greyish brown in winter. At close quarters the general body appearance is a mottled black and yellow colour with white on the extremity of the lower jaw as well as the inside of the ears and on the lower part of the tail. The colour of the more northern species *H.antisensis,* which is slightly smaller in size, is paler, with fewer dark coloured hairs about the face. The bifurcation on the antler is also closer to the coronet on the latter species. The young of both species are born without any trace of spots.

As already mentioned, the range of *Hippocamelus bisulcus* – often referred to as the Chilean Huemul – is in the southern part of the Andes chain that lies between Chile and Argentina, extending northwards to the province of Colchagua (about latitude 34°S). Formerly it reached the Atlantic coast in Santa Cruz between the River Deseado and Santa Cruz but it is now quite extinct in this area. In summer this deer is to be found high up in the mountains, whilst in winter it descends to the woods.

The range of the Peruvian Huemul *Hippocamelus antisensis,* extends southwards along the high Andes chain from Ecuador in the north (south of the Equator), through Peru and western Bolivia into northern Chile and north-west Argentina as far south as Catamarca province (about latitude 27·30°S). Throughout most of its range the Peruvian Huemul – often referred to as *taruca* or *taruga* – is scarce, and is seldom found below 13,000 feet (3,960 metres) above sea level.

During the rainy season (December to May) the Huemul move to the highest part of the Andes, attracted to eat the green pastures that grow between the rocks of the high peaks. Hunters, therefore, have to reach great heights and travel immense distances before this deer can be successfully shot at this season. In consequence the number of deer killed by white hunters in Peru alone is probably very small,

Map 8. The range of Huemul or Guemal *Hippocamelus* in SOUTH AMERICA

1. *Hippocamelus antisensis*   Northern Andes
2. *H.bisculus*   Southern Andes

The range of Marsh deer *Blastocerus dichotomus* in SOUTH AMERICA

A. *Blastocerus dichotomus*   Central Brazil to North Argentina

but the Indians who live throughout the year at these altitudes undoubtedly take a considerable toll. The deer has few natural predators, the principal one being the mountain puma which take a few fawns. On rare occasions, also, the mountain fox may take a newly born fawn. The habits of this deer are much the same as the Chilean Huemul except that it seldom enters the woods.

The date of the rut varies according to locality but in the northern part of the Andes it takes place between June and August. The fawns, normally one but occasionally twins, are born during the months of February to August depending on when the rut took place.

MARSH DEER *Blastocerus dichotomus*   Map p. 61

The largest of the South American deer is the Marsh deer, which is found throughout much of southern Brazil, Paraguay and north-eastern Argentina. It also occurs very sparingly in parts of Uruguay where it may even now have completely disappeared.

Standing about the height of a small Red deer, the Marsh deer is a bright rufous chestnut colour in summer, which turns to a browner shade in winter. The lower portions of the legs are dark and there is a black band on the muzzle and upper lip. The ears are large, and filled internally with woolly white hair. The tail is of medium length and bushy. The young are unspotted.

Although eight is the average number of points on Marsh deer antlers, 10-or 12-pointers are by no means rare, whilst abnormal heads bearing up to twenty-eight points have been recorded. A good pair of antlers, which will consist of a terminal fork on the main beam and a bifurcated brow rather similar to those of the Mule deer, will measure about 24 inches (61 cms) in length.

This deer, as its name implies, is fond of marshy ground and is seldom found far from water and an ideal terrain would be such places surrounded by mountainous country. Very occasionally it has been referred to as 'Delta' deer or 'Swamp' deer whilst other local names are '*Pantanos*' deer and '*Guazú pucú*' deer.

The stags have no fixed season for shedding or reproduction of their antlers, and it *may* well be that there is no fixed breeding season either, which would account for the belief that gestation lasts twelve months. Stags, therefore, with antlers either fully hard and developed or in various stages of growth can be seen at almost any season of the year. The majority of stags, however, do seem to rut during the months of October and November.

Apart from man, the principal natural predators are the puma and jaguar.

PAMPAS DEER *Ozotoceros bezoarticus*   Map p. 65

Considerably smaller than the Marsh deer is the Pampas deer *Ozotoceros bezoarticus,* of which three subspecies are recognised – the typical form *O.b.bezoarticus* in Brazil; *O.b.leucogaster* in Paraguay, northern Argentina, southern Bolivia and western Brazil; and *O.b.celer* in the pampas of Argentina.

The Pampas deer, which in South America is generally referred to as Guazú-tí, signifying *white deer,* was given the name by the Guaranese on account of 'the inferior parts of the animal being white' (D'Azara, 1801). At the present time in Argentina, it often goes by the name of *venado,* with the females being referred to as *gama.* The Brazilians call it *veado campeiro* (camping deer) or *veado branco* (field deer). This deer has also been called *the stinking deer* because of its strong odour which, according to Roosevelt (1914) 'can be made out at a considerable distance'.

Without doubt the Pampas deer is the most elegant of all the South American deer. Standing about the height of a Roe buck (27 inches – 69 cms – at the shoulder) the general colour of its short, smooth hair is yellowish brown, with the inside of the ears and under-parts white, and with dark brown to almost black hairs on the upper surface of the tail. According to Dr Cabrera the general colour of the upper parts of *O.b.celer* is somewhat lighter than that of *O.b.leucogaster,* being described as 'pale cinnamon buff' as compared to 'light reddish brown' of the latter. There is 'no noticeable difference' between summer and winter pelage. On rare occasions, albino *O.b.celer* have been seen.

The formation of the hairs is such that there is a whorl at the base of the neck and another on the centre of the back which allows the hair on the withers to be directed forwards. This hair formation is very evident in the new-born fawn which, like most young deer, is spotted at birth.

The Pampas deer carries a symmetrical head of six points, very similar to that of a Roe deer.

The Pampas deer (*O.b.celer*) was at one time common in the northern and central pampas zones of Argentina but today, apart from a few small colonies that are protected on private estates at General Lavalle and at La Corona, Villanueva in Buenos Aires province, and at central San Luis, it is almost extinct. A few also remain in the southern part of Mendoza, but it is described as 'very rare'. This subspecies also occurs sparingly in Uruguay.

In the northern part of Argentina and adjacent Paraguay another race, *O.b. leucogaster,* is recognised, and in particular it frequents the province of Santiago del Estero and the northern parts of the province of Santa Fé and Corrientes. Its range extends to the south Mato Grosso district of western Brazil, but does not appear east of the River Uruguay. In central and northern Brazil practically up to the Amazon River, the typical form *O.b.bezoarticus* occurs in most areas that are suitable for this deer – namely the open grassy plains.

Pampas deer are generally to be found in small groups of five to fifteen animals, except during the fawning season, when the does become more solitary. The majority of fawns seem to be born between September and November, but fawns have been reported for almost any month of the year, more particularly on the pampas to the south of Buenos Aires. Physical conditions in the pampas are quite different from those in the Gran Chaco, and this may have some influence on the subject.

However there appears to be some variation in the dates of antler shedding, and although the majority will be discarded in May, some bucks retain theirs a month or two longer and well into the South American winter. It is possible, therefore, that some bucks rut later than others, thus resulting in April fawns.

As the name suggests, this is a deer of the open plains and it avoids, as far as possible, woodlands and mountainous country. During the winter they move about singly or in pairs, but in the spring they start to collect together into small herds, and it is not unusual to see one or two dozen together. Like the *Guazú pucú* (Marsh deer) this species prefers to come out during the night to feed. During the day it remains hidden in the high grass or in some fields among the tall grass or between bushes. Early in the morning it is fond of lying in the sun, and then going down to the river to bathe, always searching for the cleanest water it can find.

PUDU *Pudu*   Map p. 65

The lower Andes is the home of the Pudu – the smallest of the South American deer – of which two species *Pudu pudu* and *Pudu mephistophiles* are recognised, the latter consisting of two races.

The range of the Pudu in western South America follows a somewhat disjointed pattern, for some 2,000 miles (3,218 kilometres) separates the two species, the range of *Pudu pudu* being in parts of Argentina and Chile, and that of *P.mephistophiles* being in Ecuador, Colombia and extreme north of Peru.

In the southern part of its range *P.pudu* occurs in the deep forests of the slopes of the southern Andes and is generally found not far from water. It is probably most numerous in the deep forests of south central Chile but nowhere can it be described as plentiful. There are also a few on the island of Chiloé, but these are confined mainly to the southern and uninhabited part of the island and are rare. It is non-migratory.

Little is known about the northern species *P.mephistophiles* which is divided into two races, *P.m.mephistophiles* in Ecuador and the extreme north of Peru, and *P.m. wetmorei* in Colombia. The deer was originally made known from a specimen taken on the paramo of Papallacta, Ecuador, very few examples of which have since found their way into collections. In Peru it occurs in the Upper Huallaga basin, where it is relentlessly hunted with dogs and guns, so it is feared that it may not survive there long. Destruction of habitat for settlement is also a serious threat.

The Pudu *P.pudu,* which the Chilean calls *venadito,* stands little more than about 14 to 15 inches (about 35 to 38 cms) high at the shoulder, and may weigh about 20 to 24 lbs (about 9 to 11 kilograms). The bucks have small spike antlers of about 3 to 4 inches (7 to 10 cms) in length.

There seems to be a certain amount of colour variation among members of the same species, for W. H. Osgood in *The Mammals of Chile* (1943) wrote:

Our specimens (which included some animals taken on Chiloé Island), taken in January, which is the season of midsummer, show wide differences in coloration probably representing two different pelages. One of these might be called a rufous pelage or phase and the other a dark brown one. The first has a broad band from the top of the head to the tail bright clear Hazel or Cinnamon Rufous, the sides being paler and finely speckled by reason of sub-apical dark bands on the hairs. The legs and feet are pale, nearly clear Cinnamon Rufous. In the other phase, which appears to be a fresh coat, the dorsal band is less defined and its color is deep Burnt Umber or Vandyke Brown inclining to blackish. The sides are only slightly lighter, owing to numerous hairs with

Map 9. The range of Pudu deer *Pudu* in SOUTH AMERICA

A. *Pudu pudu*   Chile and Argentina
B. *P.mephistophiles mephistophiles*   Ecuador and Peru
C. *P.m.wetmorei*   Colombia

The range of Pampas deer *Ozotoceros bezoarticus* in SOUTH AMERICA

1. *Ozotoceros bezoarticus bezoarticus*   Brazil
2. *O.b.leucogaster*   Central South America
3. *O.b.celer*   Argentina (Pampas)

narrow light tips. The feet and lower legs are hazel with a slight mixture of blackish in front.

The fawns are spotted.

The northern Pudu *P.mephistophiles* is slightly larger in size than *P.pudu* and its pelage is described as being reddish brown, with the body tawny coloured on the neck and almost black on the head and feet.

Pudu live in small groups and it is unusual to see single specimens. Its predators include puma, fox and condors.

Little is known about the breeding habits of this little deer, but the majority of fawns are probably born between November and January. Normally the doe produces but one fawn, but twins also occur.

EXOTIC DEER

A number of species of exotic deer have been introduced and the majority have acclimatised themselves well.

Mention has already been made on page 11 to the introduction of REINDEER *Rangifer tarandus tarandus* from Europe to Alaska and northern Canada. An attempt to acclimatise Reindeer *R.t.tarandus* in Michigan was a complete failure.

A number of years ago some European RED DEER *Cervus elaphus* were introduced to an estate in Kentucky, and by 1955 the number there was said to be about 120 head. This species has also been successfully introduced to South America and some extremely fine trophies have been taken in Argentina. The original deer from Europe reached Argentina about 1916.

SIKA DEER *Cervus nippon* has also acclimatised itself well on many estates from Michigan in the north to Texas in the south. In the latter State about fifty Sika deer range the Rickenbacker Ranch (about 2,700 acres or 1,092 hectares) near San Antonio, Texas, whilst others have been introduced to Nebraska. In Michigan Sika deer are quite capable of withstanding a winter temperature as low as 40 degrees below zero.

A herd of about fifty FALLOW DEER *Dama dama* is kept on the Rickenbacker Ranch in Texas, but the deer do not fare too well because, it is thought, of the persistent drought conditions. Fallow deer, however, have done well on the Prudenville Estate in Michigan despite the fact that winter temperatures sometimes fall to as low as 40 degrees below zero. Fallow have also been introduced to estates in Nebraska, Kentucky and Alabama, as well as to a few private estates in Argentina and Chile in South America.

Two other species of deer that have been introduced to the Rickenbacker Ranch are the SWAMP DEER or BARASINGHA *Cervus duvauceli* and the SAMBAR *Cervus unicolor*. According to Rickenbacker (*in litt.* 1955) the Swamp deer 'are frail and weak, and not good breeders, whilst the Sambar dislike the heat and spend the summer hiding in wooded canyons, coming out at night'.

AXIS DEER or CHITAL *Axis axis* have also done well in a number of places, which include the Rickenbacker Ranch already mentioned where they are said to be hardier than the introduced Fallow deer. During the 1930s some Axis deer escaped from an estate in Volusia County, Florida, and a number are now leading a feral existence. Since 1951 these feral deer have been protected by a state law.

In 1867 some Axis deer were transhipped from India via Japan to Hawaii as a gift to an Hawaiian king. Although there have been no further introductions, the species thrived, and a population of about 4,000 deer now inhabit the following three islands: Oahu, Molokai and Lanai. On Molokai, where the deer population is about 3,000, the hunting pressure is greatest and in consequence the deer only venture into the open country at night to feed, retiring into dense forest during the day for protection. On the island of Lanai the deer are frequently found in the vicinity of Algaroba trees *Prosopis chilensis* which provides them with both cover and food when the seed pods are dropped. Apart from man, their only enemy on these islands is the domestic dog.

Axis deer have been introduced to a few estates in Argentina and Brazil, but they are few in number and exist only in semi-confinement.

On 19th June 1961, and again on 12th June 1962, and 13th April 1966 a total of thirty-five MULE DEER *Odocoileus hemionus columbianus* were released on Kauai Island in Hawaii, and the population appears to be well established (Tomich 1969).

5

The Deer of Europe
and Northern Asia

Some twelve species and over forty subspecies of deer are indigenous to Europe and northern Asia – an area which can loosely be described as the Palaearctic or northern part of the Old World. In its eastern limits it includes Japan, Tibet, most of China and countries to the north. With but two exceptions, the Sika deer and Musk deer, all these deer occur approximately north of latitude 30°N. As regards the two exceptions, latitudes 16°N in Vietnam for the former and 22°N for the latter, mark the extent of their range in a southerly direction.

With the exception of the Musk deer – which is antlerless – and the Sika deer which is normally 8-tined, the antlers of all the other Palaearctic deer are inclined to be elaborate and multipointed, with pronounced palmation in two species, the Elk and Fallow deer. Even the Roe, normally 6-pointed, can be included in this category, because the pearling on many antlers, particularly from Siberia, is very pronounced.

Included among the twelve species are ten which are *indigenous* nowhere else in the world, although some of them, such as Red deer, Sika deer and Fallow deer have been introduced to countries in the southern hemisphere, which include Australia, New Zealand and South America. The range of the other three – Elk, Wapiti and Reindeer – extends into North America, where they are referred to as Moose, Elk (Wapiti) and Caribou, respectively.

The twelve indigenous species of deer in this region are as follows:

	Species		
RED DEER	*Cervus elaphus*	12 subspecies	pp. 69–73
WAPITI	*Cervus canadensis*	7 subspecies	pp. 73–6
THOROLD'S DEER	*Cervus albirostris*		pp. 76–7
SIKA DEER	*Cervus nippon*	13 subspecies	pp. 77–81
ROE DEER	*Capreolus capreolus*	3 subspecies	pp. 81–6

1(a) Fallow buck *Dama dama dama* in November

1(b) Melanistic Fallow deer *D.d. dama* in summer pelage

2(a) Melanistic Fallow buck *D.dama dama* in late autumn

2(b) Menil-coloured Fallow buck *D.d.dama*
with antlers still in velvet during July

2(c) Young white-coloured Fallow buck *D.d.dama*

3(a) Persian Fallow buck *Dama dama mesopotamica*

3(b) Persian Fallow doe *D.d.mesopotamica*

4(a) Adult bull Moose *Alces alces americana* in North America

4(b) Young bull Moose *A.a. andersoni* in Alberta

5(a) Adult bull Elk *Alces alces*
      alces in Sweden

5(b) Rear view of adult bull Elk
      A.a.alces in Sweden

6(a) Bull Reindeer *Rangifer tarandus tarandus* from Scandinavia

6(b) Woodland Caribou *Rangifer tarandus caribou* in the autumn

7(a) Barren-ground Caribou *Rangifer tarandus granti* during September in Alaska

7(b) Barren-ground Caribou *R.t.granti* in migration during July in the interior of Alaska

8(a) Red deer *Cervus elaphus scoticus* during the rut in late September

8(b) Hangul or Kashmir stag *Cervus elaphus hanglu* (from an original painting by W. H. Riddell)

8(c) Red deer stag *Cervus elaphus* in Woburn Park

9(a) Bull Wapiti *Cervus canadensis nelsoni*

9(b) Altai Wapiti *Cervus canadensis songaricus*
       (Drawn by J. Smit)

9(c) Thorold's deer stag *Cervus albirostris*
       (Drawn by J. Smit)

10(a) Japanese Sika deer *Cervus nippon nippon* during the rut

10(b) Japanese Sika deer stag in February
(front view)

10(c) Japanese Sika deer stag in February – rear view
showing white caudal patch and light-coloured
patches about the hocks

11(a) Kerama Sika deer stag *Cervus nippon keramae*

11(b) Manchurian Sika deer stag *Cervus nippon mantchuricus*

12(b) Formosan Sika deer stag
C.n.taiouanus in July

12(a) Formosan Sika deer stag
Cervus nippon taiouanus in the
autumn

12(c) Dybowski's Sika deer *C.n.*
hortulorum

12(d) Shou or Wallich's deer *Cervus*
elaphus wallichi

13(a) Eld's deer *Cervus eldi eldi*

13(b) Siamese Eld's deer *C.e. siamensis* in the Parc Zoologique, Paris

13(c) Schomburgk's deer *Cervus schomburgki*

14(a) Swamp deer hind *Cervus duvauceli duvauceli*

14(b) Swamp deer stag *C.d.duvauceli*

14(c) Chital or Axis deer stag *Axis axis axis* in San Diego Zoo

15 Chital or Axis deer *Axis axis axis* at Whipsnade Zoo

16(a) Hog deer stag *Axis porcinus porcinus*

16(b) Hog deer stag *A.p.porcinus*

17(a) Kuhl's deer or Bawean deer stag *Axis kuhlii*

17(b) Kuhl's deer or Bawean deer hind *Axis kuhlii*

18(b) Group of Ceylonese Sambar stags *C.u.unicolor*

18(a) Ceylonese Sambar stag
       Cervus unicolor unicolor

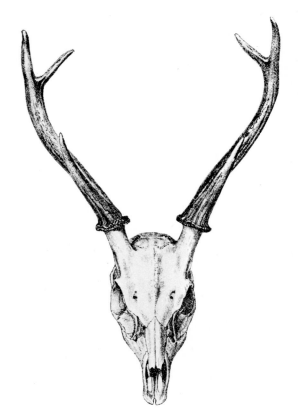

18(d) Skull and antlers of Calamian deer *Axis
       calamianensis*. All attempts to trace an
       illustration of this deer, which is briefly
       described on page 117, have failed

18(c) Malayan Sambar stag *C.u.
       equinus*

19 Moluccan Rusa deer *Cervus timorensis moluccensis*

20(a) White-tailed deer buck *Odocoileus virginianus borealis*

20(b) Albino White-tailed deer doe *Odocoileus virginianus* in Douglas County, Wisconsin

20(c) White-tailed deer buck *O.v.virginianus* (Museum specimen)

21(a) Mule deer buck *Odocoileus hemionus hemionus*

21(b) Mule deer does *O.h.hemionus* in deep snow

22(a) Pampas deer *Ozotoceros bezoarticus* in the
Field Museum of Natural History, Chicago

22(b) Pampas deer doe *O.b.celer*

22(c) Marsh deer *Blastocerus dichotomus* – mounted group in the Field Museum of Natural History, Chicago

23(a) Huemul or Guemal *Hippocamelus bisulcus*   23(b) Huemul doe *Hippocamelus bisulcus*

23(c) Brocket deer *Mazama americana* in the Field Museum of Natural History, Chicago

24(a) Pudu deer buck *Pudu pudu* in the Field Museum of Natural History, Chicago

24(b) Pudu deer doe *P.pudu*

25(a) Père David's deer stag *Elaphurus davidianus* in June

25(b) Père David's deer stag *Elaphurus davidianus* – a photograph that shows well the long tail and curious antler formation

26(a) Roe buck *Capreolus capreolus capreolus* in summer

26(b) Young Roe buck *C.c.capreolus* in early winter, with one antler cast

27(a) Melanistic Roe buck *Capreolus capreolus capreolus* in October

27(b) Siberian Roe buck *Capreolus capreolus pygargus* in late winter

27(c) Siberian Roe buck *C.c.pygargus* in summer

28(a) India
Munt
*Munt
munt*

28(b) Reev
Mun
*Mun
reeve*

28(c) Black or Hairy-
fronted Muntjac
*Muntiacus
crinifrons*

29(a) Michie's Tufted deer *Elaphodus cephalophus michianus* (Drawn by J. Smit)

29(b) Musk deer buck *Moschus moschiferus*

29(c) Chinese Water-deer buck *Hydropotes inermis*

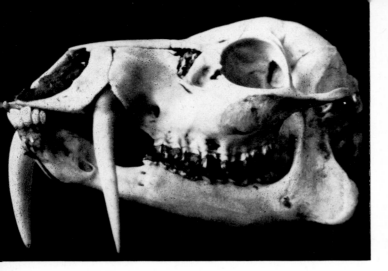

30(a) Skull of male Chinese Water-deer *Hydropotes inermis* showing upper canines of exposed length 59 mm

30(c) Dentition of Red deer – *Cervus elaphus*. Upper jaw (right) – 14 teeth, consisting of 6 molars, 6 premolars and 2 canines. Lower jaw (left) – 20 teeth, consisting of 6 molars, 6 premolars, 6 incisors and 2 lower canines. Total (top and bottom jaws) 34 (see page 2)

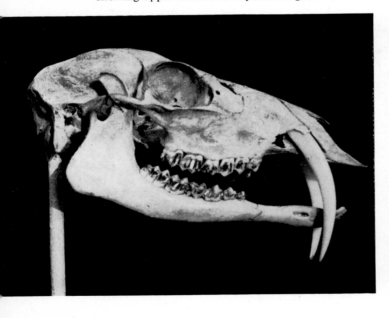

30(b) Skull of male Musk deer *Moschus moschiferus* showing upper canines of exposed length 62 mm

30(d) Reindeer-drawn sledge in Lappland

(a) The new growth starts to emerge early in May

31(b) By the end of May the antlers, covered in velvet, will be almost a foot in length

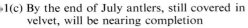

THE GROWTH OF A FALLOW BUCK'S ANTLERS

1(c) By the end of July antlers, still covered in velvet, will be nearing completion

31(d) By September, the antler growth on most matured bucks will be complete and free of velvet

32(a) The greatest deer that has ever lived – the extinct Giant deer *Megaceros giganteus* (Artist's impression by Winifred Austen)

32(b) The author in his museum, dwarfed by the skeleton of a Giant deer *Megaceros giganteus*

FALLOW DEER		*Dama dama*	2 subspecies	pp. 86–91
ELK		*Alces alces*	2 subspecies	pp. 91–4
REINDEER		*Rangifer tarandus*	3 subspecies	pp. 94–7
MUSK DEER	(i)	*Moschus moschiferus*	2 subspecies	pp. 97–100
	(ii)	*Moschus sibiricus*	2 subspecies	pp. 97–8
	(iii)	*Moschus berezovskii*		p. 99
PÈRE DAVID'S DEER		*Elaphurus davidianus*		pp. 100–1

RED DEER *Cervus elaphus* Map p. 70

The Red deer *C.elaphus*, which includes the Maral of the Middle East, the Hangul, Shou, Bactrian deer and Yarkand deer of Asia, has a wide distribution in Europe, as well as being abundant in other areas outside its indigenous range, where it has been introduced. These include New Zealand (page 144), Australia (page 139), and South America (page 66).

In Europe the Red deer occurs in almost every country from Norway and Sweden in the north to Spain and Greece in the south-west and south-east respectively. It is, however, absent from Finland, Portugal and the small Pyrenean republic of Andorra. In its European range a number of subspecies are represented: these include *C.e. scoticus* in Great Britain and Ireland; *C.e.atlanticus* in Norway; *C.e.elaphus* in Sweden; *C.e.hippelaphus* in western Europe excluding Spain where it is replaced by *C.e.hispanicus*; and *C.e.corsicanus* in Corsica and Sardinia. South and east of the Caucasus in Turkey and in Iran *C.e.hippelaphus* is replaced by *C.e.maral,* whilst in North Africa another race, *C.e.barbarus*, is recognised. Further east, between the Carpathians and Sikang in China another four races occur. In the far north-east and in North America *C.elaphus* is replaced by *C.canadensis* – the Wapiti – of which seven subspecies occur in Asia and four extant in North America.

In Britain and Ireland, where the total population falls somewhere between 180,000 to 200,000 animals, the range of the Red deer includes northern, central and part of south-west Scotland; the north-west, East Anglia and south and south-west England; whilst in Ireland isolated herds occur in north-west, the east (Wicklow) and south-west.

In Scandinavia the Red deer does not have a very wide distribution, being more or less restricted to a small area in the county of Skåne in southern Sweden, part of the western coast and islands of western Norway and in a few localities of Denmark. The species is also indigenous to the Netherlands, being found in the province of Gelderland.

Elsewhere in western Europe, apart from the countries already mentioned, the Red deer occurs in almost all areas where the habitat is suitable. In a north-easterly direction its range includes the Baltic states of Estonia, Latvia and Lithuania, whilst in an easterly direction *C.e.hippelaphus* reaches the Ukraine of western USSR.

The finest specimens, as regards weight and quality of antler, occur in the east of this range, and stags weighing 600 to 660 lbs (272 to 299 kilograms) – clean – have been killed in Poland, Hungary, Yugoslavia and Rumania. Antlers from these

F

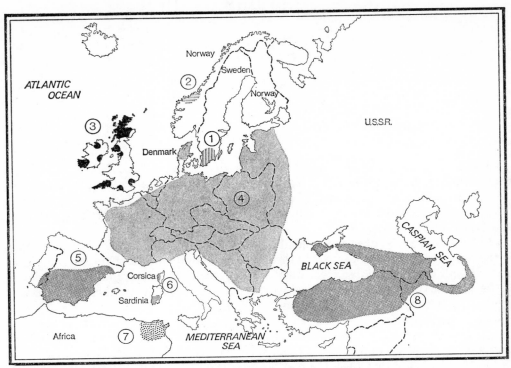

Map 10. The range of Red deer *Cervus elaphus* in EUROPE and THE MIDDLE EAST

1. *C.e.elaphus*   Sweden
2. *C.e.atlanticus*   Norway
3. *C.e.scoticus*   Great Britain
4. *C.e.hippelaphus* Europe
5. *C.e.hispanicus*   Spain
6. *C.e.corsicanus*   Corsica and Sardinia
7. *C.e.barbarus*   North Africa
8. *C.e.maral*   Asia Minor

For the remaining four subspecies of *C.elaphus* see Map 11, p. 75

 9. *C.e.hanglu*   Kashmir
10. *C.e.yarkandensis* Chinese Turkestan
11. *C.e.wallichi*   East Tibet
12. *C.e.bactrianus*   North Afghanistan, Russian Turkestan

European Red deer have been introduced to a number of areas outside Europe, and these include Australia, New Zealand and Argentina, South America

countries frequently carry twenty or more points, weigh, on frontal bone, over 22 lbs (10 kilograms) and extend to 49 inches (123 cms) in length. If one compares these weights and measurements with those of a good Scottish stag (body weight 210 lbs (95 kilograms), antler length 35 inches (89 cms) and antler weight 4 lbs (1·8 kilograms)) one can appreciate what fine specimens these European stags are. The Maral is little inferior.

In the Mediterranean islands of Corsica and Sardinia, however, a much smaller race of Red deer *C.e.corsicanus* exists, but nowhere are they plentiful. Here, due to their insular isolation, an average stag will weigh about 168 lbs (76 kilograms) clean. The Red deer of North Africa *C.e.barbarus,* of which less than 500 now remain, is also of small stature, being similar in size to a Scottish Red deer.

The general colour of the European Red deer is a rich reddish brown in summer, which becomes a greyish brown in winter. Animals which seldom, if ever, have access to woodland tend to have lighter coloured coats owing to weathering and general fading from sunlight. The caudal disc or rump patch is yellowish brown, and in some animals there is a dark dorsal stripe. Calves are spotted, but the spots are barely visible after the third month. Traces of spots, however, are sometimes visible in the region of the dorsal stripe on the adult beast. High up on the outside of the hind cannon bone there is a gland tuft, whilst at the approach of the rut the stags develop a mane and the neck swells. Colour abnormalities include white, cream and albino animals, and there is also a white-faced (bald-faced) strain which usually has some white, also, above the hooves.

In western Europe the rut takes place between the middle of September and the end of October, which results in the calves being born from late May to early July. During the rut the stag develops a lion-like roar with which he greets all challengers. Fights between rival stags often occur, and sometimes end fatally to one of the contestants. On rare occasions antlers have been known to become locked together, resulting in the death of both participants from starvation. At other seasons of the year the stag is generally silent but can, and often does, bark when alarmed. The hind also barks when alarmed. During the rut the hind makes small nasal grunts – a noise which is often imitated by hunters in order to attract a stag.

During the winter, the older stags keep very much to themselves while the hinds and younger animals form mixed herds, the female members of which will probably remain together for the rest of their lives, being visited by the stags during the period of the rut.

In Britain, apart from man, there are no serious predators to Red deer, though the fox and Golden eagle occasionally take a very young calf. In parts of Europe, however, the wolf is still a great menace to deer in winter, stalking them through the deep snow or driving them on to the ice where they can easily catch up with the slipping animals. In summer, also, wolves take a large number of calves and it has been estimated that in one reserve in the Caucasus no fewer than 60 per cent of the young deer and other ungulates are killed by this predator.

The four easternmost members of the Red deer are the Hangul or Kashmir Red deer *C.e.hanglu* of northern India; the Shou, *C.e.wallichi* of south-east Tibet; the Bactrian or Bukharian deer, *C.e.bactrianus*; and the Yarkand deer *C.e.yarkandensis* of Chinese Turkestan, all of which are now becoming rare.

HANGUL *Cervus elaphus hanglu* Map p. 75

In many respects the habits of the Hangul or Kashmir Red deer are similar to the European Red deer. Unfortunately, it is also often referred to by sportsmen as

'Barasingh' or 'Barasingha' which is apt to confuse this species with the Swamp deer *Cervus duvauceli* which is also known by the same name (page 120).

A full grown Hangul stag stands about 48 to 50 inches (122 to 127 cms) high at the shoulder and weighs about 450 lbs (204 kilograms). In winter the general colour varies from brown to liver colour, with the light area on the inner side of the buttocks being a dirty white. In the summer coat the general colour is lighter and more rufous with most of the under-parts whitish. In this season it is sometimes possible to see traces of spotting on the flanks of the hinds, and on occasions the stags too. The calves, which are born in April or May, are spotted.

The antlers, which in a typical adult stag are of ten points, consist of brow, bay, tray and fork. A feature of the Hangul antlers is that not only are the bay points often longer than the brows but the latter generally sprout from the beam about 2 inches (5 cms) above the coronet. A good head should measure at least 44 inches (112 cms) along the curve, $50\frac{1}{2}$ inches (128·3 cms) being the record for length. On rare occasions heads carrying fourteen or even sixteen points have been taken.

The stags shed their antlers in March and early April, at which time of the year they are just about to set off for their summer haunts, which is spent in the mountains at an elevation of about 9,000 to 12,000 feet (2,742 to 3,656 metres). Towards the end of September the antlers will be hard and the stags are now ready to join the hinds for the rut, which takes place in October. As is the case with the European Red deer, the stags collect a number of hinds together whose possession is disputed by rivals. By this time the stags will be roaring – a sound which is often more comparable to that made by a Wapiti than the European Red deer.

By late November the big stags will have left the hinds, and gone to the upland meadows or into the horsechestnut forests. Hard weather or an early fall of snow will force the deer down to lower altitudes.

In recent years the Hangul has declined in numbers enormously and it is doubtful if more than 300–400 deer now remain.

Man, both directly by poaching, and indirectly by over-grazing with domestic stock, has been the main cause of the decline of this fine deer, whose natural enemies include Black bear and leopard, both of which prey principally on the young deer.

SHOU *Cervus elaphus wallichi* Map p. 75

Another rare deer which is closely related to the Hangul of northern India is the Shou or Wallich's deer of south-east Tibet, but little is known of its present status. One of its former habitats was the Chumbi valley in Tibet, which was formerly part of Sikkim, and because of this the Shou was often referred to as the 'Sikkim stag'. It would appear, however, to have been extinct in this valley since about 1925 when F. Ludlow of the British Museum saw three hinds in the area of Lingmothang, for none have been reported in this locality since then. This deer now appears to be extinct except in the Tsari district of south-east Tibet.

As in the Hangul, Shou antlers – of which a few specimens have measured 55 inches (140 cms) in length – normally carry five points on each side (i.e. ten points) but the brow is apt to sprout from the main beam closer to the coronet, and the terminal fork is placed at right angles to the axis of the head, so as to face directly forward. Another feature of the antlers of this deer is that the beam bends forward at the tray tine so that the upper half is inclined to overhang the face.

In general, the colour of the Shou is rather lighter than the Hangul and the rump patch is more conspicuous. The muzzle and chin are also fawn-coloured, whereas in the Hangul these areas are whitish.

YARKAND DEER *Cervus elaphus yarkandensis*   Map p. 75

Another eastern member of the Red deer group is the Yarkand deer *C.e.yarkandensis* which is found in the basin region of the Tarim Lop Nor Lake, Sinkiang (Chinese Turkestan), and like the last-mentioned species, is now becoming exceedingly rare. This is a comparatively large-sized deer, with massive but somewhat short antlers bearing twelve points a good pair of which will measure about 40 inches (102 cms). Some opinions believe that *C.e.hanglu* and *C.e.yarkandensis* are synonymous.

BACTRIAN DEER *Cervus elaphus bactrianus*   Map p. 75

The Bactrian or Bukharian deer *C.e.bactrianus* – also referred to as the Bactrian Wapiti – occurs in the forests of the lower Syr Darya of Kazakhskaya SSR and in the Amu Darya basin of Turkmenskaya SSR, as well as in northern Afghanistan. Nowhere is it plentiful, and the world population is estimated to be about 500 animals of which three quarters occur in the USSR, the majority being located in the Tigrovaya Reserve in Tadzhikskaya SSR.

The general colour of this deer, the males of which will stand about 46 inches (117 cms) high at the shoulder, is of a light grey.

Rutting takes place from mid-September to the end of October – much the same as the Red deer in Britain. The majority of young are born in May. Hinds will normally breed at three years of age.

The Bukharian deer is an extremely strong swimmer and will tackle fast-flowing rivers such as the Vakhsh and Piarj when in flood. Near Sarai, the deer often swim across from the Afghanistan shore to the Russian side, sometimes in quite large groups, including some young deer. The deer swims with such speed that it cannot be overtaken by a rowboat.

During the summer, the deer lie down during most of the day, only rising to feed about six o'clock in the evening. At this time of year the deer are much tormented by bot flies and mosquitos. The chief predator of this deer is the tiger, their similarity of habitat bringing these two animals into frequent contact with each other.

WAPITI *Cervus canadensis*   Map p. 75

The westernmost member of the Wapitoid Group in Asia is the Tien Shan Wapiti *C.c.songaricus* which occurs throughout most of the Tien Shan mountain range from

Syr Darya in Russian Turkestan to about the Tarbagatai mountains in extreme western Mongolia.

Whilst there is little doubt that the Tien Shan Wapiti has been seriously reduced in numbers because of the demand for antlers in velvet in the Chinese markets, there appear to be still fair numbers of them in the mountains between the Chu and Naryn rivers.

Of all the Asiatic Wapitis the Manchurian race, *C.c.xanthopygus,* has the widest distribution, the habitat of this deer being the forested areas of eastern and northern Manchuria, ranging westwards and northwards into eastern Mongolia and Transbaikalia respectively, whilst in an easterly direction its range extends into south-east Siberia and extreme north-east Korea.

In Siberia its range extends west as far as Lake Baikal and east to beyond the Amur River.

The Manchurian Wapiti is similar to the North American animal except that in summer its coat is a more vivid red, whilst in winter it is darker. In summer pelage the rump patch is a similar reddish colour to that on the body with which it merges. It is less red in winter, and more of a contrast to the body colour. The antlers are relatively weak, a good pair with twelve tines will measure only about 40 inches (102 cms) in length.

The rut takes place during September, the calves being born during May and June.

Another race of Wapiti which is restricted to the Ala-Shan range of mountains that lie between southern Mongolia and northern China is the Ala-Shan Wapiti *C.c.alashanicus*. According to Flerov (1952) *C.c.alashanicus* differs from the Manchurian Wapiti *C.c.xanthopygus* in its smaller size and colour, which in winter pelage is almost completely a monochromatic greyish brown, gradually lightening towards the belly. The antlers are of the form typical for the Wapiti.

An adult male will stand about 50 to 51 inches (130 cms) high at the shoulder. Further south, in Tibet, M'Neill's deer *C.c.macneilli* occurs, its range extending into western China.

The typical locality of M'Neill's deer was originally given by Lydekker as Szechwan in western China. It would appear, however, that this animal is more typical of the Tibetan plateau, and only extends its range to the extreme western borders of Szechwan where, according to Dolan (Allen 1940), it occurs 'in the marginal forests of the Mekong, Yangtze and Yalung ranges, usually above 12,000 feet (3,656 metres), in heavy growth of rhododendron'. It is now very scarce. The reason for its decline is the demand for the antlers in velvet on account of their supposed aphrodisiac properties.

M'Neill's deer is rather similar in size and colour to the Hangul or Kashmir deer *C.e.hanglu*.

The typical antlers of an adult stag should have five tines on each side, consisting of brow, bay and tray with a terminal fork. Antlers are shed about March and by the end of September most of the big stags will have their antlers free of velvet. Younger beasts, however, will still be in full velvet.

The Kansu deer *C.c.kansuensis* is another member of the Wapiti group that frequents this part of Asia. Its range would appear to be restricted to the mountainous

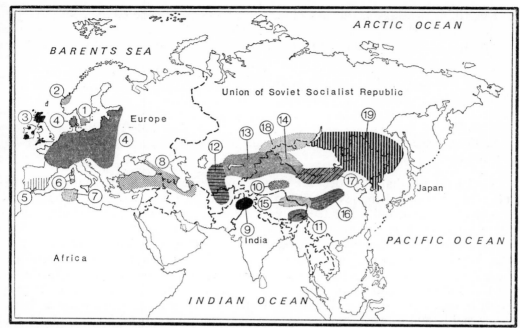

Map 11. The range of Red deer *Cervus elaphus* and Wapiti *Cervus canadensis* in ASIA

RED DEER *Cervus elaphus*

  9. *C.e.hanglu*   Kashmir
10. *C.e.yarkandensis*   Chinese Turkestan
11. *C.e.wallichi*   East Tibet
12. *C.e.bactrianus*   North Afghanistan, Russian Turkestan

For the European and Middle East range of *C.elaphus* which include *C.e.elaphus* (1); *C.e.atlanticus* (2); *C.e.scoticus* (3); *C.e.hippelaphus* (4); *C.e.hispanicus* (5); *C.e.corsicanus* (6); *C.e.barbarus* (7); and *C.e.maral* (8) see Map 10, p. 70

WAPITI *Cervus canadensis*

13. *C.c.songaricus*   Tien Shan Mountains, etc.
14. *C.c.wachei*   Western Mongolia
15. *C.c.macneilli*   Tibetan/Chinese border
16. *C.c.kansuensis*   Kansu, China, etc.
17. *C.c.alashanicus*   South-east Mongolia
18. *C.c.asiaticus*   Altai to Transbaikalia
19. *C.c.xanthopygus* Manchuria and Mongolia

For the range of *C.c.roosevelti*; *C.c.nelsoni*; *C.c.manitobensis*; and *C.c.nannodes* in North America, see Map 3, p. 41

forests of Kansu and northern Szechwan. Like other Chinese deer, this animal is faced with extinction on account of the demand for antlers in velvet for medicinal purposes.

Of the other members of *Cervus canadensis*, *C.c.macneilli* would appear to be the nearest, and indeed some consider *C.c.kansuensis* to be a synonym of it.

Describing the stags he saw in China, Wallace (1913) considered them 'as resembling Red deer in shape and build, but more uniform in colour, much larger, with the roar of a Scottish stag and the horns of a Wapiti'. Continuing, he said:

An adult stag stands about 57 inches [145 cms] at the shoulder, and weighs (approximately) 530 lbs [240 kilograms]. . . . He is in the winter brown-grey all over, and has not the distinctive dark neck and light body of the American animal [Wapiti]. The legs are darker than the body. The hinds are relatively smaller, and I was much struck by the apparently abnormal size of their ears. . . . They shed [their antlers] in April, the horns being complete in September. They are said to start roaring about the third week in October.

Wallace stated that these deer are kept in captivity by the Chinese, who saw their antlers off annually when in velvet. Many of the animals were in a wretched condition, being haltered in a stall. Confinement under these conditions often resulted in their hooves attaining a great length, rendering walking extremely difficult.

Further north in the region of Lake Baikal occurs another race of Wapiti – the Altai Wapiti *C.c.asiaticus*, whose range extends from the Baikal region of Siberia in the east to the Altai mountains of western Mongolia in the west. Included in its range are the Tannu-Ola and Vostochnyy Sayan mountains, and the upper Yenisei and Irtysh basins. In the Kobdo (Jirgalanta) district of western Mongolia another form *C.c.wachei* is said to exist, but it may be a synonym of *asiaticus*.

Harper (1945), quoting from various sources, states that the range of this deer is now quite restricted and includes the Altai, Kusnetsk Alatau and Sayan. In the lowland the animal appears only accidentally.

THOROLD'S DEER *Cervus albirostris*   Map p. 78

Thorold's deer – also known as the White-faced Tibetan or Przewalskii deer – was first described after a skin and skull of an old stag had been obtained by a member of the Third Przewalski Expedition to Kasak Kalminin on the River Koko-su, western slopes of the Humboldt ridge, Nan Shan Range, during July 1876.

The range of this deer at present includes eastern and northern Tibet, and the upper reaches of the Yangtze River and Nan Shan district of western China.

Standing just over 4 feet (122 cms) high at the shoulder, the White-faced Tibetan deer is a comparatively large animal, with the withers somewhat lower than the rump. The skull is broad, but rather short, and the whole head has a somewhat flattened appearance. The antlers are normally five-tined, i.e. ten points in all. The ears are peculiar in shape, being relatively long and narrow, lance-shaped in appearance and pointed at the end. The tail is very short, being only about 5 inches (12–13 cms) long. The hooves are high, short and wide, 'sharply different from all other deer, more resembling the hooves of the hollow-horned cattle' (Flerov, 1952).

The general colour of this deer in summer is brown, the belly and underparts being a creamier shade, with white on the groins. The nose, lips and chin are white to the throat. There is also a small white spot in the region of the ears.

In winter the hairs are long and wavy, and the colour slightly lighter than in summer pelage. A feature of this deer is the 'remarkable reversal of the hairs on the withers, which forms a kind of hump and is directed forwards' (Lydekker, 1900).

SIKA DEER *Cervus nippon* Map p. 78

The Sika deer has a wide distribution in eastern Asia, and although some thirteen different races are recognised, many of these, and in particular those present in China, are now considered endangered species.

The Sika deer, although indigenous only in eastern Asia, have proved themselves most adaptable in a feral state when introduced to other hemispheres and wild Sika herds are now present in such countries as Morocco, New Zealand, Great Britain and a few countries in western Europe which include Denmark, France, Austria and Poland. On occasions, Sika deer have interbred with the Red deer, some of the most recent instances (1967) being in north Lancashire, England.

The Sika deer are animals of medium size, varying in shoulder height from about 25½ inches (65 cms) in one of the Japanese races to about 43 inches (109 cms) in Dybowski's deer from Manchuria. The antlers of an adult stag are usually eight-tined (four and four) but antlers bearing five tines aside, and very exceptionally six, sometimes occur. The bay tine is invariably absent, and any tines in excess of the more usual number of four aside are generally located in the top which, in many instances, tend to palmate.

In summer pelage, apart from melanism in the Kerama Sika deer *C.n.keramae*, the general colour varies from a rich chestnut-red to a more yellowish brown hue, dependent on the race, and with white spots on both sides. Indeed, this deer is sometimes referred to as the Spotted deer, but as the spots in some of the more northern races are barely discernible in winter coat, this name might be considered a misnomer.

A typical feature of the Sika deer group, except those of melanistic strain, is the white caudal disc present in both winter and summer pelage. This rump patch, which can be compared to that of the Roe deer in winter pelage, is limited by a blackish stripe. Along the neck, back and extending to the tail, is a dark stripe. Below the hock on the outer edge of the rear limbs are glands covered with light-coloured hair which in some races stand out prominently. The young are spotted.

The breeding habits and period of gestation are similar to Red deer, and as mentioned above, interbreeding between Sika and Red deer can occur. During the rut the stags have a peculiar kind of whistle which may change into a high-pitched scream. The female utters a soft, low whistle in the breeding season.

The two most northern forms, the Manchurian Sika deer *C.n.mantchuricus* and Dybowski's Sika deer *C.n.hortulorum*, occur in both Manchuria and Korea, the range of the latter extending into south-eastern Siberia.

The principal distribution of the Manchurian Sika deer is in the central and southern parts of Manchuria and in particular in the depth of the Kirinand Heilungkiang forests, extending southwards into Korea. Dybowski's Sika deer is found in the eastern and south-eastern parts of Manchuria, extending its range south into extreme north-east Korea, and northwards, into south-eastern Siberia.

Dybowski's deer, which is the most spotted of the Sikas, is also the largest of the

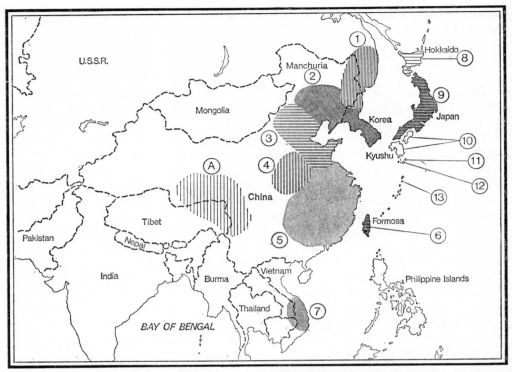

Map 12. The range of Sika deer *Cervus nippon*, and Thorold's deer, *Cervus albirostris* in ASIA

SIKA DEER. *Cervus nippon*

1. *Cervus nippon hortulorum*   Ussuri district, Manchuria
2. *C.n.mantchuricus*   Manchuria, Korea
3. *C.n. mandarinus*   Northern China
4. *C.n.grassianus*   Shansi district, China
5. *C.n.kopschi*   South-east China
6. *C.n.taiouanus*   Formosa
7. *C.n.pseudaxis*   Vietnam
8. *C.n. yesoënsis*   Hokkaido Island, Japan
9. *C.n.centralis*   Hondo (Honshu) Island, Japan
10. *C.n.nippon*   Kyushu Island, Japan
11. *C.n.mageshimae*   Mageshima Island, Japan
12. *C.n.yakushimae*   Yakushima Island, Japan
13. *C.n.keramae*   Ryukyu Islands, Japan

THOROLD'S DEER. *Cervus albirostris*

A. *C.albirostris*   Eastern Tibet, western China

Sika group, an adult male standing up to about 43 inches (109 cms) high at the shoulder. A good pair of antlers will measure up to 34 inches (86 cms) in length.

The Manchurian Sika is only slightly smaller, a good stag standing about 38 to 39 inches (96 to 99 cms) high at the shoulder. In summer the adult deer is a rich chestnut red with spots, the white caudal disc being bordered with black. In winter the colour changes to a deep brown on the body, darkening to a bluish-black on the neck. The spots are barely discernible. During antler growth, the velvet is a reddish colour. A good pair of antlers will measure up to about 26 inches (66 cms).

Further south, in China, there are three races of Sika deer, but the present-day status of all three is causing some concern. These are the North China Sika *Cervus nippon mandarinus*; the Shansi Sika *C.n.grassianus*; and the South China Sika *C.n.kopschi*. The classification of the Chinese Sika deer is, however, still a little obscure.

Formerly the North China Sika deer no doubt ranged over much of north-east China, and in particular the Shantung province. From recent reports, however, it would seem that this Sika deer may now be extinct in a wild state and may only be preserved on deer farms. No up-to-date information is available.

The Shansi Sika deer *C.n.grassianus,* which is about the size of a Scottish Red deer, is also facing extinction, the destruction of its habitat by local farmers in order to turn the land over to cultivation being one of the principal factors. The South China Sika deer – or Kopsch's deer *C.n.kopschi* – can still be found in the Lower Yangtze in Anhwei and southern Kiangsu provinces, extending its range into northern Chekiang, Kiangsi and northern parts of Kwangtung and Kwangsi. There is no doubt, however, that in former times it was considerably more plentiful than it is today, and because of constant hunting, this deer has now become exceedingly secretive in its habits. In size, Kopsch's deer is similar to the Shansi Sika deer, and compared with the more northern forms, the stripe along the back is more distinct, with the spots along the back less defined. In winter the spots are barely visible.

The only other mainland race of Sika deer is the Tonkin Sika deer *C.n.pseudaxis* which inhabits the hills of northern and central Vietnam – a race which some consider to be a synonym of *C.n.kopschi*. This deer is now becoming rare.

Opposite Fukien, on the island of Formosa or Taiwan, there is an insular race of Sika deer – the Formosan Sika – *C.n.taiouanus,* which, like some of the mainland forms, is now on the verge of extinction. Formerly the Sika deer abounded in the central or high range of mountains which are, in parts, covered with perennial snow. During the years Formosa was under Japanese rule, the deer were protected, but this is no longer the case, and the deer have declined to near extinction, and any that now remain in the wild state do so in the mountainous southern parts of the island. This deer, however, is now kept in many zoos and parks throughout the world, including small herds at Whipsnade and Woburn Park in England. Off the Chinese coast, a number of deer are raised on Lu-tao (Green Island) which lies some 18 sea miles (29 kilometres) east off T'aitung, for their antlers, a pair of which is said to be worth about 100 dollars.

Formosan Sika deer were imported about thirty years ago to Oshima – a small island which lies south of Tokyo (Honshu island), Japan. These deer subsequently escaped from Oshima zoological gardens and established themselves on the eastern slopes of the island. According to Nagamichi Kuroda (1955) their introduction had 'no effects on the original species' – presumably *C.n.centralis*.

For an island race, the Formosan Sika deer is quite large, standing as it does some 38½ inches (98 cms) high at the shoulder. During the summer the coat is a bright chestnut colour, with prominent white spots, and a rather reddish tint on the hind part of the neck. In winter, the pelage becomes more drab and the spots less prominent. The black line which borders the white rump patch and also runs down the centre of the tail is more in evidence than on the Japanese Sika deer. The metatarsal glands are of a brownish shade.

The Japanese Sika deer, which is the only indigenous deer of Japan, is well distributed throughout the islands, the following six subspecies being represented:

> *C.n.nippon* (Shikoku, Kyushu and Goto Islands)
> *C.n.centralis* (Hondo (Honshu), Sudo, Awajishima and Tsushima)
> *C.n.yesoënsis* (Hokkaido)
> *C.n. mageshimae* (Mageshima and Tanegashima)
> *C.n. yakushimae* (Yakushima and Kuchino-Erabujima)
> *C.n. keramae* (Ryukyu islands)

The rutting season takes place about mid-September to the end of October, the calves being born from the end of May to the end of June. Formerly wolves were the principal predators, but now a few deer are taken by bears during periods of deep snow. An occasional calf is also taken by the fox.

The deer live almost exclusively in the forests and only venture on to more open ground in search of food. During the spring, summer and autumn months, herds will be found up to altitudes of 8,175 feet (2,491 metres) but in winter they seek lower levels.

The typical Japanese Sika deer *C.n.nippon* of Shikoku and Kyushu stands about 31 inches (79 cms) high at the shoulder and weighs some 106 lbs (48 kilos). Its general body colour in summer is a reddish brown with numerous white spots. In winter the colour darkens and the spots disappear.

The deer of Hondo *C.n.centralis* are very similar in colour in summer pelage, but in winter the upper parts become an almost uniform blackish brown, with a prominent black line down the back. The upper margin of the white caudal disc is also edged with black. This deer is slightly larger than the typical race, standing some 33 inches (84 cms) high at the shoulder and weighing about 154 lbs (70 kilos).

The largest deer, *C.n.yesoënsis* are found on Hokkaido. Here a good stag will stand about 35 inches (89 cms) at the shoulder and weigh some 176 lbs (80 kilos). This deer in summer pelage is also very similar to that of *C.n.nippon*, or *C.n.centralis*, but is more strongly tinged with yellowish red colour, and profusely spotted. In winter the spots disappear and the coat turns a dark, reddish brown.

The smallest deer *C.n.yakushimae* are to be found on the island of Yakushima where a good stag will seldom exceed 25½ to 28 inches (65–71 cms) at the shoulder.

The deer from Mageshima – *C.n.mageshimae* – are also small but not quite so small as the last named. The colour is very similar in both winter and summer to the deer on Yakushima. The antlers, however, are much larger, a good pair measuring about 16 inches (41 cms) in length as compared to about 11 inches (28 cms) of those from Yakushima, where a head of six points (three and three) is the general pattern although 8-pointers, which is the usual number of points for Sika deer, are not unknown.

The longest antlers come from Hokkaido, where the average length from an adult stag is about 29 inches (74 cms) with occasional specimens running up to 32 inches (81 cms).

The Kerama or Ryukyu Sika deer, *C.n.keramae,* which come from the Ryukyu islands, is also a small deer. It resembles the typical Japanese Sika deer *C.n.nippon,* but in size is closest to the deer of Yakushima. Adult Kerama deer have a dark stripe extending down the spine, and lack the spots which are a feature of the other Sika deer. This deer is prone to melanism, and occasionally all-black individuals occur. Some of these melanistic deer were formerly present in Woburn Park, England, but were subsequently transferred to Whipsnade. There is no white rump patch on the melanistic specimens.

The Kerama Sika is an endangered deer, and in 1964 it was estimated that only about thirty animals remained as compared to 160 some ten years previously. These deer are all congregated on the small uninhabited island of Yakabi, which extends to some 304 acres (about 123 hectares) covered with miscanthus grass.

During the summer the principal food of the Sika deer are buds, leaves, seeds and fallen leaves of the needle-leaf and broad-leaf trees. Occasionally they raid the cultivated fields for soya beans and oats. In winter, they have resort to bark and bamboo grass.

ROE DEER *Capreolus capreolus*   Map p. 83

This small deer, *C.c.capreolus,* is present in Scotland and England, and in almost every country of western Europe. Further east, across the Ural mountains it is replaced by the larger Siberian Roe *C.c.pygargus,* and in China and Korea by *C.c.bedfordi.*

EUROPEAN ROE DEER *Capreolus capreolus capreolus*   Map p. 83

In Scotland the Roe has been present continuously since the prehistoric period. Its range, however, has not been quite so constant, and there was a period during the eighteenth and nineteenth centuries when this graceful mammal was practically extinct in all the lowland countries. Today, however, there is not a county in Scotland where one or two pairs cannot be found wherever the locality is suitable for them. In the lowlands this was mainly brought about by an introduction, at the beginning of the last century, of some Roe to the Culzean estate in Ayrshire by the Marquis of Ailsa, where they increased and quickly spread their range eastwards.

In England the history of the Roe has been even more precarious than in southern Scotland, and if we are to believe the opinion of certain eighteenth- and nineteenth-century naturalists, the Roe was, in their day, quite extinct south of the border. I am convinced, however, that this was never the case, and whilst it may have been extinct in the southern half of England there seems no doubt that a few remained in the Lake District of north-west England and possibly also in Northumberland and

Durham as well. However, attempts made during the last century to re-establish the species in the wild state met, in the majority of cases, with immediate success and today the Roe has so spread its range that it is resident in at least thirteen English counties. The most successful introductions have been to Petworth in Sussex (*c.* 1800), Milton Abbas in Dorset (*c.* 1800) and Thetford in Norfolk (*c.* 1884).

Although formerly found in many parts of Wales, it would seem that the Roe, in the wild state, has been extinct for at least 350 years and possibly longer. Remains of it have, however, been found in widely separated areas, from Anglesey in the north to Carmarthenshire in the south, and many of these are preserved in the National Museum of Wales. Their disappearance can be directly correlated with the destruction of the woods which reached its climax about the seventeenth century.

As far as Ireland is concerned, it would appear that the Roe was never an indigenous species. This view is supported by the fact that whereas innumerable antlers and bones of other members of the *Cervidae* have been found in the Irish bogs and elsewhere, no relics of Roe have yet come to light.

Although Roe were, therefore, never indigenous to Ireland, a few were introduced during the latter part of the last century, the most successful introduction being at Lissadell, County Sligo, where some of the bucks produced enormous heads, one of which had no fewer than twelve points. The introduced animals came from Duplin Castle, Perthshire, and reached Lissadell in the early 1870s.

These Roe survived in County Sligo for perhaps fifty years, and although a few spread into the adjacent County Mayo, at no place were they numerous. Early in the present century, nurseries were planted at Lissadell for re-afforestation purposes, and in consequence all the Roe were shot, and as far as I can ascertain, none now remain.

Before leaving Britain, mention should be made of some Siberian Roe *Capreolus c.pygargus* which were introduced to some woods outside Woburn Park in Bedfordshire about 1910 by the eleventh Duke of Bedford. They never increased to any great extent and by 1950, because of the disturbance of the woods during the war years by the military, only about three remained. All recent reports suggest that the species is now probably extinct.

In Europe the range of the Roe is extensive, ranging from Norway, Sweden and southern Finland in the north to southern Spain, Greece and northern Iran in the south, and from Portugal in the west to about Iran and the Ural mountains in the east where the European form is replaced by the Siberian Roe *C.c.pygargus*.

The typical European Roe stands about 25 to 29 inches (about 64 to 74 cms) high at the shoulder, and an adult buck will weigh anything from 38 to 50 lbs (17 to 23 kilograms) clean. Exceptional beasts from Poland will, however, weight as much as 80 to 90 lbs (about 38 kilograms), but such animals are exceptional.

In summer pelage the European Roe is a rich, foxy red colour with no marked white rump patch as in winter. The face is a grizzled grey. The chin is white and there is a black band which runs from the nostril to the angle of the mouth. There is no white throat patch.

In winter the pelage roughens and changes to a greyish fawn colour, flecked with yellow. Two white patches, more noticeable in some animals, develop on the throat and gullet. The rump patch becomes white, which under the influence of fear and excitement can be expanded to form a large, white disc.

The Roe has no *visible* tail although a small one is present. During the winter the doe develops a prominent anal tush – a tuft of long hair – which is sometimes mis-

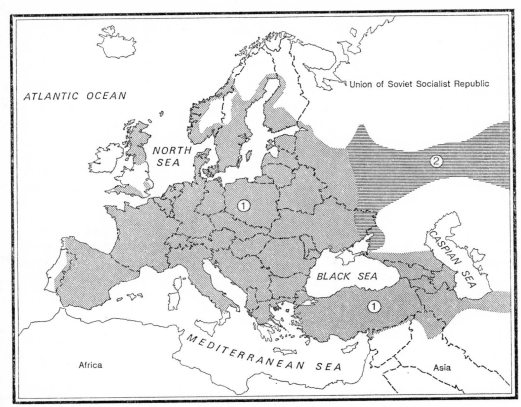

Map 13. The range of Roe deer *Capreolus* in Western EUROPE and ASIA MINOR

1. *Capreolus capreolus capreolus* Western Europe to Ural Mountains
2. *C.c.pygargus* Siberia and northern Asia

A third subspecies *C.c.bedfordi* occurs in northern China and Korea etc. (See Map 14, p. 85)

taken for a tail. This anal tush, however, is a most useful guide to help distinguish the buck from the doe when the former has cast its antlers as it does in early winter.

The newborn kid is a reddish brown with spots on the back and sides.

A few melanistic Roe occur in the Netherlands and north-west Germany, but elsewhere their occurrence would appear to be rare, as would the other colour variations which include bald-faced (white-faced), albino, black and white or brown and white.

The full head of a buck should be 6-pointed, though multi-pointed heads are met with at times. Does very occasionally grow small antlers but, more commonly,

pronounced coronets without any antler growth. Occasionally a buck which has
been injured in the testicles may grow a perruque head – a malformation which
causes the upper part of the forehead to be covered by a mass of antler, frequently
in velvet. Another name for this type of head is 'wig-antler'.

Antlers are shed from October to early December, and dependent on the date of
shedding, the new growth should be complete and clean of velvet by April or May.

Some of the strongest Roe antlers from Europe have come from Sweden, and
in particular from the Malmöhus district. Southern England has also produced
some very fine antlers, as well as Perthshire in Scotland. The best recorded antlers,
however, came from a buck killed in Hungary in 1965, which under CIC rating
gained no fewer than 228·68 points.

The bucks go to rut during late July and the first fortnight of August. Due to delayed implantation, no development of the embryo within the uterus is visible until
the latter part of December (about four months' delayed implantation). Thereafter,
development is fairly rapid and the kids will be born some time between late April
and early June. A newborn kid weighs about 4 lbs (1·8 kilograms) at birth. Twins are
fairly common, and triplets also occur at times.

The typical call is a dog-like bark, which is uttered by both sexes throughout the
year, particularly when alarmed.

Although the range of the European Roe *C.c.capreolus* does not extend beyond
the Ural Mountains two subspecies are present east of this range, the Siberian Roe
C.c.pygargus in Siberia, Mongolia and Manchuria, and the Chinese Roe *C.c.bedfordi*.

SIBERIAN ROE DEER *Capreolus capreolus pygargus*   Map p. 85

In Siberia the Siberian Roe is found south of about latitude 57°N ranging from
the Ural Mountains in the west to about the Gulf of Tartary. In the south, about
latitude 45°N can be said to be the approximate limit of range in this direction as
it follows a west-to-east course through northern Turkestan, northern Mongolia
and northern Manchuria to the sea coast of the Gulf of Tartary. It is just possible
that this race also extends its range into the extreme northern parts of Korea, but
it requires confirmation.

CHINESE ROE DEER *Capreolus capreolus bedfordi*   Map p. 85

Throughout the greater part of the Korean Peninsula the Roe is the Chinese or
Manchurian race *C.c.bedfordi* – sometimes referred to as the Duke of Bedford's
deer – and in parts it is described as plentiful. This race also occurs sparingly on
Quelpart Island (Saishu To) which lies off the southern tip of Korea.

West of Korea, *C.c.bedfordi* extends its range throughout central and southern
Manchuria into Mongolia. Further south, this deer is found in northern and western
China where in some areas, that provide good cover, it is quite plentiful. The range
of the Chinese Roe in northern China and southern Mongolia covers roughly a half-
circle round the south, east and northern perimeter of the Gobi Desert. The southern
limit of the Roe deer in China seems to be about latitude 30°N but in Sikang and

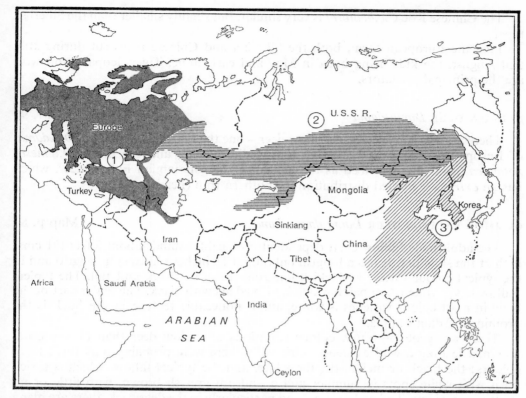

Map 14. The range of Roe deer *Capreolus* in ASIA

2. *C.c.pygargus* Siberia and northern Asia
3. *C.c.bedfordi* Northern China, Korea, etc.

The typical form, *C.c.capreolus* (1) occurs throughout western Europe. (See Map 13, p. 83)

Szechwan provinces it may extend slightly south of this latitude in the Kinsha River area.

The main differences between the Siberian Roe *C.c.pygargus* and the typical European form *C.c.capreolus* is the size, a good buck standing about 35 inches (89 cms) high at the shoulder – a good 6 inches (15 cms) higher than the western race – and weighing almost double. The antlers are also considerably larger, and are widely separated at the pedicles, the coronets never touching, as they do in the common Roe. A good pair of antlers will measure 15 or more inches (38 cms) in length, will have deep pearling, and although basically 6-tined, the posterior point of the fork will often bifurcate to give it eight points. The winter pelage is much thicker and rougher than the European race. The body colour is greyish brown, with the typical white rump patch of *Capreolus*. The summer coat is a brighter and lighter rufous colour, lacking the waviness on the neck and shoulders which characterises the European Roe.

G

The Chinese Roe *C.c.bedfordi* is very similar, but slightly smaller than the Siberian type.

Like the European form, both the Siberian and Chinese races rut during July and August, the kids being born in May and early June. Tiger, leopard and wolf are the principal predators.

FALLOW DEER *Dama dama*   Maps pp. 87, 90

There are two sub-species of Fallow deer – one the typical Fallow deer, *D.d.dama,* of Europe and countries bordering the Mediterranean, and the other, *D.d.meso-potamica,* generally described as the Persian or Mesopotamian Fallow deer, which has an *extremely* limited distribution in southern Iran (Persia).

COMMON FALLOW DEER *Dama dama dama*   Map p. 87

The adult male Fallow deer, dependent on locality, stands about 3 feet (91 cms) high at the shoulder. It has a longish tail (about 13 inches (33 cms) in length) and in the typical colour variety a blackish line runs down the back and tail. The typical Fallow has a white rump patch which is also edged with black. The under part of the belly in most colour varieties is white, and a noticeable feature in the buck is the prominent Adam's apple.

There are probably more colour variations in Fallow deer than in any other mammal leading a wild existence. Originally there were probably only three main colours: the black or melanistic, the white, and the typical fallow, which is a rich fawn with white spots in summer and a uniform greyish brown, with little or no spotting, in winter. Today, however, and particularly in the deer park, there are many colour varieties, which include menil, cream, sandy, silver-grey or blue, and sooty-dun. The menil Fallow deer are lighter in colour than the typical fallow and the spots are more prominent. In winter the spots are still visible on a greyish brown background. There is no black bordering to the rump patch and none on the tail, the upper surface of which is a light reddish brown.

In the white or cream colour variety, the deer are whiter looking in winter pelage than in summer. The fawns are also creamy coloured unless they happen to be albino, when they will be snow-white with pink eyes. The velvet on the antlers of cream or white coloured bucks is also light coloured, being a rather pretty silver-pink which harmonises very well with their general colour.

In similar fashion the colour of the velvet on the antlers of a black or melanistic buck matches the body colour of the deer. The black Fallow deer should not have white anywhere, the upper part of the body being, in summer, a beautiful glossy black with sooty-grey underparts. In winter the colour is rather greyer without the glossiness of the summer pelage. This colour type is sometimes called the 'Forest Breed'.

A very pretty colour variety is the blue or silver-grey Fallow deer. Deer of this colour may vary quite considerably, but the more common variety has the blue-grey hairs mixed with brownish hairs, producing a light roan effect. The prettiest are

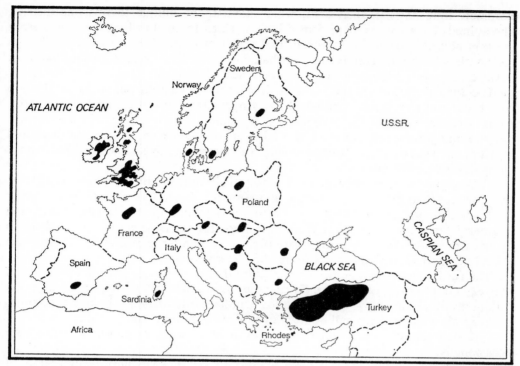

Map 15. The range of Fallow deer *Dama dama* in EUROPE

Dama dama dama   Europe and Near East*
See also Map 16 (page 90) for range of *D.d.mesopotamica*

*The original home of *D.dama dama* was the Mediterranean region of southern Europe, including Anatolia and Island of Rhodes. It has been introduced to many countries of Western Europe, although in some (marked with an asterisk) their existence has only been maintained in fenced-off reserves or parks; Austria, Belgium*, Bulgaria, Czechoslovakia, Denmark, England, Finland, France, Germany, Hungary, Ireland, Italy*, Netherlands*, Norway*, Poland, Portugal*, Rumania, Sardinia, Scotland, Spain, Sweden, Switzerland,* and Yugoslavia. It has also been introduced to Australia, Tasmania, New Zealand, North America, Africa and South America.

those which are very light in shade, with the hairs generally mixed with those of a silver-grey colour to give it the attractive blue shade. Sometimes a blue Fallow deer will have a saddle of normal colour, or other dark mark on the body.

Other colour varieties include the sandy or cream, which is a gingery-red colour with faint spots showing both winter and summer; the yellow-dun, which is a yellowish mouse dun colour in winter without any spots, and lighter in summer; the dark dun, which has a bay-brown-coloured body, light grey underparts and no spots. Occasionally, a white-faced or bald-faced Fallow deer has occurred in a park but such animals are not common.

In a wood near Ludlow in Shropshire there are a number of Fallow deer with extremely long hairs in their coat, which seem to be unique to this one district. The animals have hair perhaps 5 or 6 inches (12 to 15 cms) in length hanging from the ears and also from the forehead, and the bucks at a distance look as though their antlers have long shreds of velvet hanging from the brows. A variant like this, however, should not be considered a subspecies.

The typical antlers of the matured buck should be well palmated at the top with brow and tray tines, although the bay normally, but not invariably, is absent. Along the rear edge of the palmation there should be a number of snags with a longer point jutting back at the lower edge of the palmation. A good head should measure at least 28 inches (71 cms) in length accompanied by an inside span of about 24 inches (61 cms) or more.

Fallow bucks in Europe generally cast their antlers during April and May, early or late shedding being a matter of age or condition. Contrary to Red deer, it seems that the young bucks will clean rather earlier than the old bucks, there being a general tendency throughout the whole herd for its male members to clean in order of youthfulness. It appears, therefore, that an antler of palmated construction takes longer to grow than one of more simple construction.

The rut in European countries takes place during the latter part of October and may extend into early November. During the rutting season the buck makes a husky, rolling grunt. He may give some subdued grunts at other times. The doe sometimes barks in alarm, and when calling her fawn, gives a rather plaintive call.

The majority of fawns will be born in June or early July. Twins occur very occasionally.

The original home of *D.d.dama* is said to be the Mediterranean region of southern Europe and Asia Minor. It is the typical park deer, and at the end of the last century in England alone over 71,000 Fallow deer were being preserved in parks.

There has always been considerable doubt, however, as to whether the Fallow deer is indigenous to England, or was originally introduced by the Romans or Phoenicians. Most historians have suggested the former, but J. G. Millais in *The Mammals of Great Britain and Ireland*, Vol. III, considered it much more likely that they were brought over to our islands by the Phoenicians who were great sailors, and traded with Britain for many years before the Roman Conquest. Another theory is that the Fallow deer were only re-introduced by the Romans, having become extinct in this country before the historic period. During the Pleistocene period there was most certainly a species of deer known as Clacton or Brown's Fallow deer *Dama clactoniana* (*D.browni* being a synonym of *D.clactoniana*) which appears to have been very similar in build to the modern Fallow deer *D.dama,* the antlers differing only slightly. This deer was hunted by early Palaeolithic man in the Thames Valley.

Although Fallow deer are generally associated with the deer park there are, nevertheless, several herds in England that have for many centuries led a completely wild existence. These include the New Forest (Hampshire), Epping Forest (Essex), Dean Forest (Gloucestershire), Rockingham Forest (Northamptonshire) and Cannock Chase (Staffordshire).

At the present time Fallow deer lead a feral existence in at least nine counties on the Scottish mainland, and also occur on the islands of Islay, Mull and Scarba.

In Wales, although not indigenous, it would appear that the species has been present there for at least seven hundred years. Although most records of the animal's existence in Wales suggest that it was mainly a park animal, it would seem that by the sixteenth century a few wild deer were roaming the forest of Snowdon.

In Ireland the pattern has been the same as in England – large estates have been broken up and the denizens of their parks have been allowed to escape to form feral herds. The Fallow deer is now a well-established alien in at least half of the counties of Ireland, and although practically everyone's hand is raised against them, no deer has shown itself more capable of looking after its own skin.

At the present time Fallow deer occur in the following countries of Western Europe, although in some (marked with an asterisk) their existence has only been maintained in fenced-off reserves or parks: Austria, Belgium*, Bulgaria, Czechoslovakia, Denmark, Finland, France, Germany, Hungary, Italy*, Netherlands*, Norway*, Poland, Portugal*, Rumania, Sardinia, Spain, Sweden, Switzerland* and Yugoslavia. It also occurs in Anatolia (Turkey) and on the Island of Rhodes but would now appear to be extinct in Albania and Thrace, where it formerly appeared in parks.

Some of the best trophies have come from Hungary where the species is not as plentiful as formerly. Klampenborg Park near Copenhagen in Denmark has also produced some very fine heads, as has Schleswig-Holstein and Bayern in Western Germany.

There are wild Fallow deer on the Island of Rhodes in the Aegean Sea but whether the species is indigenous to the island is not certain. It is believed, however, that the deer originally came from Asia Minor. In the middle fifties the Fallow deer population on Rhodes was said to be about 500 head.

On the mainland of Anatolia (Turkey) Fallow deer, although formerly plentiful in many parts, are now restricted to the northern slopes of the Taurus Mountains. Several writers have suggested that the Fallow deer of Anatolia are the Persian type *D.d.mesopotamica* but it is doubtful if the range of this latter deer ever extended north of about latitude 36 degrees. Certainly none of the antlers that have come from Anatolia in the past century bear any resemblance to *D.d.mesopotamica*.

There are no indigenous Fallow deer in North Africa but about 1914 some Fallow were introduced to the Vereeniging estate in the Transvaal where they managed to acclimatise themselves. Fallow deer, along with Sika deer, have been satisfactorily introduced to the forests of Madagascar.

Since the middle of the nineteenth century European Fallow deer have also been introduced to the following countries – Australia (page 140), Tasmania (page 141), New Zealand (page 146), North America (Kentucky, Texas and elsewhere), and South America (Argentina and Chile).

PERSIAN FALLOW DEER *Dama dama mesopotamica*   Map p. 90

The Persian Fallow deer *D.d.mesopotamica*, which was first announced to zoologists in 1875 by Sir V. Brooke, has always had a rather limited distribution. Its former range included Iran (Persia), Iraq (Mesopotamia), Israel, Jordan (Palestine) and Syria and in all these countries except Iran – and *possibly* Iraq – this deer has now disappeared. It is doubtful if this deer ever occurred north of about latitude 36°N and by about 1930 was assumed to be quite extinct, for there had only been one report (in 1906) of this beast having been seen by any European.

Although Brooke was the first person to describe this deer, it was an English Vice-Consul by the name of Robertson from Basra who first drew his attention to it, for during a shooting expedition on the lower reaches of the Kurun in Persia, a

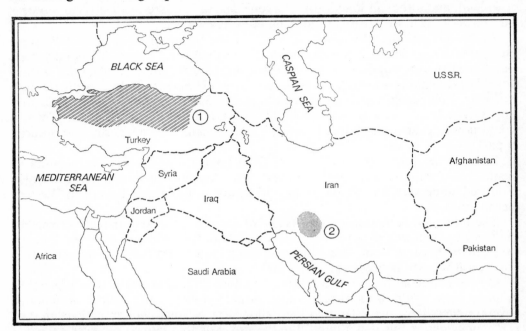

Map 16. The range of Fallow deer *Dama dama* in South-west ASIA
1. *Dama dama dama*   Turkey
2. *D.d.mesopotamica*   Iran
(See also Map 15 for range of *D.d.dama* in Europe)

buck with antlers still in velvet was shot and, along with some cast antlers, were sent to him at the British Museum in London. Brooke immediately recognised the importance of this new deer, described it and named it *Cervus (Dama) mesopotamicus*. Robertson, however, was unable to tell Brooke much about the habits of this deer.

It has often been said that history repeats itself, for just as Robertson during his hunting trip to Persia in the 1870s had first come across this Fallow deer, so did a German by the name of Herr Werner Trense some eighty years later, also during a hunting trip in the same area, hear of a deer which answered very closely to the description of a Fallow deer. On further investigation, Herr Trense discovered that this deer was, in fact, *D.d.mesopotamica* and occurred sparingly in the Khuzistan province of Iran, and in particular, two small herds, numbering about a dozen animals each, were localised in the region of the Rivers Dez and Karkheh.

In Iran the deer were found to be inhabiting the impenetrable bush forests which bordered to a width of half to two kilometres (under 1¼ miles), the rivers running through the plains from the Luristan Mountains. Much of this region is flooded each year and the tracks through the forests are only kept open by the passage of Water-buffalo which are able to force a way through the tangled area of bush-poplars, willows, tamarisk and mimosa. But for the density of these forests it is doubtful if even these few survivors would remain today.

The reason for the disappearance of this deer is much the same as elsewhere in the world – it has been hunted to extermination over most of its range and the introduction of the modern firearm has accelerated the process. However, whilst hunting pressure has come more from military personnel than from the local people, the latter have been responsible for the disappearance of much of this deer's habitat, not only by cutting down the forests but also by allowing their domestic animals, which include camels, cattle, Water-buffalo and goats, to invade the thickets. More-over, plans were started in 1966 to eliminate part of their forest habitat under a government irrigation project.

Subsequently, a few animals have been caught and then liberated in a small fenced-in reserve at Dasht-e-Naz, near Sari in the north. One or two other deer have also been transferred to Herr Georg von Opel's private zoo at Kronberg, near Frankfurt-am-Main. It is to be hoped that these small captive herds will thrive, for it is doubtful if the world population of this rare deer exceeds fifty animals.

D.d.mesopotamica is slightly larger than *D.d.dama* with antlers of a rather different pattern; for whereas the latter normally has a brow point of moderate length and no bay, the typical *D.d.mesopotamica* head has very short brows with a long tray which sprouts comparatively close to the brow (indeed in some heads it might be considered a bay tine). Where this point emerges from the main beam the antlers show marked palmation, and this second tine may be bifurcated. Palmation does occur at the top of the antlers but, compared to that on many *D.d.dama* heads, it is comparatively light.

In summer pelage the general base colour of the Persian Fallow deer is dark reddish brown with rows of white spots running on each side of the dark median line of the back. The under part of the belly is white. The transition colour from the upper flanks to the white of the belly is of a sandy tone, which is also the colour of the haunches. The head is grey in colour on the forehead with a brownish tint. The surround of the eyes is lighter coloured. The front part of the lower lip is white as also is the inner side of the ears. The tail is white in colour and is somewhat shorter than in *D.d.dama*.

ELK *Alces alces*   Map p. 93

Although the Elk, which is similar to the Moose of North America, is no longer present in the British Isles, it is plentiful in all parts of northern Europe, spreading its range eastwards as far as eastern Siberia. Throughout northern Europe only one subspecies is represented – the typical *Alces alces alces* – and this race extends its range eastwards as far as about the River Yenisei where it is replaced by *Alces alces cameloides* (page 94). In North America, where this deer is called Moose, four other subspecies of *A.alces* are represented, *A.a.americana*, *A.a.gigas*, *A.a.shirasi* and *A.a.andersoni* (pages 29–33). Moose have also been introduced into New Zealand (page 147).

Standing about six feet (183 cms) high at the shoulder, the Elk is distinguished by its large size, long legs (giving it a high shoulder appearance), short tail and broad, overhanging muzzle, the nose of which is covered with short hair except for a small bare patch, triangular in shape, situated between the nostrils. The neck is comparatively short, and from it hangs a dewlap or bell which, although well developed in North American forms, is short in the European Elk. A good bull will weigh about half a ton (508 kilograms).

In summer coat the Elk is brownish grey with lighter coloured, almost grey legs. Some animals are darker and some greyer than others. In winter, as the hairs lengthen, so does the coat become lighter. Albinos have been observed.

A typical feature of the Elk is the large palmated-type antler carried by the bulls, which in a good European head may have a spread of 48 inches (122 cms) and bear eighteen to twenty points. Antlers are dropped from November onwards, the older animals usually being the first to cast. The antlers will be clean of velvet a few weeks before the rut which extends for about a month's duration commencing in mid-September. The young calf, which is unspotted at birth, will be born about May or early June, twins being comparatively common. On rare occasions triplets have been recorded and there is also a report from Sweden of quadruplets.

The Elk is normally a silent animal, and his calls can only be heard when close at hand. The bull has a grunting noise used during the rutting season. The cow has a nasal call used all the year round when calling her calf.

The food varies from aquatic plants to shrubs and mature trees providing browse. The maximum amount of aquatic feeding takes place between mid-June and August.

From the numerous relics that have been found in the peat or superficial deposits, it would appear that the Elk was extant in Britain during the Bronze and Celtic periods and survived until at least the ninth century. The final extermination of this fine deer was due to the destruction of the forests, which formed its abode, for unlike the Red deer, the Elk cannot survive without woods.

In parts of Scandinavia, however, the Elk is still very plentiful. In Norway it is numerous in all the wooded parts of the south-east, extending its range northwards to about the Namsen River. It is similarly plentiful in most parts of Sweden except in the more mountainous districts of the north, and in the southern counties of Malmöhus and Blekinge where the population is kept as low as possible on account of crop damage. During a census taken in 1959 it was estimated that the Elk population in Sweden was in the region of 100,000 animals. There are no Elk on the island of Gotland, but when the Kalmar Sound is frozen over, animals have crossed on to Öland Island, where there is now a small resident population.

An occasional animal has also swum the Helsingør Sound south-west of Sweden to Sjaelland, Denmark, but nowhere in Denmark has the species been able to establish itself. Although formerly present, the Elk became extinct in Denmark before the tenth century.

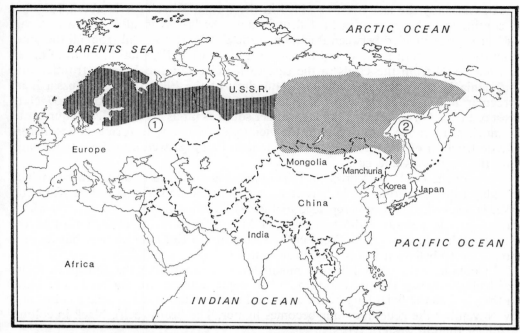

Map 17. The range of Elk/Moose *Alces alces* in NORTHERN EUROPE and SIBERIA

1. *Alces alces alces*   Northern Europe
2. *A.a.cameloides*   East Siberia, Mongolia and Manchuria

The Elk is well distributed throughout Finland. There are also a few on Aland Island which lies in the Gulf of Bothnia. Two distinct types of antler are present, those in the north and east being well palmated, whilst those in central and southern Finland show little palmation.

South of Finland across the Gulf of Finland, a few Elk still occur in Esthonia, Latvia and Lithuania which lie along the eastern seaboard of the Baltic Sea. In Latvia it is found both inland and along the coast. The position is much the same in Lithuania, the majority of deer occurring in the western part and, in particular, towards the delta of the Memel where they sometimes wade in the surf. It is possible, also, that Elk travel up into the south-eastern part of Lithuania from the marshes of Pinsk, an area which was formerly part of Poland, but is now White Russia.

Although the Elk apparently became extinct in Poland during the eighteenth century, by the end of the last century a few animals had rehabilitated the marshes of Pinsk or Pripet, doubtless having wandered in from the Minsk district of Russia.

However, during the War the Elk was again almost exterminated, and by 1945 only a few remained in the Czerwone Bagno (Red Bog) forest in the Rajgród district which was then the only remaining natural breeding place of this deer. In 1948 the Elk was afforded complete protection and since that date numbers have slowly built up again.

In Germany the last Elk was killed in the former West Prussia about 1830 but it continued to be present in East Prussia until the last War, after which this part of Europe was divided between Poland and the USSR. It is absent from all the other countries of western Europe, but in Russia it has a wide distribution south of about latitude 63°N from the Urals in the east to Karelia and the Finnish frontier and Lithuania in the west. The southern boundary of the Elk's range in Russia is an irregular line extending westwards from the Urals from about latitude 57°N to west of Pinsk. On occasions Elk may wander south as far as Stalingrad. It is numerous in much of its range, and occurs in the vicinity of Moscow. In former times, before the destruction of the forests, the Elk extended its range well into the Ukraine and into the northern Caucasus.

East of the Urals the European Elk *A.a.alces* is restricted to a narrow belt which roughly follows latitude 60°N between the Rivers Ob and Yenisei. Once the latter river is reached, *A.a.alces* is replaced by the east Siberian form *A.a.cameloides* whose range spreads eastwards through parts of Mongolia as far as Manchuria and the Sea of Okhotsk. East of the Yenisei the status of the Elk is unknown, but there is no reason to believe it is any way a rare animal.

In colour the eastern Elk is a much darker animal than the European form, particularly during the early autumn when some animals are almost black. Later in the year, as the hairs lengthen, the natural shine of the autumn pelage is lost and by November the general colour becomes lighter. The beard (bell), black in colour, is longer than in western types.

The chief predator of the Elk throughout its range is the bear, but in some areas wolves, hunting in packs, take a fair toll. In the Far East the tiger is included among its predators.

REINDEER *Rangifer tarandus*   Map p. 95

The Reindeer has a wide distribution throughout northern Europe and the USSR, ranging from Norway in the west to the Bering Sea in the east.

Opinions differ as to the number of subspecies which occur in the eastern hemisphere. Ellerman and Morrison-Scott (1951) suggest eight, five on the mainland and three insular, whereas Banfield (1961) reduces these to three, *R.t.tarandus* and *R.t.fennicus* on the mainland and *R.t.platyrhynchus* on the Spitsbergen archipelago. This latter opinion I have followed. Banfield restricts the range of *R.t.tarandus*, which he calls the Eurasian Tundra Reindeer, to a few places in central Norway, the Kola Peninsula and Yalmal Peninsula in northern USSR and then eastwards north of about latitude 65°N into Yakutsk.

During the middle and upper Pleistocene Age the Reindeer was present in Britain, and continued to exist in Scotland until at least the ninth century AD. It is apparent from the number of remains that have been discovered that the Reindeer was once abundant throughout Britain, but gradually its range became more and more limited as it retreated northwards, until finally compelled by the sea to make its last stand in Caithness.

During the eighteenth and nineteenth centuries, several attempts were made to reintroduce Reindeer to Scotland, without success. More recently, in April 1952 eight Reindeer were released on a 300-acre (121 hectares) reserve near Loch Morlich, Inverness-shire, by the Reindeer Council of the United Kingdom which had been founded in 1949. Subsequently not only were further animals added to the herd, but the size of the Reserve was increased, and the animals, now numbering about a hundred, have access to Airgiod Meall (2,118 feet or 645 metres) and other high ground.

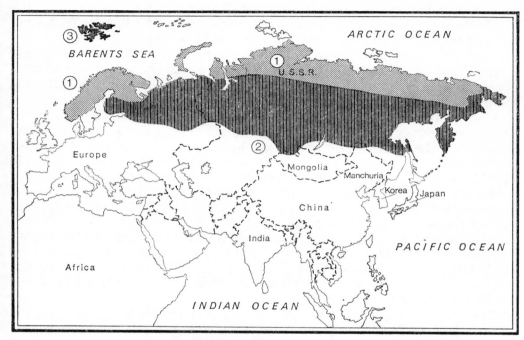

Map 18. The range of Reindeer *Rangifer tarandus* in NORTHERN EUROPE and SIBERIA

1. *Rangifer tarandus tarandus*   Norway to Russia
2. *R.t.fennicus*   European Russia, from Karelia to Sakhalin Island
3. *R.t.platyrhynchus*   Spitsbergen

In Sweden the last truly wild Reindeer was killed about 1865, but in the northern part of the country domestic herds, which in 1955 were estimated at about a quarter million animals, are herded by the Lapps.

In neighbouring Norway both wild and domesticated herds occur in many parts of the country, and in recent years their numbers have increased. The largest herds of wild Reindeer are to be found in the Njardaheim Reserve in the south, and in the Hardangervidda plateau and Dovrefjell Mountains of central Norway. There is little doubt that tame deer have at one time or another mingled with all the wild herds, and particularly those in the Njardaheim Reserve and at Hardangervidda. Over-population of range in recent years has led to a general deterioration in the class of animal. In 1954 the Norwegians commenced building a frontier fence all along the border between Norway and Finland to prevent Reindeer straying from one country to another – a total distance of about 343 miles (549 kilometres).

In Finland the position is much the same as in Sweden, the wild animal having been exterminated about 1900 although a few probably still exist in adjacent Russian Karelia. The wild Reindeer survived longest in the extreme north of the country but had disappeared in western and central Finland by the end of the eighteenth century. In place of wild Reindeer there are now in the provinces of Oulu and Lappi large herds of semi-domesticated animals which are all privately owned.

Some 420 miles (672 kilometres) north of Norway across the Barents Sea a small race of Reindeer, *R.t.platyrhynchus*, is restricted to Spitsbergen.

South of about latitude 65°N the Tundra Reindeer is replaced by the Forest Reindeer, and this woodland form ranges between about latitudes 55°N and 65°N from south-east Finland in the west through central Siberia to the Sea of Okhotsk and the Kamchatka peninsula in the east.

Many of the herds in this vast tract of country are domesticated and this has resulted in a number of local types being recognised by various observers. These include *R.t.phylarchus* in south-east Siberia, where its range extends from Kamchatka in the east to Manchuria in the west; *R.t.setoni*, which occurs only on Sakhalin Island in the Sea of Okhotsk, and which some consider a synonym of *R.t.phylarchus*; *R.t.angustirostris*, which has a very restricted range around Lake Baikal and the Barguzin Mountains; and *R.t.valentinae*, whose range extends through the forested zone of Siberia from the Urals in the west to the Stanovoi Mountains in the east, and southwards towards the Altai Mountains in northern Mongolia. All these forms have been considered by Banfield (1961) to be synonyms of *R.t.fennicus* – a subspecies which Ellerman and Morrison-Scott (1951) considered to be a synonym of *R.t. tarandus,* whose range, they suggest, extends eastwards to about the Ural Mountains, east of which it is replaced by *R.t.sibiricus.*

These latter authorities also recognise an insular form *R.t.pearsoni* on the Arctic island of Novaya Zemlya. It is possible that this deer, which is almost completely white in winter, may have been brought on the ice floes to various islands of the northern Arctic Ocean. This form is considered by Banfield (1961) to be a synonym of *R.t.tarandus* which also occurs on the Novosibirskie Islands off north Siberia.

Slightly smaller than the Caribou of North America, the average shoulder height of the European Reindeer is about 44 to 47 inches (112 to 119 cms), the females being some 4 to 6 inches (about 12·7 cms) smaller. Bull antlers generally have a palmated 'shovel' close to the face on one of the antlers, although a shovel on both antlers is by no means a rarity. The upper points are also frequently of palmated form. There is also a back tine about halfway up the main beam.

Old bulls shed their antlers about December but the new growth will not begin until the spring. The younger bulls shed their antlers towards the spring whilst it will not be until late spring or early summer, at about the time the calves are born, that the antlers on the cows will be cast. Indeed, the annual growth of the antlers of the cows is about six months out of phase with that of the antlers of the adult bulls, which will have their antlers fully developed and clean of velvet by the end of August or early September. A good pair of Scandinavian antlers will measure about 50 inches (127 cms) in length and may bear twenty-eight or more points.

The colour varies considerably, especially among those animals with a tame admxture. The colour may therefore range from a dark, greyish brown to a completely white animal. The underparts are white. Old bulls have a whitish neck, and by winter will have developed a long white mane. The nose has no naked part, being completely covered by short fur to the lips.

The rut takes place during the latter part of September and early October. At this time of the year the bulls utter a grunting sound. When a herd is feeding there is a continuous low 'barking' going on among the cows, calves and possibly young bulls. Another characteristic sound associated with the passage of a herd of Reindeer is the loud clicking of the foot bones. It is believed that this peculiar noise may have some social significance, helping to keep the herd together.

The calves, normally one but occasionally twins, are born from about the last days of April until the middle of June. Like the Elk calf, Reindeer calves have no spots, being a uniform brown colour, tending to darken along the back.

The largest of all the Palaearctic Reindeer, however, is the Okhotsk Reindeer – considered by some authorities to qualify as a separate subspecies *R.t.phylarchus* – which in winter coat is somewhat similar to the typical deer but considerably darker. It would appear that this Reindeer occupies an intermediate position between the Tundra and the Forest deer. The Reindeer of Sakhalin Island is also very similar to the Okhotsk Reindeer. The deer of the Barguzin Mountains is also a large animal and its coat, particularly in summer, is dark coloured.

However, in Reindeer and Caribou herds there seems to be no *fixed* shade of pelage, and there are many depths of shade between individual animals.

The European Reindeer, in domesticated form, has been successfully introduced to both North America and to South Georgia in the south Atlantic Ocean, the deer in this latter area having reversed their breeding seasons to fit the Antipodes (see page 13).

MUSK DEER *Moschus*   Map p. 98

The Musk deer, represented by three species, two of which are divided into two subspecies, has a wide distribution in eastern Siberia and throughout much of Asia. It prefers forests and scrubland at elevations of about 7,000 to 11,000 feet (about 2,130 to 3,350 metres).

The typical race *Moschus moschiferus moschiferus* is found in the Himalayas of northern India extending its range eastwards to about northern Burma, where it is replaced by *M.m.sifanicus*. The Siberian Musk deer *M.sibiricus sibiricus* has a wide distribution ranging from the Altai Mountains in the west to the Kolyma Mountains in the east, being absent, however, from Kamchatka. South of Transbaikalia this latter deer extends into the forestal areas of northern and eastern Manchuria. It also extends westwards from northern Manchuria into the extreme eastern parts of Mongolia. In western Mongolia the Musk deer occurs only in the mountains of the upper Yenisei basin, and in that region practically every peasant house is adorned

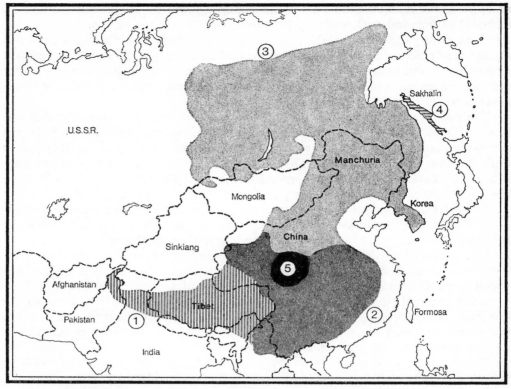

Map 19. The range of Musk deer *Moschus* in ASIA

1. *Moschus moschiferus moschiferus*   Northern India, Himalayas, etc.
2. *M.m.sifanicus*   West, central and southern China
3. *M.sibiricus sibiricus*   Siberia, north Mongolia and Korea
4. *M.s.sachalinensis*   Sakhalin Island
5. *Moschus berezovskii*   Szechwan, China

with skins. To the south, the Gobi Desert forms a barrier between the Musk deer of northern Mongolia and the Kansu or West China Musk deer *M.m.sifanicus,* which occurs throughout the mountains along the Tibetan–Chinese border as far south as northern Burma where, according to Brooke Dolan (in G. M. Allen, 1939), they range 'from comparatively low altitudes to the highest growth of dwarf rhododendron. Their favourite habitat is probably at about 12,500 feet (3,808 metres) in rhododendron, spruce or prickly oak. It is principally there that they are trapped by professional musk hunters, but their salvation seems to lie in the fact that there is a reserve in higher altitudes where the native hunters cannot trap them profitably.'

In the Amur and Ussuri districts of south-eastern Siberia Heptner and Tsalkin (1947) suggest that a fairly localised race, *M.m.turowi,* occurs, extending its range into Manchuria, but Flerov (1952) considers *M.m.turowi* to be a synonym of *M.s. sibiricus.* Flerov (1952) also suggests that the Musk deer of the high forested mountains of north and central Korea, which he himself at one time designated to be a subspecies *M.m.parvipes*, is likewise a synonym of *M.s.sibiricus*. Musk deer are reported from the whole length of the Korean peninsula, and in particular their occurrence is noted in the mountains near Mokpo in south Tscholla province of southern Korea. It is said to be extremely shy and retiring in its habits.

The Musk deer which occurs in the Yakutsk district of north-east Siberia, in an area which includes the Verkhoyansk, Taskhayakhtakh and Kolyma Mountains, is considered by some authorities to constitute a subspecies of its own – *M.m.arcticus*. It is, however, probably a synonym of *M.s.sibiricus*. It is absent from the Kamchatka peninsula. On the Island of Sakhalin or Karafuto in the Sea of Okhotsk an insular form *M.s.sachalinensis* occurs, but it appears to be very rare and during the inter-war period was stated to be 'threatened with destruction'.

The third species *Moschus berezovskii* appears to be restricted to Szechwan and southern Kansu, in China.

When Sakhalin was governed by Japan, the Musk deer was protected by game laws, but what the position is today under Russian rule is unknown. The usual method of taking this deer is by snaring, using twigs of *Betula ermani* and a wire ring.

Over its range the Musk deer have a number of natural predators which include leopard, lynx, wolf and wolverine.

All species and races of Musk deer are somewhat similar in appearance. The Musk deer is one of the two genera of deer in which neither sex produces antlers. Instead the males are furnished with long, upper canine teeth which extend far below the upper lip and descend considerably lower than the chin. In adult males this sabre-like tooth may reach 70 mm or more in length (say $2\frac{3}{4}$ to $3\frac{1}{2}$ inches). In females the canines are relatively small and never protrude beneath the lower lip. The canines are moveable on the alveoli of the males and may point forward or backward.

A musk gland in the abdomen of the male (three years of age or more) secretes a brownish wax-like substance which is used extensively in the manufacture of perfume and soap. About 28 to 30 grammes of this secretion can be obtained from a single male. Unlike other *Cervidae*, Musk deer possess a gall-bladder.

An adult Musk deer stands about 20 to 22 inches (about 53 cms) high at the shoulder, the height at the rump being some 2 inches (5 cms) higher. Adults weigh approximately 20 to 22 lbs (9 to 10 kilos).

Colouration appears to be quite variable, possibly as a result of age and season. Generally it is a rich, dark brown colour mottled and speckled with light grey above and paler beneath. The chin, inner borders of the ears, and inside of the thighs are whitish and there may be a spot of white on each side of the throat. The Siberian Musk deer *M.s.sibiricus* is somewhat darker in colour than *M.m.moschiferus*, whilst the Sakhalin Musk deer *M.s.sachalinensis* is the darkest race of all. It is also somewhat smaller than *M.m.moschiferus*.

It would appear that mating takes place about January; the birth of the fawn, usually one, but rarely two, occurring in June.

Solitary by habit, it is seldom that one can see more than two or three together. They feed mostly at daybreak and in the evening, their spring and summer diet consisting of a variety of vegetation such as grass, moss and tender shoots. In winter they have to rely mainly on twigs and lichens.

Apart from a loud hiss uttered when disturbed, and a plaintive scream when wounded, this deer is normally silent.

Amongst the native names for this deer are *Kastura* and *Kabanga*.

PÈRE DAVID'S DEER *Elaphurus davidianus*   Map p. 104

The story has often been told of the discovery, in 1865, of this deer, hitherto unknown to science, when the French missionary and explorer Armand David succeeded in being the first foreigner to see what lay inside the 45-mile (72 kilometres) wall of the Imperial Hunting Park of Nan-Hai-Tze just south of Peking. Its native name would appear to have been *Mi-lu, Mi-lou* or *Ssu-pu-hsiang*.

The Mi-lou, which has since been found in sub-fossil deposits, perhaps became extinct in the wild some two or three thousand years ago. Just how it came to be preserved in the Imperial Hunting Park is not known, and probably never will be.

Anxious to secure some specimens for the Paris Museum, Père David made arrangements with some of the park keepers to obtain for him the hides and bones of a pair of deer for which he paid twenty *taels*. It was, apparently, not without some difficulty and danger that the transaction was completed, for not only did each party mistrust the other, but it was strictly against orders for specimens to leave the park. However, one dark January night in 1866 the specimens were duly handed over the wall to Armand David, and the keepers received their reward.

The discovery of this new deer, quite naturally, aroused the interest of the Zoological Society of London and in due course, through the good offices of M. Henri de Bellonet, *Chargé d'Affaires* of the French Legation in Peking, a living pair was placed at the disposal of the Society. Unfortunately both died before reaching London. Eventually, in 1869, after several other unsuccessful attempts, a pair reached London alive, but within twelve months both had died, leaving no progeny.

During the next ten years other deer reached various zoos in Europe, but it was not until 1898 that a pair of young deer reached Woburn from a zoo in Paris, and in due course began to breed. By this date tragedy had descended on the Nan Hai-Tze herd, for in 1894 a river, which flowed through the park, breached the wall in several places and, through the gaps thus made, the bulk of the deer escaped to be killed and eaten by the famine-stricken peasantry. It is believed, however, that a small remnant managed to survive and remained in the park until about 1900 when, during the Boxer outbreak, it was broken into by troops marching to the relief of the foreign legations in Peking, and the deer were either killed or captured, a few being shipped to Europe.

About this date the eleventh Duke of Bedford, realising the very serious plight of this unique deer, managed to persuade the European zoos to let him have as many specimens as possible to release in his spacious park at Woburn. In this way about eighteen Père David's deer were assembled, and by the outbreak of war in 1914 the herd at Woburn had increased to eighty-eight. During the 1914–18 War, mainly due to the fact that it was illegal to buy extra winter feed for the deer, the numbers fell to about fifty – a figure which represented the total world population of Père David's deer, for it was now completely extinct in its native China and none of the European zoos retained any.

After the First War, the herd quickly built up again, and by the outbreak of the Second World War in 1939, numbered about 200. It now (1972) numbers just over 300 deer. Since the War Père David's deer have been sent to over thirty zoos and collections throughout the world, including China. The future of this fine deer, which is probably the only living mammal in the world which no man has ever claimed to have seen living in an entirely wild state, is now assured.

Its physical attributes are unique. For a deer, this animal – which stands nearly 4 feet (122 cms) high at the shoulder – carries a remarkably long tail and its hooves are wide and somewhat similar to those of a Reindeer, which suggests they were designed to travel over snow. The antlers appear to be worn back-to-front, for instead of any forward-pointing tines there is an extremely long back tine which appears to be of more use domestically than as a weapon of offence, being particularly useful as a 'back-scratcher', or for anointing the deer's back with mud.

Gestation lasts about ten months – about six weeks longer than that of a Red deer. The calves are a light yellow-red colour at birth with yellowish-white spots. The calf, once it has found its feet, becomes independent, and apart from joining its mother at meal times, soon forms little nursery parties with other calves, numbering at times perhaps twenty or thirty beasts.

During the summer months the general body colour of the adult is a bright red with a blackish stripe running down the spine. In winter, this colour will have changed to a dark iron grey with fawn shading. The winter coat has an underlayer of soft beige-coloured wool entirely different to the coarse hair of the winter coat.

The call of the stag consists of two or three gutteral braying roars, of which the last is lower in tone than the previous one. The challenge, often made on the run, takes the form of a series of grunts.

During the rut stags often festoon their antlers with long grass which gives them the appearance at times of carrying a loose bale of hay on their heads.

It will be seen, therefore, that the Père David's deer is a remarkable animal. No other deer is quite like it, yet it carries the peculiar characteristics of many. It was all these peculiarities that led the Chinese to giving it the name *Ssu-pu-hsiang* which means, literally, 'not like four – like, yet unlike the horse; like, yet unlike the ox; like, yet unlike the deer; like, yet unlike the goat'.

H

6

The Deer of Southern Asia and the Far East

No fewer than fifteen different species and over fifty subspecies are found in this area which can best be described as the Oriental Region, stretching from the East China Sea in the east to the Arabian Sea in the west, and includes India, Burma, Malaya, the Philippines and Indonesia. India has the largest number of different species – namely eight, which includes two in Chapter 5 – and of these the Axis deer or Chital *Axis axis* and the Swamp deer *Cervus duvauceli* occur nowhere else in the world as an indigenous species. The total number of extant species in this area could have been sixteen but it seems almost certain that the beautiful Schomburgk's deer *Cervus schomburgki* of Thailand (Siam), was exterminated some time before the 1939 War.

A feature of the deer from this area is that apart from Eld's, Swamp and Schomburgk's deer, the adult antlers of twelve of the other species *normally* carry but six (three a side) or fewer tines. The bucks of the remaining species – Chinese Water-deer – never produce any antlers.

	Species		
SAMBAR	*Cervus unicolor*	16 subspecies	pp. 103–10
RUSA DEER	*Cervus timorensis*	6 subspecies	pp. 110–12
CHITAL or AXIS DEER	*Axis axis*	2 subspecies	pp. 112–15
HOG DEER	*Axis porcinus*	2 subspecies	pp. 115–17
CALAMIAN DEER	*Axis calamianensis*		p. 117
BAWEAN DEER	*Axis kuhlii*		pp. 117–18
ELD'S DEER	*Cervus eldi*	3 subspecies	pp. 118–20
SWAMP DEER	*Cervus duvauceli*	2 subspecies	pp. 120–3
SCHOMBURGK'S DEER	*Cervus schomburgki*	(extinct?)	pp. 123–4
TUFTED DEER	*Elaphodus cephalophus*	3 subspecies	pp. 124–5
CHINESE WATER-DEER	*Hydropotes inermis*	2 subspecies	pp. 126–7

MUNTJAC	(i)	*Muntiacus muntjak*	15 subspecies	pp. 127–32
	(ii)	*Muntiacus reevesi*	2 subspecies	pp. 129–30
	(iii)	*Muntiacus crinifrons*		pp. 129–30
	(iv)	*Muntiacus feae*		p. 129
	(v)	*Muntiacus rooseveltorum*		p. 129

SAMBAR *Cervus unicolor*   Map p. 104

Of all the species of deer in southern Asia, the Sambar *Cervus unicolor* is not only the largest but also the most widespread in its distribution, for its range stretches from the Philippine Islands in the east, through Indonesia, southern China, Burma, to India in the west. Sambar have been introduced to New Zealand and now flourish in the North Island (page 149). Throughout its range sixteen subspecies are recognised.

In Ceylon the Sambar *Cervus unicolor unicolor* – which is often referred to as Elk – is well distributed, ranging from the sea coast right up to altitudes of 7,000 to 8,000 feet (2,285 metres). Early in the century the species was much persecuted on account of its hide which was used for shoe-making. However, a Ceylon Game Protection Society was formed which was followed (1909) by the proclamation of the Dried Meat Ordnance which effectively curbed the activities of the lowland poachers. From this date, therefore, the commencement of any protection for the game of the low country can be said to have started.

In India, the Sambar *C.u.niger* has a wide distribution also, being found in all suitable localities right up to the foothills of the Himalayas, where, on occasions, it has been found at altitudes as high as 9,000 feet (2,742 metres). It does not occur in the barren plains of the Punjab or Sind. It is absent, also, from Baluchistan, and like the Chital, it can be said that about longitude 74°E marks the limit of its range in a westerly direction.

The Sambar, *C.u.equinus,* also has a fair distribution in Burma where it is often referred to as *connai,* being found at all elevations where there is sufficient cover for it. It seems to avoid open scrub-land and the heaviest types of evergreen forest. Further to the south-east it is described as 'rather common' in all suitable localities in both Thailand (Siam) and Vietnam (Indo-China).

In a southerly direction, the range of *C.u.equinus* extends down the Malay peninsula into Malaya and across the Strait of Malacca into Sumatra (Indonesia). It also occurs on numerous islands around Sumatra but on Borneo it is replaced by *C.u.brookei.*

In China *C.u.equinus* is found throughout most of Yunnan and southern Szechwan and eastwards along the south Chinese border with Vietnam through Kwangsi and Kwang Tung to the south-east coast and Hainan Island. It is also plentiful across the border in Vietnam. The local name for this deer in Szechwan is *Hei-lu* whilst in Hainan it is called *Twahé,* which means, literally, the 'mountain horse'. Another race, *C.u.dejeani,* also occurs in southern China – and in particular in Szechwan. It is stated to be very similar in form and colouration to the Formosan race *C.u.swinhoei,* but as large as the Indian Sambar from which it differs by the more sombre brown colour, and the longer and bushier tail (Lydekker, 1915).

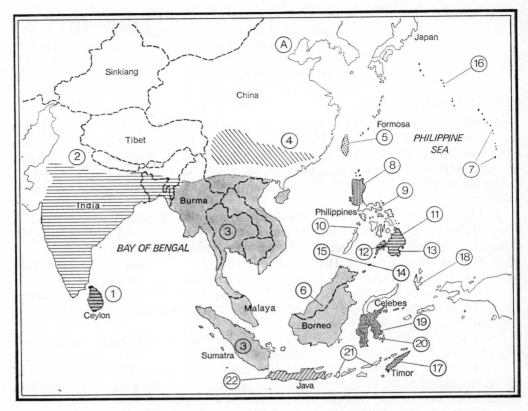

Map 20. The range of Sambar *Cervus unicolor* and Rusa deer *Cervus timorensis* in ASIA
Also former range of Père David's deer *Elaphurus davidianus* (A) in CHINA

SAMBAR *Cervus unicolor*

1.	*Cervus unicolor unicolor*	Ceylon
2.	*C.u.niger*	India
3.	*C.u.equinus*	Burma, southern China, through to Sumatra
4.	*C.u.dejeani*	South-west China
5.	*C.u.swinhoei*	Formosa
6.	*C.u.brookei*	Sarawak, Borneo
7.	*C.u.mariannus*	Guam Island, Marianne Group (probably extinct)
8.	*C.u.philippinus*	Luzon, Philippines
9.	*C.u.alfredi*	Central Philippines
10.	*C.u.barandanus*	Mindoro Island, Philippines
11.	*C.u.francianus*	Mindanao Island, Philippines
12.	*C.u.nigellus*	West Mindanao Island, Philippines
13.	*C.u.apoensis*	South-east Mindanao Island, Philippines
14.	*C.u.basilanensis*	Basilan Island, Philippines
15.	*C.u.nigricans*	Basilan Island, Philippines
16.	*C.u.boninensis*	Bonin Island (probably extinct)

Sambar have also been introduced to Australia and New Zealand.

In Sumatra the Sambar is locally abundant both on the mainland and on numerous islands which include Bengkalis and Rangsang in the Malacca Strait; North Pora or Siberut, South Pora, Pageh or Pagai Islands and Nias, off the west coast. Sambar are also present on Pulau Siuntjal in the Sunda Strait and on Billiton Island which lies between Sumatra and Borneo. As on Malaya, breeding seasons on Sumatra are variable.

Although the Sambar of peninsular India, *C.u.niger,* is slightly larger than the Ceylon form, both are very similar. Generally speaking, this deer is a uniformly large, dark brown animal with a yellowish tinge under the chin, inside the limbs, between the buttocks and underneath the tail. When running, this light colouring inside the limbs and buttocks is very noticeable. The hinds and calves are lighter in colour and the latter at birth never have spots. Some of the old stags often appear quite black and this dark colouring is often due to the beast having recently indulged in a mud wallow – a habit to which this deer has a strong addiction. The hair is coarse, especially on the neck, which in both sexes carries a small mane. The ears are large and the tail short, and rather bushy. The face glands below the eyes are large and during the rut often emit a strong-smelling secretion. A full-grown Sambar stag will stand about 52–6 inches (132–42 cms) high at the shoulder, and weigh about 600 lbs (272 kilograms), although exceptional animals have weighed as much as 700 lbs (318 kilograms).

The Malayan Sambar, *C.u.equinus,* is almost as large as the Indian type which it closely resembles. A good stag from Burma will weigh about 500 lbs (227 kilos). Some animals, particularly from Burma, appear to have a bare patch at the base of the neck, the cause of which is unknown though it may be due to some parasitic infection. In colour *C.u.equinus* is rather darker and a more sombre brown than the Indian deer. Breeding dates are variable.

Typical Sambar antlers consist of a terminal forward-facing fork and two fairly long brow tines coming off at an acute angle from the beam. There seems to be no fixed pattern for the fork – sometimes the inner tine may be the longest, sometimes the outer, whilst in some heads the two may be even.

RUSA DEER *Cervus timorensis*

17. *Cervus timorensis timorensis*	Timor and adjacent islands
18. *C.t.moluccensis*	Molucca islands
19. *C.t.macassaricus*	Celebes island
20. *C.t.djonga*	Muna and Buron islands (Celebes group)
21. *C.t.floresiensis*	Flores and Lombok islands, etc.
22. *C.t. russa*	Java

Rusa deer have also been introduced to south-east Borneo, New Guinea, Hermit and Ninigo islands (Bismarck Archipelago), New Caledonia, Australia and New Zealand

The former range of Père David's deer *Elaphurus davidianus* in CHINA

A. *Elaphurus davidianus*	Imperial Hunting Park, Peking*

*Preserved at present in Woburn Park, England, and in many zoological gardens throughout the world.

Abnormal Sambar heads are comparatively common, and may range from a typical switch head of but two points, to a multi-pointed 'monstrosity' bearing, perhaps, twelve or more points. Such heads are generally produced by a bifurcation of each point.

The record length for a Sambar head is $50\frac{1}{8}$ inches (127·3 cms). These antlers came from a beast killed in territory adjoining Madhya Pradesh (Central Provinces). Most of the best heads have come from this part of India, where a good average pair of antlers should have a length of 40 inches (102 cms) and a beam of 6 inches (15·24 cms). Both Ceylon and Burmese heads are slightly smaller, and anything over 28 inches (71 cms) in length in either place would be good. The record for Ceylon is $32\frac{1}{2}$ inches (82·5 cms) in length. Whilst a good Malayan head will only measure about 23 inches (58 cms) some very massive heads have come from Thailand, and it appears that the antlers from here may be nearer the Indian than the Malayan type. The best Thailand head measures 37 inches (94 cms) with a span of 31 inches (78·7 cms) and was taken in the teak country.

In central India most Sambar shed their antlers towards the end of March or in early April, but as in some other species of deer in this part of the world there is a certain amount of variation in the dates. In Burma the shedding is somewhat later, and most stags will be losing their antlers between the months of May and July and will be in hard antler by the end of the year. Further south, in the Malayan peninsula, the shedding becomes more irregular and several writers have suggested that they carry their antlers for two years or more. There is, of course, a close connection between breeding seasons and the shedding of antlers by the stags. As there does not seem to be any well-defined breeding season in the Malayan peninsula, it seems probable that because stags with hard antlers can be seen at times with those in full velvet, it has been *assumed* that these stags have not shed in that particular year. The same thing has often been suggested regarding the Sambar of central India.

By the time the rains have set in, the majority of antlers are in velvet and will continue to develop during the rainy season. At this time of year the stags lead a secluded life, and are generally found lying up in some grassy plot on top of a small hill in preference to deep forest where trees may damage the growing antler.

In central India most of the rut takes place during December but, as already mentioned, the dates are very variable. The cold weather is also the usual period for the rut in Burma. In the hills of Ceylon the rut generally takes place during October and November, but in the plains it is less fixed.

Prior to the rut the stag selects his territory and issues a challenge by bellowing for any stag to come forward and dispute possession of territory. There is no attempt to round up a herd of hinds, but any hinds in the area selected by any particular stag as his territory are attracted to him by his call. Dunbar Brander (1923) suggested that the 'powerful odour emitted by his facial glands' may also help to attract the hinds. It is, however, only for a brief period that the stags will be found in company with the hinds, and as a rule the number will seldom exceed six or eight. As soon as the rut is over the big stags return to a solitary existence but the immature beasts will generally remain with the hinds. Even so, the big stags continue to resent intrusion of their territory by a visiting stag and will often fight to retain ownership just as savagely as they would have done before the rut.

Sambar are seldom found far from water and drink every night at forest springs and streams. At all times of the year, but particularly previous to and during the rut, the stags are fond of wallowing in mud. Even in winter, when the ground is covered by frost, one will often see Sambar lying in a pool of water. Generally speaking, the habits of the Sambar are chiefly nocturnal, and unless disturbed they are seldom, if ever, seen about in the middle of the day.

Apart from man its principal predators include leopard, jackal, tiger, python and crocodile. A number of Europeans have heard and also seen tigers – generally the male but in at least one instance the female – mimicking the call of the Sambar. It has been shown that a tiger's Sambar mimicry is often employed when there is no Sambar in the vicinity, and some hunters consider it to be solely a call of alarm or suspicion when suddenly disturbed. *Shikaris* and nearly all aboriginal tribes have always affirmed, however, that tigers mimic deliberately in order to lure the Sambar and although a difference is generally detectable, there are many reports of Sambar having been heard to answer the call, thus suggesting that the mimicry is evidently sufficiently good to deceive the Sambar.

The Sambar of Borneo *C.u.brookei,* which is a slighter smaller animal than *C.u. equinus,* is well distributed throughout the mainland and on some of the adjacent islands, which include Pulau Laut off the south-east coast, and Banggi and Balambangen in the extreme north.

On the mainland it is locally abundant, especially in the south-east, in the district of Kandangar, and in west Borneo in the districts of Sarawak and Landak. The type locality of this race is said to be Monat Dulit, Sarawak. In the Kulei district of east Borneo the deer are said to be slightly smaller than elsewhere in Borneo. In 1940 two game reserves were formed in the south at Kota Waringin, extending to some 100,000 hectares (247,000 acres) and at Sampit (205,000 hectares or 506,350 acres).

The Sambar occurs at all altitudes from sea level up to about 10,000 feet (about 3,000 metres) on Mount Kinabulu. It is frequently seen swimming in the sea. Its habits are mainly nocturnal and although it may be seen feeding in the morning and evening, it grazes mainly at night when it visits small patches of cultivation. It feeds on grass, especially the greener grass near water, and various wild fruits, of which it is very fond. It also browses on shoots and leaves of trees.

As elsewhere in Indonesia, the breeding habits of the Borneo Sambar are very variable, but most rutting activity probably occurs between July and October or November.

The Sambar of Formosa *C.u.swinhoei* is found in most of the forests that lie between 1,000 and 12,000 feet above sea level (304 to 3,656 metres) but is most frequently encountered at elevations between 4,500 and 7,500 feet (1,371 to 2,285 metres). It is fond of grassy slopes near pools or ponds. The present status of the deer, which is restricted to Formosa, is unknown, but during the early thirties it was described as 'plentiful'. Its local name is *Tsui-roku*.

The Sambar of Formosa is stated by Lydekker (1915) to be 'closely allied' to the Sambar of Sarawak, Borneo *C.u.brookei,* from which it appears to be distinguished by its shorter head and concave profile, relatively longer legs . . . and the somewhat smaller size. In winter general colour uniform reddish black-brown, with the head and ears reddish yellow-brown. . . . In summer the general colour light yellowish red-brown, darker in front than behind, and lightest on under-surface. . . . Good antlers measure from 16 to $19\frac{3}{4}$ inches (41 to 50 cms) in length, with a girth of from $3\frac{1}{2}$ to $4\frac{1}{2}$ inches (9 to 11·4 cms).

In the Philippines no fewer than eight races are represented. However, the taxonomy of the Philippine deer is, up to the present time, still in a state of confusion. Nobody has really settled down to collect sufficient numbers of the different races from the various islands in the Philippine archipelago and work through a monograph of the group.

As a rule, all the larger islands have, or used to have, deer except Palawan. The following islands are included in the distribution of the various races in the Philippine archipelago:

		Islands
(i)	*Cervus unicolor philippinus*	Luzon
(ii)	*C.u.alfredi*	Leyte
		Masbate
		Panay
		Negros
		Samar
(iii)	*C.u.nigricans*	Basilan
(iv)	*C.u.barandanus*	Mindoro
(v)	*C.u.basilanensis*	Basilan
(vi)	*C.u.francianus*	Mindanao
(vii)	*C.u.nigellus*	Mindanao
(viii)	*C.u.apoensis*	Mindanao

C.u.alfredi, often referred to as the Philippine Spotted deer, is the only true Spotted deer in the Philippines, there being a regular row of whitish spots on each side of the back, but distribution elsewhere is less regular.

This race, in addition to the above-mentioned islands, has been recorded also from the islands of Cebu and Guimaras but due to excessive hunting and total deforestation of the two islands, the species is now extinct there (D. S. Rabor, *in litt*. 10.11.1953).

C.u.nigricans – the smallest of all the Sambar races, with a shoulder height of only about 24 to 26 inches (61 to 66 cms) – is restricted to Basilan Island, on which a larger deer, *C.u.basilanensis*, also occurs.

C.u.nigricans was described by Dr Steere as 'occupying the higher parts of the island, in a country of steep, rocky ridges, covered thickly with timber and thick undergrowth. In the valleys were shallow streams. I took it rather for a mountaineer than a swamp-inhabiter, though the whole country was dripping with moisture at the time of my visit, and the highest lands in the Philippines are always swampiest . . .' (quoted by Lydekker, 1898).

C.u.basilanensis is also, apparently, restricted to Basilan Island from which it takes its name.

On Mindanao Island three races occur, but integration must surely take place. Of the three races, *C.u.francianus* is the commonest, its principal habitat being the lowlands. During the Philippine Zoological Expedition (1946–7) seventeen specimens of this deer were collected from the two southern provinces of Cota Bato and Davao. Lydekker (1915) considered this deer 'nearly related to *C.u.philippinus*'.

The range of *C.u.nigellus* on the island of Mindanao is said to be rather restricted, the typical locality being Mount Malindang on the west side of the island where it occurs up to about 8,000 feet (2,400 metres).

The third race occurring on Mindanao is the dark coloured *C.u.apoensis* which is described by Sanborn as being related to *C.u.nigricans* of Basilan Island, and to *C.u.nigellus* of western Mindanao. *C.u.apoensis* is, however, separated from *C.u. nigellus* by about 190 miles (305 kms), for whereas the typical locality of *C.u.apoensis* is given as Mount Apo in the south, that of the latter is Mount Malindang in the west, the two districts being separated from each other by areas of low-lying country. Signs of deer were noted on Mount Apo from about 2,500 feet (760 metres) right up to an altitude of about 9,600 feet (2,900 metres) near the summit.

Part of the range of *C.u.apoensis* at lower altitudes is shared with *C.u.francianus* so it is probable that intermediate types occur where their range overlaps.

Deer were heard calling on Mount McKinley between the 22nd October and 21st November 1946 by members of the Philippine Zoological Expedition (Sanborn, 1952) which suggests that rutting occurs during this period. It is unlikely, however, that the rut is restricted to that period.

C.u.philippinus, which occurs on Luzon Island, is according to Lydekker (1915),

... nearly allied to *C.u.swinhoei,* but smaller; height at shoulder about 28 inches (71 cms); general build stout and massive, with the hind-quarters not specially elevated, and the form that of a small Malay Sambar; general colour rich, ruddy brown, darkest on back and lightest on the neck; forehead and cheeks rufous fawn ... chin white; underparts uniformly brown ... antlers very similar to those of the Malay race, massive, nearly straight, with a long brow-tine, and the inner tine of the terminal fork markedly shorter than the outer one. ...

Before leaving the Sambar, mention should be made of two other races which now appear to be extinct: one which occurred on the Bonin or Ogasawara Gunto islands which lie some 700 miles (1,126 kilometres) east of Kyushu (Japan) in the Pacific Ocean, and classified by Lydekker in 1905 as *C.u.boninensis*; and the other *C.u.mariannus* on the Marianne group of islands east of the Philippines in the Pacific Ocean. It would appear that the deer were introduced to Bonin about 1850, but the island is now clear of deer.

Little information is available concerning the deer *C.u.mariannus* of the Marianne or Ladrone group which include the islands of Guam, Rota and Saipan. It has been suggested that the Sambar were brought to the Island of Guam from Luzon (Philippine Islands) but the evidence is by no means conclusive. If so, then the race would be *C.u.philippinus*.

Sambar has been introduced to Australia and occurs in a wild state in Northern Territory in the Knocker Bay country. This deer has also been introduced to the North Island of New Zealand where it has acclimatised itself in the west coast area.

RUSA DEER *Cervus timorensis*   Map p. 104

The most widespread species of deer in the Indonesian archipelago is the Rusa deer *Cervus timorensis,* of which a number of insular races are represented. A medium-sized deer, the Rusa deer very much resembles the Sambar and formerly a number of zoologists considered these two as belonging to the same species.

The principal distribution of Rusa deer in Indonesia is as follows:

	Islands
C.t.timorensis	Timor
	Flores
C.t.floresiensis	Flores
C.t.russa	Borneo
	Java
*C.t.renschi**	Bali
C.t.moluccensis	Moluccas
C.t.macassaricus	Celebes
C.t.djonga	Muna (Celebes group)
	Butung (Celebes group)
*C.t.laronesiotes**	Meeuwen

It is by no means certain that all these deer are indigenous to the above-named islands, for it is known that a considerable importation of deer seems to have taken place into some islands of the archipelago previously uninhabited by deer.

It is known that deer have been imported to Obi (1930) and Aru (1855) as well as to the western part of Onin peninsula of New Guinea (1913), and it is believed that the deer of Amboina are the descendants of seventeenth-century importations of *C.t.russa* from Java and *C.t.macassaricus* from Celebes. The latter deer appear to be restricted to Celebes and possibly also the islands of Banggai and Salajar which lie off the east and south coasts respectively.

It seems probable that racial crosses have occurred in the northern part of Celebes, and in particular in the Minahassa district. The deer in this area are possibly a cross between *C.t.macassaricus* and *C.t.russa,* the latter having been imported, perhaps, into northern Celebes from Java. Apart from hunting pressure, the deer seem to have few natural predators, native dogs running wild probably killing a few fawns.

Another race, which is restricted to the islands of Muna and Butung situated off the south-east tip of Celebes, is *C.t.djonga.* It is one of the smallest representatives of the species, being equal in size to *C.t.floresiensis* of the Flores Island group.

C.t.moluccensis occurs in a number of the Moluccas group of islands, which

*Probably insular forms of *C.t.russa.*

include Ceram, Batjan, Halmahera, Banda, Sula and Parapottan. They have also been imported to the island of Belang-Belang of the Obi group, as well as to New Guinea.

In the northern Moluccas deer are known to inhabit forest, perhaps mostly used for cover. During feeding, they often prefer coconut plantations, especially those which have been neglected for a long time, and where shrubs and herbs offer plenty of food. On Aru Island there seems to be a preference for open plains. Deer have also been observed, at times, swimming in the sea.

An adult Moluccan stag will stand about 38½ inches (98 cms) high at the shoulder, the hinds being some 4¾ inches (12 cms) less.

The largest of the Rusa deer, *C.t.russa*, come from Java with the shoulder height in adult stags measuring up to 43¼ inches (110 cms) which is about the size of a good Highland Red deer stag.

This deer, both now and formerly, appears to be less common in west Java than in the eastern part of the island. Even in the large Game Reserve of Udjung Kulon, which covers an area of about 37,500 hectares (about 92,600 acres) in the most western peninsula of Java, deer have never been plentiful. On the other hand, the deer in the Jang Highland Reserve of eastern Java, prior to Japanese occupation in 1942, rapidly increased from about 100 animals in 1906 to about 12,000. However, because of the War, and the chaotic conditions which followed, it was not long before their numbers in the reserve had sunk to less than 500.

Just over a century ago it was recorded that there were no fewer than 50,000 deer on the Jang Highland. Sixty-two years later, as already stated, their numbers had been reduced to only about 100, and it was only due to the drastic measures taken by the Ledeboer brothers that their numbers were able to recover to their pre-war status of over 10,000 head.

The deer on Java seem to show a marked preference for parkland and grass plains. Woods – or bush country – are mostly used for shelter, and the deer may be encountered anywhere from sea level up to a height of 1,600 metres (5,250 feet). It seldom, if ever, occurs in close forest. Generally speaking they are nocturnal in their habits, although on the high Jang plateau they are frequently seen grazing in the daytime.

Dr van Bemmel observed that although the deer of east Java are distinguished by smaller measurements from those of west Java, their antlers are, on the other hand, heavier and east Javan heads are the best. One of the best heads ever recorded from Java had an antler length of 43¾ inches (111·5 cms).

Natural predators on Java include panther and wild dog. A few tiger occur in the Udjung Kulon Reserve.

On the adjacent islands to Java, *C.t.russa* occurs on Nusa Barung Island, Kangean Islands, Sepandjang Island and Karimon Java Isles. Rusa deer also occur on Meeuwen Island in the Sunda Strait, but there are conflicting views as to whether the race represented here is an acceptable subspecies (*C.t.laronesiotes*). Similar doubt exists concerning the race of Bali Island which Sody (1933) considered a subspecies of its own, namely *C.t.renschi*.

During the seventeenth century Rusa deer *C.t.russa* from Java were introduced to south-east Borneo, and soon increased to enormous herds that occupied the grassy plains near Pula Lampej and in the Tareh Laut near Bandjarmasin. Little is known of this deer in Borneo, but according to van Bemmel (1949) *Rusa timorensis* still occurred in the Martapura district – an area which, presumably, is shared with *C.u.brookei* (page 107).

C.t.floresiensis, one of the smallest representatives of the species, is typical of Flores. Its range spreads east as far as Solor Island and west to Lombok Island. Included in this range as well as Flores are the islands of Sumbawa, Komodo, Rintja, Adonare and Sumba.

Very extensive areas of these islands are covered by grass, so that the food of the deer may be assumed to be nearly exclusively grass which, during at least seven months of the year, must be consumed in dried form because there is only some rain during two or three months of the year. The deer can often be seen in company with the wild Water buffalo – particularly on Komodo Island – but seldom accompany the latter when they go to water.

Wild dogs are probably the chief predators. A number of young deer are also taken by the Komodo lizards (*Varanus komodoensis*).

According to van Bemmel (1949) *C.t.floresiensis* is distinguished from the western races by smaller size, lack of sexual and age differences in colour, thin coat without mane, palmate brow tine at old age and deviating markings. Distinguished from north-eastern races principally by smaller size and thinner coat, from *timorensis* by lighter colour and less-developed mane.

Commenting on the antlers, van Bemmel stated, 'Antlers do present a geographical difference. The best heads are found in Sumba. . . . The population from Komodo offer the next best heads.'

The range of the Timor Rusa deer *C.t.timorensis* includes the islands of Timor, Rotti, Semau, P. Kambing, Alor, Pantar and the small island of Pulau Rusa, which lie west of Pantar. This deer has also been introduced to the Hermit and Ninigo Islands which lie to the north of New Guinea in the Bismarck Archipelago.

Native dogs gone wild are the chief preators on Timor.

As regards the rut of the Rusa deer in Indonesia, there seems to be no fixed pattern and calves have been recorded in almost every month of the year. During one day in January 1948 Lapré recorded a roaring stag, two stags in velvet and a calf of three months old (*C.t.floresiensis*).

In Java the birth dates of *C.t.russa* varied between March and September, whilst in Flores (*C.t.floresiensis*) most births seem to occur between October and November. In Timor, the majority of hinds killed between July and December were found to be pregnant, whilst births of *C.t.macassaricus* in Celebes were observed in almost every month of the year.

In addition to localities already mentioned above, Rusa deer have been introduced to New Caledonia (page 134), Australia (page 138) and New Zealand (page 148).

AXIS DEER or CHITAL *Axis axis*   Map p. 113

There are two subspecies of this beautiful Spotted deer, the typical *Axis axis axis* of India, and *A.a.ceylonensis* of Ceylon.

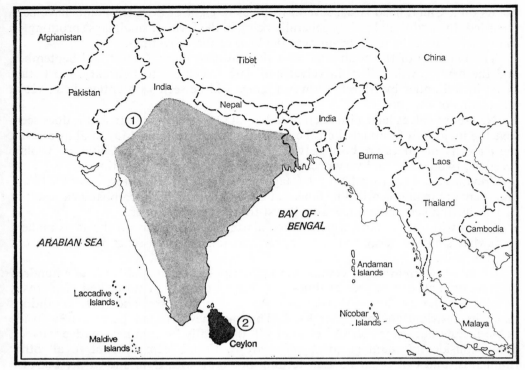

Map 21. The range of Axis deer *Axis axis* in ASIA

AXIS or CHITAL DEER. *Axis axis*

1. *Axis axis axis*   Peninsular India
2. *A.a.ceylonensis*   Ceylon

The general colour of the Chital is rufous fawn, covered in both winter and summer pelage with white spots. There is no marked seasonal change in colour. A good average-sized Chital stag from Madhya Pradesh (formerly the Central Provinces) will stand about 36 inches (91 cms) high at the shoulder, and will weigh about 190 lbs (86 kilos). Further south, the animal is somewhat smaller both in body size and antler, whilst the race on Ceylon, *A.a.ceylonensis*, is also very similar in appearance to the Chital of southern India. The ground-colour of this latter race is, however, yellower and purer fawn, while the white spots on the body are smaller and may be described as flecks rather than spots.

The antlers of the adult Chital are reddish brown in colour. The beam, which curves backwards and outwards in a lyre-shaped formation, is usually about 30 inches (76 cms) long and any antlers measuring in excess of 38 inches (96·5 cms) are extremely good. The record head, which came from Kumaon Terai, had an antler length of 40 inches (101·6 cms) and bore seven points. The longest antlers of a Ceylon deer measured 36¼ inches (92 cms) but these were exceptional and the majority of heads measure under 30 inches (76 cms) in length. Although the usual number of points on a Chital head is six, several trophies of eight or even ten points have been recorded, the additional points generally being in the form of small jags sprouting on the upper side of the main beam near the base of the brow tines.

The majority of the adult stags cast their antlers about August and September, and the new growth will be in velvet until late December to February, most stags being in full antler by March. However, stags will be seen with antlers in velvet at all seasons of the year.

New-born calves have also been found at all seasons of the year, but it does seem that the majority of animals join the rut during late April and May, and as a result the majority of calves are born between October and December. Chital are prolific breeders, two calves, and very occasionally three, being born at a time.

Previous to and during the rut the stags frequently fight for possession of the hinds, and there are many recorded instances of a stag having died in combat as a result of its ribs having been punctured by a thrust from its rival's antler.

Chital will utter a shrill whistle when alarmed. During the rut the stags make a somewhat similar sound, but it is longer and louder. Both sexes will scream out when in pain.

Chital are comparatively common in many parts of India, and herds of a hundred or more animals can be seen at times. The near proximity of water and also covert in which to lie up during the day is essential for this deer, and these conditions make its distribution somewhat local. They are never found permanently inside dense forests but being tolerant of man will frequently be seen near native villages, doing considerable damage to standing crops. Chital seem tolerant to all other ruminants, and can often be seen feeding not only with domestic cattle, but also Black buck, Swamp deer, Nilgai and pig, etc.

As is the case with many animals associating in large herds, Chital are rather more diurnal than some species, and will often be seen feeding for several hours after sunrise, and be on the move some time before sunset. They both graze and browse, and being good swimmers, take readily to water.

The principal predators of the Chital are leopards and wild dogs, but on occasions deer will be taken by crocodile and python.

The Chital *A.a.axis*, although less numerous than formerly, is still well distributed throughout the peninsula of India, occurring in all suitable localities south of about latitude 25°N. North of this line it occurs in parts of Uttar Pradesh, and extends right up to the confines of Jammu in the north-east.

The Ceylon race *A.a.ceylonensis* also has a wide distribution, being common in all the more sparsely inhabited districts on the island and in particular in the north-eastern part where it is drier. It shuns the heavy forest, and rarely ascends over 1,500 feet (457 metres).

Shortly after the 1914–18 War some Chital were introduced to the Andaman Islands in order to create a source of meat for those who have to live and work in the forests. They increased rapidly and by the end of the Second World War had become a pest, and were destroying the seedlings of valuable commercial species in the regeneration areas. To counteract them two leopards were introduced during the year 1952–3, but in order to ensure that no breeding took place, both were females.

Chital have also been successfully introduced to a few other parts of the world, including the Hawaiian Islands and to the island of Brioni on the Adriatic. Generally speaking, however, their introduction to northern European countries has not been too successful, as they seem incapable of regulating their breeding habits to suit the climate. Although the attempt to introduce Chital to New Zealand met with failure, this deer has been successfully established in Queensland, Australia (see page 136).

HOG DEER *Axis porcinus*   Map p. 116

Another deer of the same genus as the Chital but with a wider distribution is the Hog deer or Para, of which two subspecies are recognised. The typical race *A.p.porcinus* is restricted to Ceylon and the low alluvial grass plains of the Indus and Ganges valleys, where it ranges from Sind in the west (about longitude 67°E) through the Punjab, Uttar Pradesh (United Provinces) and Bengal to Assam in the east, and thence into Burma. About latitude 24°N and the Himalayan foothills might be said to mark the extent of its range south and north respectively in India. In Burma, however, the Hog deer occurs as far south as Tavoy in Tenasserim (about 14·7°N) whilst in the north it reaches the Pidaung Plains of Kachin State (about 25°N). Further south in Thailand, a slightly larger race, *A.p.annamiticus,* occurs and this deer spreads eastwards into Vietnam. It does not, however, spread south along the Malay peninsula into Malaya, or northwards into China.

Hog deer stags stand about 26 to 29 inches (66 to 74 cms) high at the shoulder, and will weigh about 80 lbs to 100 lbs (36 to 45 kilograms). The build is low and heavy, with legs and face comparatively short. This appearance, together with their characteristic habit of rushing rather than bounding through the grass in the manner of a wild pig, has earned for them the title of Hog deer. Despite their small size, the stags carry good trophies, and a really good pair of antlers bearing six points will measure about 20 inches (51 cms) in length. The average length of antler for Hog deer in India is about 15½ inches (39 cms) whilst in Burma the average is slightly better – about 17 to 18 inches (44 cms). The record head (length 24 inches (60·9 cms), beam 3½ inches (8·8 cms) and inside span 14 inches (35·5 cms)) came from the Irrawaddy Valley district of Burma. Antlers are generally shed during the months of March to early May.

The general colouration of the Indian Hog deer is brown or yellowish brown, the under surface of the body being a darker shade than that above. Old stags may be a very dark brown colour, but there is some seasonal variation in the shade of the coat. Calves are spotted, and faint white spots are also sometimes visible on younger stags and hinds, particularly during the early months of summer pelage. The tail is of medium length, well haired but not bushy. The face glands are small and the metatarsal tufts are slightly lighter in colour than the rest of the leg.

At one time the Hog deer was extremely common, particularly in parts of Bengal, but excessive shooting has thinned its ranks in many areas, and cultivation of many of its former haunts has reduced its range. However, it is still quite plentiful in parts of India where the grass lands remain uncultivated. It never ascends into the hills.

In Ceylon it is scarce and seldom seen, being confined to a strip of country lying

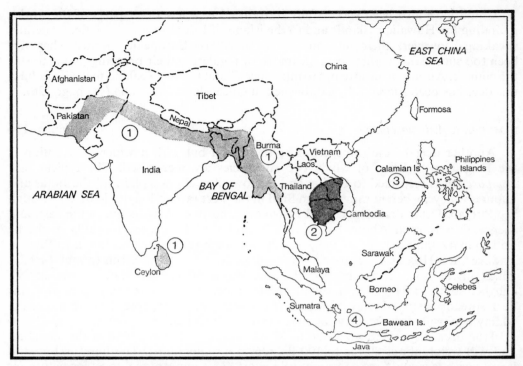

Map 22. The range of Hog deer, *Axis porcinus*; Calamian Deer, *Axis calamianensis* and Bawean deer, *Axis kuhlii* in ASIA

HOG DEER. *Axis porcinus*

1. *Axis porcinus porcinus*   North India, Burma and Ceylon
2. *A.p.annamaticus*   Thailand and Indo-China

CALAMIAN DEER. *Axis calamianensis*

3. *A.calamianensis*   Calamian Islands

BAWEAN DEER. *Axis kuhlii*

4. *A.kuhlii*   Bawean Island

near the south-west coast in the Southern Province. The Hog deer is not indigenous to Ceylon, having been introduced, it is believed, by the Dutch during the sixteenth century. It is fond of lying up in the paddy fields – a habit which has earned for it the name of 'paddy-field deer'. It is also sometimes referred to as the 'swamp deer' in Ceylon; but of course the true Swamp deer is *Cervus duvauceli* which occurs in northern India.

In Burma, too, the Hog deer, which was once very abundant in certain parts, has decreased enormously in recent years, being confined to the grassy plains, never entering the heavy hill forests. Much of what used to be the Hog deer terrain has now been turned over to cultivation and, on account of the damage the deer do to crops, they are slaughtered ruthlessly by the natives.

In Vietnam, as well as in neighbouring Laos and Cambodia, the Hog deer is well distributed although its appearance in any one area is local rather than general. It is particularly fond of swampy plains and plateaux in which there is adequate long grass to give it cover.

Unlike the Chital, Hog deer are not found in herds and it is rare to see parties of more than three or four animals together. As often as not they are found singly or in pairs.

Their food consists mainly of grass, leaves and young shoots, but they are also very fond of grain and rice plant, and, when the paddy is high enough to afford concealment, they will enter the crops even during the daytime.

When alarmed, Hog deer make a whistling sound. They will also give a warning bark. The rut takes place mainly during the months of November and December and the calves, generally one, but occasionally two, are born about eight months later. The rut for *A.p.annamaticus* would appear to take place about two months earlier.

The natural predators are much the same as for the Chital, and in particular leopards, wild dogs and crocodiles.

Hog deer have been introduced to Australia where they have established themselves in the south-east coast area of Victoria (see page 136).

CALAMIAN DEER *Axis calamianensis*   Map p. 116

Apart from the Sambar, the only other deer to be found in the Philippine group of islands is the Calamian deer *Axis* (*Hyelaphus*) *calamianensis* which is restricted to the Calamian group of islands and in particular to the islands of Busuanga and Culion.

Few specimens have been examined, but Lydekker (1915) stated 'this species is clearly a *Hyelaphus* and not a *Rusa* . . .'. Continuing he stated,

> this deer is distinguished from the type species by the shorter and more stunted face, shorter and more rounded ears, and the following details in colouring: the white on the under-side of the lower jaw, instead of being restricted to the chin, extends backwards to form a largish patch on the throat; the fore part of this throat-patch being separated from the jaw-patch by a narrow bar of fawn; there is a white moustache-mark, and more white on the insides of their ears and at their roots than in the typical Hog deer; the legs are a darker brown, and the back is bright golden brown, passing into orange on the buttocks.

A deer at Woburn Park early in the century, presumed to have come from the Calamian Islands, was subsequently presented to the British Museum by the Duke of Bedford in 1905.

BAWEAN DEER *Axis kuhlii*   Map p. 116

The Bawean deer – sometimes called Kuhl's deer – is restricted to the Bawean Island, which lies in the Java Sea between Borneo and Java. It was first discovered by

I

Salomon Müller in 1836, not on the island of origin, Bawean in the Javan Sea, but in Tuban, a small town on the north coast of Java, where the local Indonesian governor kept a small herd of these little deer in his garden.

Dr van Bemmel (1953) believes this deer prefers secondary forest and its range is restricted to certain areas of the island, 60 per cent of which is more or less cultivated. Because of the deforestation that has taken place on Bawean, he expressed grave concern about the future survival of this deer. Recent reports, however, suggest that its present status is satisfactory.

Rather similar in appearance to the Hog deer, an adult Bawean deer stag stands about 27 inches (68·5 cms) high at the shoulder. It has a comparatively short face, with the antlers supported on relatively long pedicles, not much longer than the head. Its general colour is one of uniform brown, without a dark stripe on the back. The tail is moderately long and bushy. The young are unspotted.

Little is known of the biology of this deer. In Amsterdam Zoo antlers were shed in February and the rut took place between August and September.

ELD'S DEER or THAMIN *Cervus eldi*   Map p. 122

Another deer of southern Asia which is becoming scarce is the Thamin or Eld's deer – sometimes called Brow-antlered deer – *Cervus eldi,* of which three subspecies are recognised: *Cervus eldi eldi* from Manipur; *C.e.thamin* from Burma, Tenasserim and adjacent parts of Thailand, and *C.e.siamensis* from Thailand, whose range also extends into Vietnam and Hainan Island.

The name Eld's is generally applied to the Manipur type, the native name for which is *sangai,* which means, literally, 'the animal that looks at you'. *Thamin* or *thameng,* on the other hand, are the native names for this deer in Burma.

Standing about 45 inches (114 cms) high at the shoulder, the summer pelage of the stags is fawnish red above the pale brown of the underparts. In winter the colour is uniformly dark brown above, and whitish underneath. There is some white on the chin, around the eyes and margins of the ears. At all seasons the hinds, which are smaller and more lightly built than the stags, are slightly paler. In both sexes a few light spots may be visible near the middle line of the back. According to Lydekker (*The Game Animals of India, Burma, Malaya and Tibet,* 1924) 'The Siamese thamin (*C.e.siamensis*) is more rufous-coloured, and Hainan specimens have a number of light spots on the body. In general bodily form these deer are like Swamp deer, having the same short tail, but retaining more or less distinct traces of the metatarsal gland and tuft.' The calves are spotted at birth.

The most noticeable feature of this deer is the antlers of the stags which in adult specimens differ from those of all other species of deer in that the long brow, which is set at right angles to the pedicle, and the beam form one more or less continuous bow-shaped curve. This formation has given this deer the name of Brow-antlered deer. For the greater part of its length the beam is undivided, having at first a backwards, then an outwards and finally a forward curvature. Towards its termination the beam forks, and in older stags there will be a number of small jags sprouting from the upper surface of the outer tine of the terminal fork, which may vary from two or three to at least ten. In this respect, however, there is considerable local variation. There may also be a few jags sprouting on the upper surface near the base of the brow in similar fashion to those on Axis deer (page 114). A good pair of Eld's deer antlers will measure about 38 to 40 inches (about 99 cms) in length (excluding length of brow tine) – with the record trophy from Upper Burma having a length of 44 inches (111·7 cms) and bearing sixteen points. Several heads of over twenty points have been obtained, and in the British Museum there is one with sixteen points on one antler and nineteen on the other – a total of thirty-five points. In good trophies the brow tine is about 15 inches (38 cms) long. The colour of the antler varies from a light golden yellow to dark brown.

A peculiarity of *C.e.eldi* is that the foot has been modified to enable the deer to walk on swampy ground, which is its principal habitat in the Manipur Valley. The Sitatunga antelope of Africa also inhabits very swampy ground, but in its case a sufficiently large surface of support is afforded by a lengthening of the hooves. With *C.e.eldi,* however, the hooves remain the normal length, but extra support is obtained by the animal walking on the under surface of the hardened pasterns.

E. P. Gee in *The Wild Life of India* (1964) describes two visits he made to Logtak Lake in Manipur, the last remaining haunt of *C.e.eldi* which as recently as 1951 was thought to be extinct in Manipur. 'The first thing I found', he wrote, 'was that the ten-square-mile [2,590 hectares] "swamp" in which the deer live, is not an ordinary swamp. It is a floating one, consisting of a thick mat of humus and dead vegetation which actually floats on the water of the lake. About one-fifth of this mat is above, and four-fifths are below, the surface of the water. And on the mat grow reeds and grasses up to fifteen feet [4·5 metres] in height. This mat of humus is called *phumdi* by the Manipuris and its thickness varies from a few inches to about five feet.'

During the first visit made in 1959, owing to the thickness of the vegetation, it was very difficult to see the animals closely, so Gee returned to the Logtak Lake in March 1961. After boating along a channel cut through the *phumdi* just as the sun was rising he reached an observation hillock from which, with the aid of binoculars he saw, first a stag and hind, and then in another place, two hinds, each with a three-quarter-grown calf.

In Burma and other parts of its range, the Brow-antlered deer cannot tolerate heavy forests or hills, and their mode of life is very similar to that of the Swamp deer, congregating for at least a portion of the year in large herds, and frequenting low, flat country. To a great extent they are grazing animals, feeding largely on wild rice, but they also browse on the leaves of certain trees.

The rut takes place between the middle of March and the middle of May, the calves being born during the last three months of the year. Usually there is only one calf at birth. Brow-antlered deer do not seem to have any special call at rutting time but the alarm cry of both sexes is a barking grunt, that of the stags being louder and longer.

In Manipur the stags begin to shed their antlers towards the end of June, but in Lower Burma the shedding is deferred until the latter part of August or early September. By the end of the year or early January, therefore, all the big stags will have their new growth of antlers complete and free of velvet.

The big, matured stags live solitary lives during much of the year, except during the rutting season, when they rejoin the herds of hinds. During the rutting season, and in particular during the night, the stags fight frequently for possession of the hinds. The stags are also fond of wallowing.

There is no doubt that all three subspecies of this deer are rare. In Manipur, E. P. Gee, after discussing the situation of *C.e.eldi* with local forest officers and villagers, came to the conclusion that 'there were probably about 100 Brow-antlered deer . . . in the ten-square-mile sanctuary' of Logtak Lake, but concluded by saying that 'the authorities of Manipur have undertaken to do their best to preserve these deer in their floating sanctuary'.

In Burma, before the introduction of guns and rifles, the Thamin *C.e.thamin* was extremely numerous but now it is doubtful if the total population exceeds 4,000 animals, with the largest remaining population being found in Shwebo, Meiktila and Minbu Forest divisions. Some sanctuaries have been provided, and inside the forest reserves and sanctuaries the Thamin is holding its own, or even increasing in some areas, but elsewhere it is being poached and rapidly decreasing in numbers.

The plight of the Thailand Brow-antlered deer, *C.e.siamensis*, is a little obscure. In Thailand itself, it is believed that only a few herds of four or five head now remain at Nang Kong in the north-east, and at Chieng Karn in the north. In Cambodia, where it was at one time relatively common, the deer suffered heavy losses as a result of the war. Since then the Forest Department of Cambodia has proclaimed it a protected species, and several reserves have been established for its protection. These reserves are situated in Phnom-Priech in the Kratie Province, in Koulen Promtep in the Siemreap/Kompong Thom region, in the Cardamons, in the Pursat and Battambang Provinces. This subspecies also occurs sparingly in Vietnam and also, possibly, still on Hainan Island, but as long ago as 1923 it was described as 'not abundant'. Thomas (1918) gave the Hainan Brow-antlered deer the racial status of *C.e.hainanus,* but it is probably an insular form of *C.e.siamensis.*

SWAMP DEER *Cervus duvauceli*   Map p. 122

Another deer which has a limited distribution in the world is the Swamp deer, which is found only in central and northern India and in southern Nepal. In northern Uttar Pradesh, where this deer is also known as *gond,* and also in Assam, the name Swamp deer is very descriptive for it is hardly ever found out of swamps. In Madhya Pradesh (the old Central Provinces) there are no swamps for it to frequent so this name is a complete misnomer. In this part of India the Swamp deer is often referred to as Barasingha on account of its fine antlers, but as mentioned on page 72 Bara-singha is also used to describe the Hangul or Kashmir stag, so care must be taken not to confuse the two species.

Standing about 47 to 49 inches (119 to 124 cms) high at the shoulder and weighing about 380 to 400 lbs (172 to 181 kilograms), with exceptional beasts scaling consider-ably more, there are two subspecies of Swamp deer – *C.d.duvauceli* in Assam, Uttar Pradesh and south-west Nepal; and *C.d.branderi* in Madhya Pradesh. A good des-cription of this latter deer is given by A. A. Dunbar Brander (1923).

The ordinary colour of the animal is brown, shading to yellowish brown on the lower parts. Females are lighter in colour, the hair is moderately fine and often woolly in texture. The necks of the stags are maned. There is often a darker dorsal line and it is common to see master stags so dark all over as almost to appear black in the distance. The under side of the tail is white or light yellow. There is a marked seasonal change in the colour both in this animal and the Sambar. As the hot weather advances they become much lighter, the stags being reddish brown and the does yellowish brown. At this season also they develop spots. These spots are arranged in precisely the same manner as those of the Chital; they are not white but the hair is merely somewhat lighter in colour, or may even only be apparent when viewed at an angle, when they appear as water marks. . . .

So far as the Swamp deer at Woburn Park, England, are concerned, their summer pelage is a beautiful golden brown colour, with no apparent spots being visible. In winter, the coat loses much of its gilt, becoming a fairly dark brown without any yellowish tint, paling towards the underparts.

As is the case with many other species of deer, young Swamp deer at birth are well spotted. Normally only one calf is born but twins are not unknown.

There is considerable variation in the form of the antlers, which usually bear ten to fifteen points, although heads with up to twenty have been obtained. Two distinct types are recognised with a wide range of intermediary patterns. In one case, the beam is a regular curve in the shape of a scythe curving backwards from the skull and then forwards so as to bring the uppermost point in line with the tip of the brow. At intervals along the beam and commencing about two-thirds of the distance up, tines project, the first one frequently bifurcating with one or two additional small points or snags.

In the second type, which produces a more attractive head, the brow tine is set at right angles to the beam, which grows with an outward curve giving the antlers a wide spread. At the place where the first point emerges, the beam curves abruptly forward, and the effect is that the last foot or so of it is almost horizontal. The upper tines, some of which may bifurcate, grow vertically and undoubtedly add to the beauty of this fine trophy.

A good average pair of antlers will measure about 35 inches (89 cms) in length, with exceptional trophies reaching the 40-inch (102 cms) mark. Occasionally one sees a stag bearing antlers of only six points, and resembling very much those produced by the Sambar.

There is a variation in the dates of shedding the antlers between the northern and central types, and the season of the latter deer also seems to have changed slightly during the last forty years. In central India the majority of stags shed their antlers about May – about three months later than the Swamp deer of Assam.

During growth the antlers are covered with a beautiful red coloured velvet which combines very well with the golden brown coat of summer. In cleaning their antlers the stags rarely resort to fraying against a tree, but prefer to use small shrubs or long grass, which at this season of the year – August to September – is almost head high.

The actual rut is an ill-defined period, but the chief period would seem to be

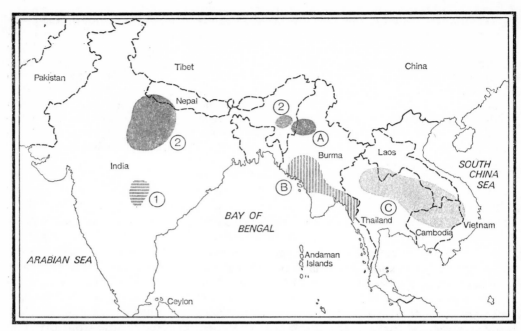

Map 23. The range of Swamp deer *Cervus duvauceli* (1 & 2) and Eld's Deer *Cervus eldi* (A, B & C) in ASIA

SWAMP DEER. *Cervus duvauceli*

1. *Cervus duvauceli branderi*   Madhya Pradesh, central India
2. *C.d.duvauceli*   Northern India and south-west Nepal

ELD'S DEER. *Cervus eldi*

A. *Cervus eldi eldi*   Manipur
B. *C.e.thamin*   Burma, Tenasserim
C. *C.e.siamensis*   Thailand, Indo-China and Hainan Island

between mid-December and mid-January.* The master stag collects together a harem of hinds which may number up to thirty or so, for the possession of which he fights in the same way as the European Red deer stag. During these fights antlers are frequently broken or disfigured through tines being snapped off.

During the rut the stags roar frequently, uttering a sound which has been compared to the '*ee on ee on*' of a donkey. This call may last about a minute and can be heard after the termination of the rutting season. Also, when alarmed, the Swamp deer will scream loudly with a shrill-sounding bray, and other animals in the vicinity may take up the chorus.

When the rut is over the big stags leave the hinds, and small parties, consisting of six or eight large stags, may be seen banded together, past enmities forgotten.

* At Woburn Park, England, the rut takes place between August and early October, the calves being born in May or early June.

The oldest and largest beasts, however, may be even more exclusive and with perhaps one companion of similar age, retire to a more secluded *maidan* for their retreat.

A characteristic of the Swamp deer is that, except during the rutting season, they go about in herds or schools of the same age or sex group. This habit is rather similar to that of the Père David's deer (see page 101).

Swamp deer are less nocturnal than the Sambar and it is not unusual to find them grazing as late as ten o'clock in the morning, after which they will lie down in the long grass. However, if undisturbed, the deer become exceedingly regular in their habits, often frequenting the same field day after day until the grass becomes much trampled down and in consequence forms little cover. Whilst resting the deer are constantly attended by the Indian minas birds which settle on them and remove the ticks with which their coats are infested.

Swamp deer have a fairly strong smell which resembles that of the European Red deer.

The favourite habitat of the southern race – *C.d.branderi* – is a large grassy plain or *maidan* on which the deer can graze and rest, preferring to live in or on the edge of these plains and only penetrating the jungle-clad hills to a short distance. This is in contrast to the northern race *C.d.duvauceli* which, as already mentioned, is a dweller of the swamp lands.

The recognised method of hunting Swamp deer is by stalking, and if this can be done from the back of an elephant so much the better, for not only are the deer accustomed to seeing elephants and are unlikely, therefore, to stampede, but the hunter from his high perch will have a better chance of seeing his quarry over the high grass. Unlike many species of deer, the Swamp deer seldom interfere with crops. Nevertheless it has been exterminated over large areas where it formerly existed. Fortunately the Swamp deer has been able to find refuge in the Kanha National Park, and a few other places, and *provided* its present status can be maintained is in no immediate danger.

Swamp deer from India have been introduced to a few parks in other parts of the world, notably to Woburn in England.

SCHOMBURGK'S DEER *Cervus schomburgki*   Map p. 125

Since early in the century Schomburgk's deer, a native of Thailand (Siam), has been on the verge of extinction, and all evidence would suggest that this has now taken place. Its last stronghold seems to have been on the great swampy plains around Paknam Po (Nakhon Sawan) in Central Thailand, and possibly also in the Muang Petchabun area. The last recorded specimen seems to have been a stag killed in 1931 by an officer of the Siamese police.

Standing about 40 to 41 inches (about 103 cms) high at the shoulder, the Schomburgk's deer was of a uniform brown colour with the underparts and lower jaw whitish. In winter the hair became rather long and coarse. The antlers are probably the most beautiful of all species of deer, being moderately large and extremely complex in formation. A feature of the Schomburgk'santler is the forking of all the main tines, which results in some trophies having as many as twenty or more points. A good head would measure about 27 inches (69 cms) in length along the outer curve, the longest recorded specimen in the British Museum measuring just over 30 inches (76 cms).

TUFTED DEER *Elaphodus cephalophus*   Map p. 125

The range of the Tufted deer is from extreme north-east Burma into south and central China as far north as about latitude 35°N. Opinions differ as to whether one or more different subspecies are represented. Flerov (1952) and Walker (1964) suggest one, Lydekker (1915) four, and Ellerman and Morrison-Scott (1951) three, namely the typical race *E.c.cephalophus* from north-east Burma and south-west China; *E.c.michianus* in eastern China and *E.c.ichangensis* for Hupeh district of central China. It may well be that this last-named race is an intermediate one between the eastern and western forms and should, therefore, not be considered a valid race. In addition to south-west China and north-east Burma, the range of *E.c.cephalophus* extends into eastern Tibet. Its range in China includes Szechwan, from which the type specimen came, Sikang and northern Yunnan. This race, the largest of the Tufted deer, frequents the high valley jungles and mountain forests up to about 15,000 feet (4,570 metres) above sea level. It is sometimes referred to as the West China Tufted deer. In Burma it is found in Hpimaw, Hpare, Zuk Lang and Lauklaung subdivisions of Myitkyina district, from where it extends its range into the adjacent districts of south-west China. The native name for this deer in Burma is *Chik Naw* whilst in China it goes by the name of *Hei Chi-tze*.

The range of the central China (Ichang) Tufted deer, *E.c.ichangensis,* includes the Ichang district of Hupeh, from which it gets its name, and eastern Szechwan. It may also include northern Hunan and Kiangsi.

Michie's (coastal) Tufted deer *E.c.michianus* is found in the coastal provinces of south-east China, from the valley and estuary of the Fuchun Kiang (Tsientang) River in northern Chekiang south to and including Fukien Province and northern Kwang-tung (or Canton) Province. This – or the preceding race – also occurs through much of Kiangsi.

Tufted deer are very similar to, but slightly larger than, the Muntjac, an adult buck from south-west China standing up to about 25 inches (63·5 cms) high at the shoulder. The other two races are slightly smaller. Its dentition is also similar to the Muntjac, with upper canines of comparable length. The antlers, however, are much smaller and are sometimes completely hidden by the tuft of hair on the forehead which gives the deer its name. The antlers grow from bony pedicles which, however, are shorter and less pronounced than those on the Muntjacs.

The general colour of the upper parts is deep chocolate brown, the underparts are white and the head and neck are inclined to be grey. There are white markings on the posterior tips of the ears, and also on the underside of the tail. The coastal form, Michie's Tufted deer, is smaller and rather lighter in colour, with less white on the tail. Similar in size to Michie's, the general colour of the central form – Ichang Tufted deer – is described by Lydekker (1915) as being 'dark brown, passing into

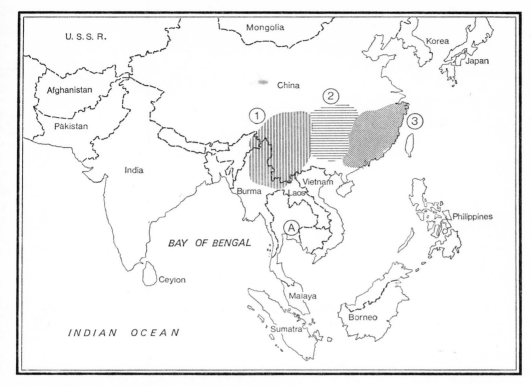

Map 24. The range of Tufted deer *Elaphodus* in ASIA

1. *Elaphodus cephalophus cephalophus*   Southern China, northern Burma
2. *E.c.ichangensis*   Central southern China
3. *E.c.michianus*   South-east China

The former range of Schomburgk's Deer *Cervus schomburgki* in THAILAND

A. *Cervus schomburgki*   Thailand (probably extinct)

blackish on the limbs; tail wholly white at tip, with only the basal two-thirds of the upper surface dark'.

Both male and female bark during the mating season or when alarmed. According to Walker (1964) the rut 'is during April and May, followed by a gestation period of about six months after which one or two young are born. The young are coloured like their parents but have a row of spots along each side of the mid-line of the back'. A female Tufted deer, however, was shot at Pudtze in West Hupeh (China) in early April that contained a large foetus which would suggest an October or November rut.

When feeding, Tufted deer carry their tails high. When bounding off, their tails flop with every bound, displaying the white underside in much the same manner as the White-tailed deer (*Odocoileus virginianus*).

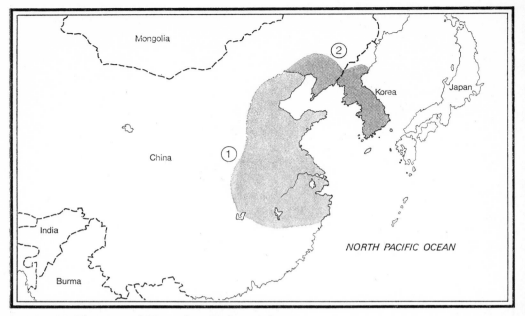

Map 25. The range of Water-deer *Hydropotes* in ASIA

1. *Hydropotes inermis inermis*   East China
2. *H.i.argyropus*   Korea

It is not known where the line of demarcation between the two subspecies occurs.

CHINESE WATER-DEER *Hydropotes inermis*   **Map above**

Another deer in which neither sex produces antlers is the Chinese Water-deer *Hydropotes inermis inermis* which is sometimes referred to as the Yangtze River deer, having been first described from a specimen from this river area. Its distribution ranges from the Yangtze River northwards to Korea.

In Korea, where a separate subspecies *H.i.argyropus* is recognised, it is plentiful in the reed-grown swamps and grasslands along the lower reaches of all the large rivers, excluding those in the extreme north-east. Its northern limit of distribution is probably about latitude 42°N.

In China it occurs plentifully in most of the central and eastern valleys between latitude 28°N and 35°N and east of longitude 111°E. It is particularly plentiful in the great reed-beds of the deltas and estuaries of the Fuchun Kiang and Yangtze Rivers. This deer, despite its abundance, seldom congregates and is generally seen alone or in pairs.

Adult bucks of this deer, which has an extremely short tail, stand about 20 to 21 inches (about 52 cms) high at the shoulder, the does being an inch or two (about 3·8 cms) smaller. Bucks will weigh about 25 to 30 lbs (11 to 13·6 kilograms), the does weighing about 5 to 7 lbs (about 2·7 kilograms) lighter. Like the Musk deer, the buck has a pair of long, sharp tusks which will average about 70 mm (2¾ inches) in length. The upper canines on the does are very short.

The summer coat of the adult is of a reddish brown colour, which as winter advances becomes a dull brown faintly flecked with grey which in some individuals – particularly the bucks – is lighter than in others. The hair of the winter coat is inclined to be coarse in texture and rather loose. The fawns, which are born during the summer months, are of a dull brown colour, some more reddish than others, with two distinct rows of yellowish white spots and a few others less regimented visible. The rut takes place in winter. Twins and triplets are common and up to six fawns have been recorded. The doe, however, only has four mammae.

The alarm cry is a harsh bark. The bucks, when fighting, often make a 'chittering noise' which may be produced by clicking the tusks. When retreating in alarm, it usually progresses by a series of leaps and bounds rather like a hare.

Chinese Water-deer have been successfully introduced to England and now lead a feral existence in the area near Woburn and Whipsnade.

MUNTJAC *Muntiacus*   Map p. 128

The Muntjacs, which include five species and over fifteen subspecies, have a wide distribution in southern and south-east Asia, ranging from India in the west to south-eastern China and Formosa in the east, whilst in the south, its distribution includes Sumatra, Java and some other islands of Indonesia.

In India, three races of *Muntiacus muntjak* – generally referred to as the Indian Muntjak – have been recognised as follows:

(i) *M.m.vaginalis* in the north, including Kashmir, Nepal, Uttar Pradesh, Bengal, Sikkim, Bhutan and Assam. This race extends its range eastwards into the northern parts of Burma, Thailand and Vietnam, as well as to the extreme southern parts of Yunnan and Kwangsi Provinces in south-western China.
(ii) *M.m.aureus,* which has the widest distribution in India, being found throughout central and much of southern peninsular India.
(iii) *M.m.malabaricus,* which is restricted to southern India from about latitude 15°N southwards. This race, which is the largest of the Indian Muntjacs, also occurs in Ceylon.

In the southern part of Burma, *M.m.vaginalis* is replaced by *M.m.grandicornis* whose range includes parts of Tenasserim and adjacent Thailand. It seems unlikely, however, that its range in Thailand is more than marginal and probably does not even reach the Mai-ping River. In a southerly direction its range does not extend into the Federation of Malaya where two races of *M.muntiacus* occur, *M.m.peninsulae* and *M.m.robinsoni,* the latter being restricted to the Rhio-Linga archipelago including Bintan Island.

In addition to *M.m.vaginalis* and *M.m.grandicornis,* a third race of *M.muntiacus* occurs in the central and southern parts of Thailand, namely *M.m.curvostylis,* but its northern limits of range are not very clear. Eastwards, its range does not seem to penetrate into Laos or Vietnam, where it is replaced by *M.m.annamensis* in the south, and in the northern and central districts of Vietnam by *M.m.nigripes* – often

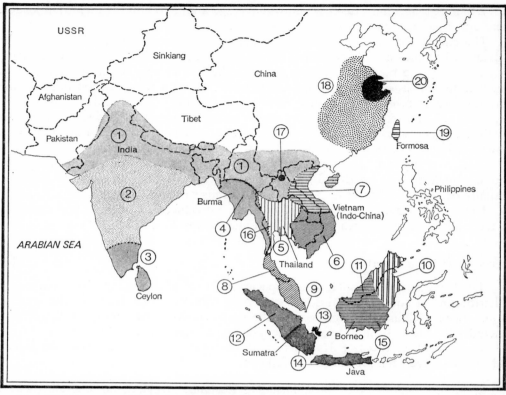

Map 26. The range of Muntjac *Muntiacus* in ASIA

MUNTJAC. *Muntiacus muntjak*
  1. *Muntiacus muntjak vaginalis*   Northern India to south-west China
  2. *M.m.aureus*   Peninsular India
  3. *M.m.malabaricus*   Southern India and Ceylon
  4. *M.m.grandicornis*   Burma
  5. *M.m.curvostylis*   Thailand
  6. *M.m.annamensis*   Indo-China
  7. *M.m.nigripes*   Vietnam and Hainan Island
  8. *M.m.peninsulae*   Malaya
  9. *M.m.robinsoni*   Rhio-Linga archipelago
 10. *M.m.rubidus*   North Borneo
 11. *M.m.pleiharicus*   South Borneo
 12. *M.m.montanus*   Sumatra
 13. *M.m.bancanus*   Billiton and Banka islands
 14. *M.m.muntjak*   Java and South Sumatra
 15. *M.m.nainggolani*   Bali and Lombok islands

FEA'S MUNTJAC. *Muntiacus feae*
 16. *Muntiacus feae*   Tenasserim and Thailand

ROOSEVELT'S MUNTJAC. *Muntiacus rooseveltorum*
 17. *M.rooseveltorum*   Indo-China

referred to as the Black-legged or Black-footed Muntjac. This latter deer is also found on Hainan Island which lies to the east across the Gulf of Tongking.

An unusual specimen of Muntjac collected at Muong Yo in northern Laos has been named *Muntiacus rooseveltorum* by Osgood (1932). Its size is intermediate between *M.muntjac* and *M.reevesi,* but in colour it is slightly redder than the latter. Its distribution would appear to be confined to the northern part of Vietnam, in which *M.muntjac vaginalis* is also found.

In addition to the various subspecies of Indian Muntjac *Muntiacus muntjak* just described, another species known as Fea's Muntjac *Muntiacus feae* occurs sparingly in Tenasserim and south-western Thailand. In the former area, where it is sometimes referred to as the Tenasserim Muntjac, it is restricted to the Thaton, Amherst, Tavoy and Mergui districts.

An adult male Indian Muntjac stands about 22–3 inches (about 57 cms) high at the shoulder, the does being some 3 inches (7·6 cms) less. In summer, the body colour is a deep chestnut, darker on the back, toning down to almost white on the belly. In winter, the colour is slightly darker.

The Burmese Muntjac *M.m.grandicornis* is larger than the Indian forms and has more massive antlers, a good pair measuring about 6¾ inches (17 cms) in length.

Fea's Muntjac *M.feae* is similar in size to the Indian form but is slightly darker in colour, being a uniform dark brown except for some yellow hairs in the centre of the crown around the pedicles and base of ears. A black line runs up the centre of each pedicle.

In central, eastern and southern China three species are represented – Reeves's Muntjac *Muntiacus reevesi reevesi* in south-east China, with a subspecies *M.r.micrurus* present in Formosa; the Black or Hairy-fronted Muntjac *M.crinifrons* which is also in eastern China, but a little further north in Chekiang Province; and two races of *M.muntiacus,* namely *M.m.vaginalis* in the extreme south-western part of China, and *M.m.nigripes* on Hainan Island.

Of the above species and races, the Reeves's Muntjac – which is sometimes referred to as the Chinese Muntjac – has the widest distribution, its range extending from the sea coast and south China as far north as Anhwei Province and southern Shantung. Lower Szechwan is probably its limit in the west.

In the south-western part of its range there is apparently a strip of country extending from the coast of southern Kwang-tung in a north-westerly direction, which separates *M.r.reevesi* from the larger Indian race *M.m.vaginalis.* In the north-east, however, its range is adjacent to that occupied by the rare Black Muntjac *M.crinifrons* in Chekiang. This deer is also known as the Hairy-fronted Muntjac.

The Black Muntjac is one of the rarest and least known of the Chinese deer,

---

REEVES'S MUNTJAC. *Muntiacus reevesi*

18. *Muntiacus reevesi reevesi*   South-east China
19. *M.r.micrurus*   Formosa

BLACK MUNTJAC. *Muntiacus crinifrons*

20. *Muntiacus crinifrons*   East China

and only about three specimens appear to have been recorded. Two of these were secured from Ningpo, Chekiang, in 1885 and 1886, and another one was taken at Tunglu, not far from Ningpo, in 1920.

The Black Muntjac has been described by G. M. Allen (1930) as being 'a large Muntjac . . . of a general dark blackish brown colour, including the dorsal surface of the tail, but the head and neck very slightly mixed with ochraceous . . . antlers short (65 mm [about 2½ inches]) with a small projection of the inner side at the base'.

The height at the shoulder of this Muntjac, which has a longer tail than other members of the group, is about 24 inches (61 cms) which is some 8 inches (20 cms) higher than the typical Reeves's Muntjac.

The general colour of Reeves's Muntjac is a reddish chestnut, with the limbs a more blackish brown colour. There is generally a distinct black stripe along the nape. The forehead, between the black pedicle-streaks, is rufous in colour. Chin and throat white, as also underside of tail, which is long. The Formosan form *M.r.micrurus* is 'distinctly richer and darker in colour' than the mainland race of this species (Lydekker, 1915).

The south-western form *M.m.vaginalis* is slightly larger than Reeves's Muntjac but not as big as *M.m.grandicornis* of Burma (page 129).

With regard to the two races that occur in Malaya, *M.m.peninsulae* is a large Muntjac whilst a feature of *M.m.robinsoni* is the long and slender pedicles that support the antlers.

Across the Strait of Malacca in Sumatra a further two races are found – *M.m. muntjak* and *M.m.montanus* – the former also occurring on the adjacent island of Java as well as on some of the smaller islands off the west coast of Sumatra, including Nias.

On Sumatra *M.m.muntjak* is well distributed in the south. In the west its range extends as far north to at least the Kerintji Valley whereas on the east side it may occur as far north as Deli. This Muntjac is fond of thick jungle, and wherever this occurs the deer is likely to be found right down to sea level.

In the west and north-western parts of the island, which is principally mountain terrain, we find the other race, *M.m.montanus*. In parts of the range of these two deer overlapping must occur, so intermediate specimens presumably exist in the zone of contact.

Slightly smaller and darker in colour than *M.m.muntjak,* the range of *M.m. montanus* covers the greater part of northern Sumatra, from the Kerintji Mountain region north as far as Atjeh and Deli. Included in this range are Mount Ophir and Mount Indrapura. This race is reported from altitudes of 7,095 feet (2,160 metres) on Mount Kerintji and 7,920 feet (2,412 metres) on Mount Ophir, and although primarily a mountain race it also occurs at low levels.

The antlers of *M.m.montanus* show poor development and generally consist of only simple spikes.

The natural predators of the Muntjac on Sumatra include the tiger and native dogs. An occasional deer is also taken by the python.

Before the war the Muntjac *M.m.muntjak* was a very common animal throughout the whole of Java and it probably still is today. It occurs from sea level right up to

7,425 feet (2,262 metres) above sea level, but seems to have a slight preference for the hills. They are, in fact, retiring into the hills more and more since the lowland jungle is rapidly vanishing. Contrary to the Rusa deer, *C.t.russa,* which also occurs in Java (page 111), the Muntjac (locally called *kidang*) is very much a woodland dweller, though it does not seem to differentiate much between whether the forests are teak or not, provided there is plenty of undergrowth to provide them with food and shelter. Occasionally they come out of the forests onto the fields, but they seldom touch grass, preferring herbs, leaves, fruits, mushrooms and bark, etc. Sometimes they can be found in coffee, rubber or sugar cane plantations. Their browsing and barking habits cause considerable damage to the young trees (mahogany, segawe, nagka) and their attentions to other cultivations are unwelcome. They tend to lead a solitary life, moving about singly or in pairs, although on rare occasions up to seven have been seen together.

The Muntjac frequently falls victim to native snaring. It can also be called success-fully. On Java, the predators are much the same as on Sumatra. Fawns often fall victims to the Wild boar.

There is no fixed breeding season but possibly the greatest activity occurs during the first six months of the year, which results in the majority of fawns being born during the latter part of the year.

In addition to these two deer on Sumatra and Java, four other races of Muntjac are found in Indonesia, two in Borneo, *M.m.pleiharicus* and *M.m.rubidus,* and two insular races, *M.m.bancanus* and *M.m.nainggolani,* the former occurring on the islands of Billiton and Banka (Bankag) which lie between Borneo and Sumatra, and the latter on Bali and Lombok which lie due east of Java.

In Borneo, the distribution of *M.m.pleiharicus* is throughout the south and south-west, whilst *M.m.rubidus* is more or less confined to the north and eastern parts of the country, extending south as far as the eastern slopes of the Meratus and Kusan Mountains. In Sarawak there seems to exist some overlapping of the two races, as well as in the vicinity of Klumpang Bay. The latter race, which is slightly darker in colour than *M.m.pleiharicus,* also occurs on Mata Siri Island, one of the Laut Islands off the south-east coast.

There seems to be no fixed breeding season, but births have been recorded in Sarawak in December and January, and from south-east Borneo in early February.

The race on the islands of Banka and Billiton, *M.m.bancanus,* is one of the smallest in Indonesia. Nothing is known of the biology of this deer which, according to descriptions, does not show much variation in colour from the typical Javan race, *M.m.muntjak.*

The deer on Bali and Lombok *M.m.nainggolani* is also similar in many respects to *M.m.muntjak.* It has a wide distribution on both Bali and Lombok occurring in all suitable localities from sea level right up into the mountains. It has a marked preference for secondary forest surrounding the fields which are temporarily used for rice and other crops, and also for young forests surrounding the native villages in slightly hilly country.

Lombok Island marks the eastern limit of any race of Muntjac in Indonesia, the species being entirely absent from both the Celebes and Moluccas groups of islands. It has been suggested that Muntjac were imported into Lombok from Bali by the Balinese Rajahs, but it seems that more evidence is required before this should be accepted as fact.

The antlers of all races of Muntjac emanate from long pedicles which extend down the face of the deer giving it the name Rib-faced deer. Both sexes have canine teeth in the upper jaw, those of the male extending to just under one inch (2·5 cms) in length. These canines are used by the males for fighting.

A loud, sharp bark similar to that of some dogs, describes the call of this deer, and this is uttered both during the rutting season and when alarmed. On account of this call, the Muntjac is often referred to as the Barking deer.

About 1900 the eleventh Duke of Bedford introduced some Indian Muntjac *Muntiacus muntjak* to the woods outside his park at Woburn in Bedfordshire where, for a number of years, they thrived and multiplied. Eventually it was decided to kill off the Indian Muntjac and introduce the smaller Reeves's Muntjac *Muntiacus reevesi* in its place. This was never achieved, with the result that in some instances the Indian has bred with the Reeves's.

Muntjac are now firmly established in central southern England, and are slowly increasing their range. There seems to be no fixed rutting season of this little deer in England, with the result that the fawns, normally one, are born at any time of the year.

7

The Introduced Deer
of Australasia

Despite the wealth of deer throughout the Far East, it is surprising to find that not a single species of indigenous deer exists in the whole of Australasia, Melanesia and Polynesia. During the past one hundred and sixty years or so, however, many exotic species of deer from both eastern and western hemispheres have been introduced to some localities, and in the majority of cases have established themselves in a wild state. The principal introductions have been as follows.

NEW GUINEA AND ADJACENT ISLANDS

Deer that occur in New Guinea and adjacent islands are all descended from introduced stock. Very few records have been retained of their introductions and identification of these species in certain districts is far from satisfactory. One species, however, the Rusa deer *Cervus timorensis,* has firmly established itself, and two races, *C.t.timorensis* and *C.t.moluccensis,* may be represented – the former being restricted to the Hermit and Ninigo group of islands which lie in the north. The original deer came to the Hermit Islands at the beginning of the present century.

German settlers were also responsible for introducing the deer to the island of Ninigo, but whether any remain there today is not known.

The Moluccan Rusa deer *C.t.moluccensis* has been introduced to several districts of New Guinea. In 1913 Raedt van Olderbarnevalt introduced some deer from Ceram Island on to the Onin peninsula, and today the species occurs along the north-west coast of Geelvink Bay in the vicinity of Manokwari, Momi and along the Muturi River (van Bemmel, 1949). Their presence is also noted on Rumberpon or Roemberpon Island in Geelvink Bay, the original stock there having been introduced by Lulofs from Halmahera in 1920. In the same year Lulofs also introduced some Halmahera deer to Hollandia near the north coast of New Guinea.

In the south, deer are reported to be plentiful on the coast of Dutch New Guinea

K

between the Fly River and Merauke. Identification has not been firmly established but they are probably Rusa.

About 1910 some Rusa deer, which appear from a photograph to be Moluccan Rusa, *C.t.moluccensis,* were liberated near Rabaul in New Britain and appear to have increased slightly since the war in the Rabaul-Kokopa area.

There appears to be some confusion concerning the origin and race of Rusa deer – generally referred to as New Caledonian deer – which inhabit the New Caledonia group of islands, and descriptions of the deer are so conflicting that it is possible two races and an intermediate type are represented. However, it seems fairly certain that some Javan Rusa *C.t.russa* were liberated there in about 1870, and the introduction was not only a success but within thirteen years there were complaints of serious deer damage to crops, etc.

Prior to the late war, when the deer population was estimated at about 225,000 head, some 46,000 hides were being exported annually. A more recent estimate (1951) suggests that their numbers have decreased slightly to about 200,000 head with a correspondingly smaller export of hides – about 25,000 to 30,000.

Other reports have suggested that not only have Rusa deer from Molucca and Sambar from the Philippines been introduced, but also Red deer from New Zealand to northern New Caledonia, but none of these liberations have been confirmed.

Some 750 miles (1,200 kilometres) to the east of New Caledonia in the Pacific Ocean lie the Fiji Islands and one of these, Wakaya, is inhabited by deer, the exact identification of which is a little uncertain, but from the description and photograph of a stag shot about 1954, they would appear to be Rusa. Wakaya, which extends to about 2,000 acres (800 hectares), is privately owned and operated as a plantation.

AUSTRALIA

Formerly there were no deer in Australia, but following various introductions that have taken place since about 1800, there are now at least six different species of deer leading a wild existence in various parts of the country.

Nevertheless, until 1967 when Arthur Bentley's *An Introduction to the Deer of Australia* was published, deer had been quite neglected by naturalists recording the wild life of Australia, and not only was there little or no information available in any of the fauna books of the country, but official records of the numerous introductions that had taken place were sadly incomplete or lacking altogether. His book, therefore, has been an invaluable source of reference.

The majority of the liberations were made by the various Acclimatisation Societies which were founded about the middle of the last century. One of the first to be formed was that of New South Wales, which was founded in 1861 by Edward Wilson who, in the same year, was also founder and first president of the Victoria Society. Grounds were acquired at Parramatta Park near Sydney, where the deer were retained for a period prior to their liberation. In 1880 a depot was established at Moore Park near Sydney, and Zoological Gardens were laid out there. The Society was then organised and re-named the Zoological and Acclimatisation Society of New South Wales. The gardens at Moore Park were opened in 1884. It was not until

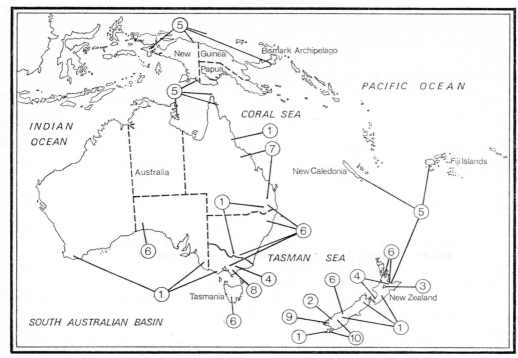

Map 27. Range of introduced deer of AUSTRALASIA

1. Red deer	*Cervus elaphus*	Australia, New Zealand (widespread distribution)
2. Wapiti	*Cervus canadensis*	New Zealand (South Island)
3. Sika deer	*Cervus nippon*	New Zealand (North Island)
4. Sambar	*Cervus unicolor*	Australia, New Zealand (North Island)
5. Rusa deer	*Cervus timorensis*	Australia, New Zealand (North Island), New Britain, New Caledonia, New Guinea, Fiji Islands, Hermit Island, Ninigo Island
6. Fallow deer	*Dama dama*	Australia, New Zealand
7. Axis deer	*Axis axis*	Australia
8. Hog deer	*Axis porcinus*	Australia
9. Moose	*Alces alces*	New Zealand (South Island)
10. White-tailed deer	*Odocoileus virginianus*	New Zealand (South Island, Stewart Island)

A number of other species of deer have been – or are supposed to have been – introduced to Australia, but no authentic information is available (See p. 141)

1916 that the collection was moved to its present location at Taronga Park, Sydney.

Various species of deer, including Swamp, Japanese and Formosan Sika, were liberated by the Acclimatisation Society in Victoria, whilst a number of other varieties were held in the Society's grounds from time to time. It is almost impossible, unfortunately, to find out what became of some of the deer held by the Society, for after 1870, in order to safeguard the deer from the irresponsible hunter, all liberations were carried out in secret.

The Queensland Acclimatisation Society was founded in 1865, which was followed, thirteen years later, by the formation of a similar society for South Australia. This latter Society, however, had little if anything to do with the introduction of deer into the State.

The Western Australia Acclimatisation Society was established in 1895 and, with the help of private individuals, was responsible for the liberation of a number of species of deer, including Red, Fallow, Hog and Rusa. The Gilruth Administration was responsible, in 1912, for liberating Fallow, Swamp and Sambar in the Northern Territory.

AXIS DEER *Axis axis*   Map p. 135

The very first deer to reach Australia seem to have been some Chital or Axis deer from India. The exact date of their arrival in New South Wales is not known but a herd of about 400 animals was firmly established on Dr John Harris's property near Bathurst by 1813.

Since that date Axis deer have been introduced to a number of localities in Australia but in Queensland only does the species appear to have survived in a wild state with any certainty. Elsewhere in Australia, Fallow deer have been frequently mistaken by hunters for Axis deer!

Probably the largest concentration of deer in Queensland is that centred about the Maryvale Creek Valley, near Charters Towers. These Axis deer (*Axis axis ceylonensis*) are descendants of those introduced from Ceylon by William Hann in 1866. A stag and two hinds were turned out, and despite the undoubted ravages of the dingoes, a fine herd was soon established. In 1953 the deer in this area were estimated at 600 animals.

A number of other Axis deer liberations were made in both Queensland and Victoria, but apart from a few animals still surviving in the vicinity of Toowoomba in Queensland, the others have all failed, and any recent reports have been a case of mistaken identity, in the form of a Hog deer.

HOG DEER *Axis porcinus porcinus*   Map p. 135

Hog deer, which were obtained from both India and Ceylon about 1870, were introduced by the Acclimatisation Society of Victoria, to a number of localities in the coastal region of south-eastern Victoria and included Gippsland, Wilson's Promontory, Snake Island and possibly the adjacent islands of Little Snake and St Margaret's. They did well and the species is now plentiful in these localities, particularly so on Wilson's Promontory and Snake Island.

The original stock of deer released in Victoria was presented to the Acclimatisation Society by the Rajah Rajendro Mullick, Mr A. Grote of Calcutta and Mr C. P. Layard of Colombo.

In 1965 the Nooramunga State Wildlife Reserve – which extends to approximately

24,600 acres (about 9,960 hectares) and includes several islands in the eastern water of the Corner Inlet, one of which is Sunday Island – was formed. This 2,500-acre (1,010 hectares) island was purchased by the Para Park Co-operative Game Reserve Limited Society, who in co-operation with the Victorian Fisheries and Wildlife Department, intend to carry out some research work on the Hog deer.

It appears likely that, in the past, the Hog deer on Wilson's Promontory will have crossed with the Axis deer which were also introduced to this National Park. Snake Island is outside the National Park, but the island and a thirty-mile (48 kilo-metres) radius therefrom is set aside as a deer sanctuary where the carrying of fire-arms is forbidden. In 1953, however, the Management Committee of the National Park decided that the Hog deer on Wilson's Promontory were thriving to the detri-ment of the native fauna. In accordance with this decision, the Victorian Fisheries and Game Department organised an experimental hunt which took place on the 12th–13th of December of that year, and resulted in thirty-four deer being shot. Included in this bag were two stags, one bearing a head of eleven points and the other nine – both an abnormal number for a deer which normally has but six points. At the time it was estimated that there were about 500 deer in the area hunted. A repeat hunt was conducted in the following year.

SAMBAR *Cervus unicolor*   Map p. 135

About 1861 the Acclimatisation Society of Victoria obtained Sambar from Ceylon (*Cervus unicolor unicolor*) and India (*Cervus unicolor equinus*) and introduced them to several districts of Victoria, which included the Grampians and the timbered country around Mount Cole in the western district of Victoria, Gippsland in the south-east coast area and the islands of Snake, which lies east of Wilson's Promon-tory, and French, which is some forty miles (64 kilometres) south of Melbourne.

In all these districts the deer thrived, and at the present time are described as 'plentiful' in West Gippsland, 'fairly plentiful' around Mount Cole and the Gram-pians, and 'some' on French Island. Their status on Snake Island is a little obscure but as the island is now a sanctuary a few may still survive there.

Some years ago two Sambar were seen on Phillip Island which lies off the Victorian coast some twenty-five miles (40 kilometres) south of Melbourne, and it is believed they had swum there from the mainland. They lived for some time in Rhyll Swamp but were eventually shot.

In 1912 the Gilruth Administration included three Sambar in the consignment of deer sent from Sydney for release on the Coburg Peninsula near Port Essington in Northern Territory and reports suggest that a few may still remain in the area.

The Sambar in Victoria is largely nocturnal, although the short nights of summer cause them to move about to a certain extent during the daylight hours. The country they inhabit is hilly with plenty of deep cover. During the winter the Sambar tends to move down from the higher ground and, like most deer, is greatly attracted to crops and cultivations, showing a particular aptitude to potatoes, oats, turnips and orchard trees.

Apart from those enjoying the protection afforded all game in the National

Parks, there is no close season for the species in Gippsland or in the Mount Cole district. The deer is usually hunted with hounds, the hunter following on foot until the deer is brought to bay, when it can be shot. One hunter, the owner of possibly the most successful pack of hounds in Gippsland, recently killed about 500 Sambar in the space of five years – an average of 100 per annum. Another hunter killed forty-seven in 1948. At the present time about seven packs of hounds hunt consistently in west Gippsland, and each will probably average about twenty-five Sambar a year – a total of some 175 deer. These are by no means the only packs hunting. Foxhounds, bloodhounds, a cross between these two, and beagles are the hounds normally employed for Sambar hunting. The Sambar, its habits and the country it frequents, may very well account for the almost universal use of hounds.

There does not seem to be any fixed rutting season and in consequence calves will appear during any month of the year.

RUSA DEER *Cervus timorensis*   Map p. 135

The first mention of the presence of Rusa deer in Australia came in 1868 in a Report of the Acclimatisation Society of Victoria, which mentioned that a number had been imported and were breeding. Others followed and in 1890 some were released on the ranges at Gembrook.

In 1912 a number of Rusa *C.t.moluccensis* were brought from the Moluccas by the late Mr R. A. C. Hockings, OBE, and liberated on Friday Island, which lies off the Cape York Peninsula in northern Queensland. They increased rapidly and a number swam to the much larger adjoining Prince of Wales Island, where they are now well established. No up-to-date population figures are available for either of these two islands, the former of which is only about 1,280 acres (about 518 hectares) in extent, whilst Prince of Wales Island is about 60,800 acres (24,605 hectares).

In 1914 Mr H. N. Hockings, a nephew of Reginald, caught up a number of deer on Friday Island and shipped them to Possession Island which lies to the east of Cape York, from which it is separated by a number of smaller islands. This island also proved favourable to them and the species is now well established there.

In 1952 Mr Fred Gray, an English missionary on Groote Eylandt which lies in the Gulf of Carpentaria off the east coast of Northern Territory, shipped a number of deer from Friday Island to his mission station on Groote, and one can assume that they will do as well there as on the other islands.

All the islands off the Queensland coast are sanctuaries under an Act protecting native fauna. The deer, however, are frequently hunted and shot by people from the small craft variously engaged in these northern waters.

There are several other reports of Rusa deer from various localities, but in some instances there is little doubt that this deer has been confused with Sambar, and *vice versa*. There are a number of reasons for this. In Victoria, for instance, the two species were liberated in much the same areas, and there seems little doubt that hybridisation has taken place. The two deer are also very similar and to an inexperienced observer, a fleeting glimpse in the bush could easily lead to confusion.

RED DEER *Cervus elaphus scoticus*   Map p. 135

Red deer are to be found in the following five states: Queensland, New South Wales, Victoria, South Australia and Western Australia.

The first Red deer to reach Australia were six animals from Windsor Great Park which Prince Albert presented, in 1860, to a Mr Thomas Chirnside who wished to start a herd at Werribee Park, which lies some twenty-five miles (40 kilometres) west of Melbourne in Victoria. Two years later Prince Albert sent some further deer from his park at Windsor as a gift to the Melbourne Hunt. The Hunt also imported a few animals from Knowsley Park, near Liverpool, belonging to the Earl of Derby who also supplied, in 1888, three deer to the Acclimatisation Society of Victoria. Deer from these newly formed herds were shipped to other parts of Australia, and some during the years 1901–3 to New Zealand as well. The Red deer in Victoria today certainly owe their origin to them, and to Werribee in particular. At the present time their principal haunt is the country stretching from the Grampians and Ararat in the west, to Ballarat and about twenty miles (32 kilometres) south of it, in the east. The species is also reported from the Otway Ranges, which lie south of Ballarat near the coast and also in west Gippsland, but only in small numbers. In recent years a few deer have wandered into east Victoria from New South Wales along the Snowy River. A few white animals have been seen in this district.

In 1873 Queen Victoria presented the Queensland Acclimatisation Society with two stags and four hinds. A further presentation was made by Lord Lamington, who was governor of Queensland about that time. The deer, the former of which came from Windsor Great Park and the latter, it is believed, from Scotland, were turned out on Mr McConnell's station at Cressbrook. They increased rapidly and spread into the ranges. Red deer are now plentiful in the mountainous country around the head of the Brisbane River.

About 1900 two stags and two hinds were turned out on Hinchinbrook Island which lies just north of Halifax Bay within the Great Barrier Reef in order to form a herd which was intended to provide food for persons who might some time be shipwrecked on the island. In 1915 a further stag and hind were released. This island is uninhabited, and although there are no recent reports of their status there, there is evidence that they may have crossed to the mainland. The distance between the mainland and the island at the nearest point would be just over a mile (about 1·75 kilometres). Hinchinbrook Island is about thirty miles (48 kilometres) long and has an average width of about five miles (8 kilometres). Many of the deer in Queensland are in poor condition from tick infestation.

In the south-eastern part of New South Wales Red deer are moderately abundant in an area known as the Quidong – that is, the country bounded in the east by a line Dalgety–Bombala–Delegate, south by the Victoria/New South Wales boundary and north by the Snowy River. The deer in this area are descendants of those liberated on Aston Station near Bombala by the late Mr J. R. Logan. The deer were enclosed on the station, but from time to time animals escaped into the bush. Then, in 1918 when the property was sold, the remaining deer were liberated. There is now evidence that the deer in this district are extending their range south and have already reached the Snowy River country and into eastern Victoria.

In South Australia their range is limited to a small area of scrub country in the vicinity of Naracoorte which is in the extreme south-east corner near the Victoria border. It is feared they may not survive long in this area.

Their status in Western Australia is equally precarious and indeed it is possible that the once well-established herd near Pinjarra, which lies near the coast some fifty miles (80 kilometres) south of Perth, may even now be approaching extinction. In 1960 a very fine 12-pointer stag was shot near Pinjarra by one of the local farmers, so it is evident a few may still remain in this area. The original deer at Pinjarra came from the Chirnside herd at Werribee Park, Victoria.

Although antlers of up to 43 inches (109 cms) in length have been killed in South Australia, heads generally are disappointing, having a narrow span and seldom achieving more than eleven or twelve points.

The breeding cycle of the Australian Red deer is about six months out of phase with that of the European Red deer, the rut occurring about the end of March and calves being dropped during November and December.

FALLOW DEER *Dama dama dama*   Map p. 135

There are wild Fallow deer in four, and possibly five, States. The exact year of their introduction is not known, but as the source appears to have been mainly Tasmania (see page 141), which received its initial stock of Fallow from England about 1850, it must have been after this date. The Acclimatisation Society of Victoria was founded in 1861. Before this Society came into being it is known that Fallow were already established in two or three localities in Victoria by the efforts of private settlers. In other states, also, private individuals were mainly responsible for the early introduction of Fallow deer, but during the closing years of the nineteenth century the various Acclimatisation Societies distributed them. It is also quite probable that they may have imported some deer from sources other than Tasmania. In 1867 four Fallow deer were sent to New Zealand at the request of the Otago Acclimatisation Society.

There were several releases in Queensland but their numbers are not great and their range is limited. At the present time there are herds in the Toowoomba district which is some sixty miles (96 kilometres) west of Brisbane, at Maryvale, and at Pikedale Station west of Stanthorpe.

In New South Wales Fallow deer are reported as being 'fairly plentiful' in the New England Range near Glen Innes where their origin is comparatively recent. They date from the introduction of six animals in about 1924 by the late Mr Colin Campbell, but where he obtained them is not recorded. Recent reports also suggest that Fallow deer are numerous in the National Park and adjacent areas, and there are also a number to the east of Lake George which is situated north-east of Canberra. The herd here started from a buck and a doe liberated in 1886 by the Lamb family of Rooty Hill. An estimate of 200 animals made in 1910 was thought to be accurate. In this state, however, Fallow are, perhaps, most numerous in the district of Albury and surrounding timbered country, which runs along the boundary with Victoria. In Victoria their status in south Gippsland is somewhat similar.

In South Australia Fallow are plentiful in the extreme south-eastern part of the state, but in the hills about Adelaide they are rarely seen.

In 1912 about fifty Fallow deer were liberated on the Coburg Peninsula which is the northernmost point of Northern Territory, but little is known of their present status. It is said that the natives will not hunt them, so there is every possibility that a small herd may be established there.

As in Australia, there were no deer in Tasmania prior to the last century. All the importations appear to have been made by private people despite the fact that an Acclimatisation Society was formed in 1862.

Probably the first deer to reach Tasmania were some Axis deer brought in by Captain Edward Dumaresq and Anthony Kemp in 1829. The majority of these animals appear to have either escaped into the bush or been worried by dogs, and what became of the survivors is not recorded. It seems certain that there are no deer of this species on the island today.

During the next twenty years a number of Fallow deer from England were imported by Mr John Bisdee and kept in Hutton Park, about thirty miles (48 kilometres) north of Hobart. They were intended for hunting, and during some of the hunts a number of bucks escaped into the bush.

At the present time the species is reported as being quite plentiful in many parts of the eastern midlands, and included are three herds all white in colour, the largest of which belongs to Mr A. F. B. O'Connor at Avoca.

The rutting season in Australia and Tasmania takes place between February and April, the fawns being born at the end of the year.

A number of other species of deer have been, or are supposed to have been, introduced to Australia but authentic information is sadly deficient.

Some hunters always refer to the deer on Wilson's Promontory in southern Victoria as 'Japanese Hog-deer'. It *may* be that the word Japanese is all that is now remembered of a liberation of Japanese Sika deer *Cervus nippon nippon* in this area. These deer are said to be slightly larger than the normal Hog deer, and as mentioned on page 137 in 1953 two stags, one carrying nine points and the other eleven, were killed. They were described as being 'quite red in colour with white spots down the flanks, the spots being about the size of a threepenny bit'.

Axis deer were, of course, liberated in this area during the last century so the colour description could apply to this species, or a cross between Axis and Hog deer. Although it is rare for either of these species to grow more than six points, malformed heads bearing more than this number have been recorded. Sika deer, on the other hand, although normally carrying but eight points, are more likely to develop in excess of this number. So this factor alone and the word 'Japanese' does, possibly, suggest a Sika introduction to this area, although documentary evidence records *only* the liberation of Hog and Axis deer on Wilson's Promontory. It is a fact, however, that the Acclimatisation Society of Victoria did introduce some Japanese Sika deer, but where they were liberated is not recorded.

Five Swamp deer or Barasingha *Cervus duvauceli* were included among the consignment of deer which the Gilruth Administration introduced to the Coburg Peninsula, Northern Territory, in 1912. Whether any remain is uncertain. In 1867–8 an unknown number of Swamp deer were presented to the Acclimatisation Society of Victoria by a Mr A. Grote of Calcutta and bred successfully in the Society's grounds. It is believed that these deer were liberated between 1871 and 1885 'in the mountainous parts of Gippsland' and it was reported some years later that 'they had penetrated deeply and thrived to a limited degree'. What their present status may be is unknown, but the species is probably extinct.

A number of attempts have been made to introduce Roe deer *Capreolus capreolus* into Victoria but there is no account of the species ever having been liberated in a wild state. Six were presented to the Acclimatisation Society of Victoria by HRH Prince Albert but what became of them is not known. In 1875 a pair of Roe arrived in the ship *Shannon* but died before they could be landed. About 1948 a man claims to have shot one with a bow and arrow near Blackwood, some fifty miles or so west of Melbourne (Bentley, 1967). The same writer also records that Water-deer (*Hydropotes inermis*) were said to be established somewhere on the South Australian coast. This story appeared to have some authenticity at the time but it was never confirmed. It was said that a ship which was carrying some of these deer was wrecked somewhere off Yorke Peninsula and that the animals had been released, or had otherwise found their way ashore. The story was that they 'were established in difficult swampy country'.

NEW ZEALAND

Prior to 1851 there were no deer of any description on either the North or South Islands of New Zealand. In that year two Red deer *Cervus elaphus scoticus* were introduced to the Matai Valley, Nelson, and thus for the first time the *Cervidae* became a resident member of New Zealand's fauna. Since that date, many liberations have been made in both islands, not only of Red deer but several other species as well, and the result has been that at present no fewer than eight different species are completely acclimatised and leading a wild existence there.

Whilst some of the earlier introductions were made privately the majority of liberations were effected by Acclimatisation Societies. In the final stages of acclimatisation, however, the Tourist Department of the government was the responsible party. The majority of the liberations met with immediate success, and as a result all but one of the following eight species of deer are now *firmly* established in a wild state, the one exception being the Moose in South Island.

North Island	South Island
Fallow deer *Dama dama*	Fallow deer *Dama dama*
Red deer *Cervus elaphus*	Red deer* *Cervus elaphus*
Sika deer *Cervus nippon* (2 subspecies)	Wapiti *Cervus canadensis*
Rusa deer *Cervus timorensis*	Moose *Alces alces*
Sambar *Cervus unicolor unicolor*	White-tailed deer* *Odocoileus virginianus*

* Also on Stewart Island.

Attempts, however, to acclimatise Mule deer *Odocoileus hemionus* and Heumul *Hippocamelus bisulcus* failed completely. For a time it appeared that the Axis deer *Axis axis* had managed to establish itself, but latest reports suggest that the species is now extinct.

In contrast to the New Zealand Government's former desire to populate their country with as many game animals as possible, the reverse is now the case and there are many who regret that deer and other game animals such as Tahr and Chamois were ever allowed to set foot in New Zealand. Many of the introduced species and of the *Cervidae,* Red deer in particular, increased to such an extent that they were considered pests, and so in 1930 protection was removed from the game mammals, and in the following year the first government control operations were commenced by the newly formed Deer Control Section of the Department of Internal Affairs. Until this date periodic culling had taken place by the Acclimatisation Societies who were responsible for the management of the herds. In 1956 responsibility for the control of introduced animals was transferred to the New Zealand Forest Service. Between 1931 and the 31st March 1967 the total number of deer killed on official operations was 1,048,566. This figure excludes some hundreds of thousands of Chamois, Tahr, pigs and goats that have also been killed over the same period. Nor does it include the number of deer shot by either sportsmen-hunters or commercial cullers. Numerous attempts to estimate the annual 'hunter kill' have been made, but without factual supporting data; such efforts have generally produced only hypothetical results. At best, it can be estimated that the yearly kill by sportsmen exceeds 100,000 animals (all species).

Likewise, the total number of deer killed annually by commercial meat exporters is difficult to obtain. The only figure available is for the total weight of venison exported and for the year 1966–7 this amounted to 5,962,622 lbs. Estimating the average processed carcase weight at 80 lbs this indicates something to the order of 75,000 deer.

From all sources of control, therefore, it would appear that something approaching 150,000 to 200,000 deer are being killed annually by sportsmen, meat exporters and Forest Service cullers.

Not all culling is done by shooting. A few years ago an attempt was made to kill by an airdrop of carrots that had been treated with 1080 poison. Although this method was directed more against Chamois and Tahr than deer, an unknown number did succumb. The disappointing results of this operation did not warrant the high cost involved and it has not been pursued. More recently, culling with the aid of helicopters has produced some spectacular results, but as deer stocks get less, this method will also have to be abandoned on grounds of economy.

Describing this method, Mr Newton McConochie writes:

The larger exporting companies generally use two helicopters which go low into the bush country at a point where the tall timber verges on to the Alpine scrub, and scared by the noise of the machines, the deer are driven up towards the open clearings. Deer cannot travel fast for any great distance uphill, and they soon start to tire, with the machines operating like two sheepdogs just above tree level. Eventually, the deer, tired out by their uphill climb, soon stand, and it is then the time for the shooters in the helicopters to start work. The majority of them are very skilled in their work, and as the pilot navigates the machine at ranges varying from a few yards to fifty from the deer, the deer are shot down one after another to near extermination.

Continuing, he writes,

As you know, the deer is a highly intelligent animal, and although it does some foolish things at times, it will not be long before an old hind, who is acting as leader, will turn back to the tall timber rather than face the open scrubland above. Indeed, I understand that one or two hinds have already adopted this manœuvre.

After the deer have been shot the skinners move in, and having completed their task, the carcases are flown back to base on hooks that are suspended under the helicopter and supplied for that purpose. Three small animals, or two large matured stags, can be taken out on each trip by this method. At first, when they first started to operate and the deer were more plentiful, a hundred or even more a day was a satisfactory kill, but this tally is slowly dwindling as time goes on and the deer get less. It obviously cannot persist indefinitely, and the time will come when the companies operating the scheme will either have to pull out or face bankruptcy.

Mr McConochie, and others, believe that good will eventually come out of an operation that must, unfortunately, result in a number of wounded animals being left in the bush. With fewer deer and less erosion, the feed will increase, and conditions generally will become more favourable for the deer, and this will result in a better-class animal – the type of animal that once produced some of the best trophies in the world. It is to be hoped that New Zealand will have learned something from past experience and that every effort will be made in the future to prevent, once again, the deer herds erupting to become not only a menace to forestry and farming, but also to themselves through over-population causing insufficient keep.

RED DEER *Cervus elaphus*   Map p. 135

The first Red deer to reach New Zealand were two animals, a stag and a hind, which Lord Petre sent in 1851 from his herd at Thorndon Park, Essex, as a present to his brother in Nelson, South Island. These were released in the Matai Valley but unfortunately the hind was shot shortly afterwards. The stag, however, remained in the vicinity of Motueka. In 1854 a further pair of deer was despatched from England, but on arrival in Wellington the hind had died. The stag was liberated on the hills at the mouth of the Waimea.

In 1861 Lord Petre again supplied some deer from Thorndon Park, and on this occasion a stag and two hinds reached the South Island safely and were liberated on the hills behind Nelson. The progeny of these animals increased and rapidly spread themselves over a great part of the high country in the provincial districts of Nelson and Marlborough – eventually spreading into North Canterbury and over towards the west coast. Thus it was not until ten years after the first liberation of Red deer into New Zealand, that any breeding took place.

During the next fifty years further consignments of Red deer were shipped to

South Island from England, the source of supply being not only deer parks such as Warnham (Sussex), Woburn (Bedfordshire), Stoke (Buckinghamshire), Windsor (Berkshire), Raby (County Durham), Duncombe (Yorkshire) and Knowsley (Lancashire) but also wild Scottish blood from Invermark deer forest (Angus), the last mentioned being released in southern Otago in 1871.

As a result of these and other introductions, Red deer are now well spread throughout all suitable localities in South Island, the heaviest concentrations being in the south-west. They are also present on Stewart Island, the original source of supply in about 1900 being some deer from the introduced herds in North Island and Werribee Park, Australia (introduced).

The species is also well established in North Island, the first members of which reached the island in 1862 as a present to Governor Weld from the Prince Consort. These deer, three in number from Windsor Park, England, were subsequently liberated on the Tarataki Plains, Carterton, in Wellington. Shortly after their release, the deer crossed the Ruamahanga River and took up their abode on the Maungaraki Ranges, where they rapidly increased. In this fashion the 'Wairarapa herd' had its origin, from which some of the finest heads in New Zealand have been secured. In 1869 the herd was said to 'number upwards of twenty'; by the end of the century it ran into many thousands and 'on one station alone the owner made contracts for the destruction of a minimum number of three thousand deer annually for several years in succession' (Donne, 1924).

The acclimatisation and expansion of this great herd, which by the beginning of the century had spread over an area embracing hundreds of square miles of mountainous forest country is, perhaps, the most spectacular of all the deer liberations in New Zealand, for so far as is known, apart from the three original Windsor Park deer released in 1863, no other liberations from outside were made in the Wellington district prior to 1908. In that year, four animals which had been obtained from Warnham Park, Sussex, were released at Paraparauma.

Between 1895 and 1914 a number of liberations were made in North Island, but the deer never spread to quite the same extent as they did in South Island. At the present time, therefore, the range of Red deer in the North Island is almost restricted to the main divide and accessory ranges with the main reservoir in the central part of the island. There are none north of the Bay of Plenty whilst the main trunk railway running north to Auckland from Palmerston North marks roughly the extent of their range westwards. The subspecies would appear to be principally *C.e.scoticus*.

In both North and South Islands the rut takes place from late March to the end of April – about six months out of phase with the deer of their homeland in western Europe. Calves are born from late November to the end of January.

WAPITI *Cervus canadensis*   Map p. 135

In 1905 eighteen Wapiti, ten of which had been purchased from a Mr H. E. Richardson of Brookfield, Massachusetts, and the remainder received from the National Zoological Park, Washington, in exchange for some Roe deer from England, were liberated by the Tourist Department in the Fiordland National Park at the head of George Sound on the south-west coast of South Island. Presumably these Wapiti were either *C.c.nelsoni* or *C.c.roosevelti*.

One of the cows died shortly after release, but the remainder quickly acclimatised themselves and bred. In April 1921, they were reported to have crossed over into the Lake Te Anau district. As a result of this liberation in Fiordland, Wapiti are now concentrated in western Southland in an area west and north-west of Lake Te Anau.

Unfortunately, Red deer in considerable numbers also occupy the same area in Fiordland as the Wapiti, and interbreeding has obviously taken place to the detriment of the latter. In recent years, however, there has been a vigorous culling campaign to try and eliminate as far as possible the Red deer in Fiordland, and as a result, recent reports suggest that there has been some improvement in the quality of the Wapiti.

In South Island the Wapiti rut takes place from about mid-March to mid-April, the calves being born just before Christmas.

FALLOW DEER *Dama dama dama*   Map p. 135

The first introduction of Fallow deer to the North Island was made about 1870 when Sir George Grey introduced some to Kawau Island which lies in the Haukari Gulf off the east coast of Auckland. About the same time other deer were introduced to Motutapu Island which lies south of Kawau Island. These liberations were successful and the species is 'still present' on both islands. There are also a few Fallow deer on nearby Rangitoto Island which lies off the east coast of Auckland, but here they are almost shot out.

Early in the century some Fallow deer were introduced to Selwyn or Kaikoura Island – an island of about 1,100 acres (about 445 hectares) lying to the west of the Great Barrier Island. Until about 1950 the deer were numerous on Selwyn, but when new farmers moved in, shooting parties reduced the stock almost to extinction. Three bucks escaped from the island by swimming to the mainland, but they were soon rounded up and killed.

The first liberation on the mainland was made in 1877 by the Auckland Acclimatisation Society, who turned out eighteen deer on the Maungakawa and Matamata Ranges, Waikato. These deer were part of a consignment of thirty deer which Mr Falconer Larkworthy imported from England, the majority of which had been supplied by Carshalton Park, Surrey. All but three of the deer survived the five months' journey from London, so the remainder were available for the Wellington Acclimatisation Society to liberate near Wanganui.

The deer released at Waikato increased rapidly, and by 1937 had become so plentiful that drastic culling operations had to be undertaken. In 1937, 440 were killed but this number was trebled during the 1945 cull. A few years later the herd appears to have been shot out, and only a few remain.

The liberation at Wanganui was equally successful, and a number still remain in this area. From the herds at Waikato and Wanganui deer were caught up for release in fresh areas. Thus today there are herds of Fallow deer at Tauranga and on the Coromandel Peninsula, both of which lie on the east coast of Auckland.

Other liberations have been made on the North Island where the deer live mainly on the farm lands, in patches of native bush and manuka scrub (tea-tree), from which they emerge at night to feed upon the farms. Thus, while being well fed, they suffer heavy execution in most localities and a head is seldom allowed to mature. Some of the deer on the Kaipara Head have taken to living on the sand hills along the west coast, but although similar country is available to the Fallow on the Manukau Peninsula, they appear to shun it.

The majority of deer in North Island are the black coloured variety. A few white animals, however, as well as the normal spotted variety, have occurred in the Waikato herd.

Fallow deer were first introduced to South Island in 1864, when three animals, which had come from Richmond Park, Surrey, were liberated in the Aniseed Valley near Nelson and acclimatised well. Other deer were released in the Takaka Valley. Descendants of these liberations are still be to found in the northern parts of Nelson, Mount Arthur and the Aniseed Valley being their principal haunts.

In 1867 the Otago Acclimatisation Society obtained four Fallow deer from Australia and these were released on the Blue Mountains, Tapanui. Two years later these deer were joined by twelve others which had recently arrived from England. In 1870 another deer was released in the same area, and these formed the forerunners of the present herds in this district. Between 1893 and 1903 licensed stalkers were killing some two hundred bucks per annum on the Blue Mountains. By 1926 control measures were in force, and according to the State Forest Service annual reports, 3,890 deer were killed in that year and 2,000 in the following year. Fallow deer are still quite plentiful in this area.

Other liberations of Fallow deer to South Island included the Lake Wakatipu area with deer from Tasmania, the Herbert State Forest in north Otago, the Albury Range area in south Canterbury and the Totara Flats near Greymouth.

As in North Island, the majority of deer introduced to South Island which, so far as is known, were either imported direct from England or from other herds of English stock, were the black variety. Colour variations do occur, however, particularly in the Blue Mountains.

The Fallow deer go to rut from about mid-April to mid-May, the fawns being dropped in December and January.

MOOSE *Alces alces*   Map p. 135

Although no attempts have ever been made to introduce Moose to the North Island, in 1899 the government obtained fourteen young animals from the Hudson Bay Company in Canada with the intention of liberating them in South Island. Unfortunately only four survived the journey and these, consisting of two bulls and two cows, were released in the Hokitika Valley, Westland. It is not known the exact source of these Moose in Canada but presumably the subspecies was either *A.a. americana* or *A.a.andersoni*. Little is known of the fate of the Moose released on this occasion nor is there any evidence to suggest that any of these animals bred.

In 1910 the government made a second attempt and on this occasion obtained ten animals from Saskatchewan in Canada, which were liberated on the shores of Dusky Sound in the Fiordland National Park, Southland. This liberation was more successful and breeding undoubtedly took place. In March 1923, the government issued two licences to kill each one bull moose, but it was not until 1929 that anyone was able to secure a trophy. In that year Mr E. J. Herrick shot a bull.

During the next twenty-two years, despite efforts by various sportsmen to secure trophies, only two Moose were officially shot – a bull in 1934 by Mr E. J. Herrick and a diseased cow by the same sportsman. Proof that the herd was still extant was forthcoming in 1951 when a cow was killed by Mr R. V. Francis Smith. This animal was obtained in the country bordering Wet Jacket Arm watershed and it was estimated that a herd of about thirty animals was frequenting this district. More recent reports suggest that the Moose is slowly dying out and may soon be extinct in New Zealand. The existing subspecies is thought to be *A.a.andersoni*.

SIKA DEER *Cervus nippon*   Map p. 135

In 1905 the eleventh Duke of Bedford presented to the Government of New Zealand three pairs of Manchurian Sika deer which had been bred at Woburn from animals imported from Manchuria seven years previously. In a letter to T. E. Donne, His Grace wrote: 'If no other Japanese deer have been imported into New Zealand it will be interesting, as you will then have none but the pure-bred Manchurian type.' It is not known whether these deer were *C.n.mantchuricus* or *C.n.hortulorum*, which some consider to be indistinguishable. Unfortunately, the Duke's claim that the original stock were all 'pure bred' Manchurian does not appear to have been confirmed by the present stock which shows considerable variation, both as regards size and colour. It appears, therefore, that there is an admixture of Japanese Sika blood (*Cervus nippon nippon*) in some of the animals.

The deer from Woburn, which numbered seven on arrival, because a calf was born during the voyage, were released at Taharua, Northern Kaimanawa Ranges, which lies to the south-east of Taupo Lake, North Island.

There is still a fair number of Sika deer in the Kaimanawa Forest district, and there is evidence that a few have spread outside the area, stray stags having been killed in Northern Hawke's Bay – about sixty miles (96 kilometres) from the forest. More recently (*c.* 1953) a young stag was shot near Te Whaiti whilst another was killed at Te Aroha which is some hundred miles (160 kilometres) north of their main habitat.

The Sika rut during May, the calves being born the following January.

RUSA DEER *Cervus timorensis*   Map p. 135

In November 1907 eight Rusa deer were obtained from Noumea in New Caledonia and released at Galatea, which lies to the south-east of Rotorua in Auckland. Two of these deer were imported by the New Zealand Tourist Department whilst a Mr H. R. Benn was responsible for the remainder. Several hundred deer still remain in this area, the only one in New Zealand in which the species is to be found.

It would appear that these deer have always been referred to as the 'New Caledonian Sambar'. However, as noted on page 134 the original deer introduced to New Caledonia appear to have been Javan Rusa, *C.t.russa*, so they are probably of this species and race. A significant point is that the rut of the Rusa deer in New Zealand takes place during the same period (July and August) as in New Caledonia, whereas the rut of the Sambar *Cervus unicolor* occurs in New Zealand some seven months later. Rusa calves are born in New Zealand during April and May – which is autumn time. No liberations of Rusa deer have been made in South Island.

SAMBAR *Cervus unicolor unicolor*   Map p. 135

On the 1st June 1875 Mr Falconer Larkworthy obtained a pair of Sambar (*Cervus unicolor unicolor*) from Ceylon which he released on his estate at Carnarvon in the Rangitikei district of Wellington. This pair bred, and by 1894 a herd numbering some thirty animals had been built up. During the next few years the herd increased rapidly and in 1900 was reported to number about one hundred. There are still fair numbers in this district today.

About 1920 some Sambar were released in the vicinity of Mount Tarawera and Ruatoki, east of Rotorua, and a recent report suggested that the deer in this area, much of which falls within the Kaingaroa State Forest, were not only holding their own but slowly spreading to new areas.

The Sambar go to rut in North Island during March and April, the calves being born some eight months later. There have not been any liberations of Sambar in South Island.

WHITE-TAILED DEER *Odocoileus virginianus*   Map p. 135

The first White-tailed deer to reach South Island were two pairs that were liberated in the Takaka Valley, Nelson, in 1901. Four years later a buck from a consignment of nineteen deer recently arrived from New Hampshire, USA – which were probably *O.v.borealis* – were released in the same area but it appears that this herd failed to establish itself. The remainder of the 1905 consignment were equally divided for liberation in new areas, nine going to Stewart Island and nine to the western head of Lake Wakatipu, Otago. In both districts the deer thrived but only to a limited extent at Lake Wakatipu. In this latter district their principal haunts are the valleys Rees, Dart and Routeburn, at the head of Lake Wakatipu. Unlike Stewart Island, where the deer quickly spread throughout the island, this area is only partially forest clad.

On South Island the rut takes place during April and May, with the fawns being dropped from late October to mid-November.

Of the failures the AXIS DEER, *Axis axis axis*, probably met with nearest success, but despite three attempts in the North Island and at least two in the South Island to introduce the species, all have ended in failure. The Axis deer introduced by the Otago Society in 1867 to the Goodwood Bush area, which lies between Oamarn

L

and Palmerston South did, however, establish themselves and increased, but unfortunately proved so troublesome to the farmers' crops that they were shot out about 1895. These deer originally came from Melbourne, Victoria, in Australia.

The MULE DEER *Odocoileus hemionus* also met with partial success. In 1905 five Mule deer, probably *O.h.hemionus*, which were obtained from Santa Fé, New Mexico, were imported by the Tourist Department and liberated at Tarawera, in the Hawke's Bay district of North Island. Ten years later, the Hawke's Bay Society reported that they were 'increasing'. Some years later a few were reported in the Tarawera area, but there have been no recent reports of their existence anywhere in North Island.

In 1905 nine Mule deer were liberated in the Rees Valley, near Lake Wakatipu, South Island, by the Southland Acclimatisation Society, but the species failed to establish itself.

Reference to the introduction of HUEMUL or GUEMAL *Hippocamelus bisculcus* to the South Island is brief, and it seems probably that the Auckland Society, who received three of these South American deer in 1870, never attempted any liberation in the wild.

Appendix

CLASSIFICATION OF THE CERVIDAE

FAMILY CERVIDAE

The family *Cervidae* consists of seventeen genera, which are sub-divided into forty species and just under two hundred subspecies, as follows:

	Common Names included in Genera	Number of Species	Number of Subspecies*
Alces	Moose, Elk	1	6
Axis	Axis, Chital, Hog, Kuhl's, Bawean, and Calamian deer	4	4
Blastocerus	Marsh deer	1	–
Capreolus	Roe deer	1	3
Cervus	Red, Wapiti, Sambar, Thorold's, Schomburgk's, Swamp, Eld's, Rusa and Sika deer	9†	65‡
Dama	Fallow deer, Persian Fallow deer	1	2
Elaphodus	Tufted deer	1	3
Elaphurus	Père David's deer, Milu	1	–
Hippocamelus	Huemul, Guemal	2	–
Hydropotes	Water-deer	1	2
Mazama	Brocket	4	26
Moschus	Musk deer	3	4
Muntiacus	Muntjac	5	17

* If a genera consists of, say, two species, one of which is divided into two subspecies, the number in this column would be 2, although 3 deer of racial differences are represented.
† includes 1 recently extinct.
‡ includes 2 extinct forms.

	Common Names included in Genera	Number of Species	Number of Subspecies
Odocoileus	White-tailed, Black-tailed, Mule deer	2	49
Ozotoceros	Pampas deer	1	3
Pudu	Pudu	2	2
Rangifer	Reindeer, Caribou	1	9*
		40	195

Amongst living *Cervidae, Moschus* and *Hydropotes* stand apart from the remainder on account of their lack of antlers. The same can be said for *Rangifer,* for in this genus *both* male and female normally possess antlers.

The common name, where possible, has been given also. The range of each deer given in the Classification is only approximate, and does not include areas to which an exotic species has been introduced.

Sub-family MOSCHINAE

Genus MOSCHUS Linnaeus, 1758

MUSK DEER
Three species (a) *Moschus moschiferus*
two subspecies
(b) *Moschus sibiricus*
two subspecies
(c) *Moschus berezovskii*
species only

Flerov (1952), who considers *M.m.parvipes* Hollister, 1911, *M.m.arcticus* Flerov, 1929 and *M.m.turowi* Zalkin, 1945 to be synonyms of *M.s.sibiricus* Pallas, 1779 has been followed. Ellerman and Morrison-Scott (1951) did not recognise *M.sibiricus* as a distinct species, and considered *M.m.parvipes, M.m.arcticus* and *M.m.turowi* as well as *M.s.sachalinensis* all to be races of *M.moschiferus.* They did not recognise *M.berezovskii* as a species, and considered only one species, *Moschus moschiferus.*

(a) *Moschus moschiferus* Linnaeus, 1758
    Moschus moschiferus moschiferus Linnaeus, 1758
        Northern India etc.
    Moschus moschiferus sifanicus Büchner, 1891
        Western, central and southern China
(b) *Moschus sibiricus* Pallas, 1779
    Moschus sibiricus sibiricus Pallas, 1779
        Eastern Siberia, northern Mongolia and Korea
    Moschus sibiricus sachalinensis Flerov, 1929
        Sakhalin Island
(c) *Moschus berezovskii* Flerov, 1929
        Szechwan, China

* includes 2 extinct forms.

Sub-family HYDROPOTINAE

Genus HYDROPOTES Swinhoe, 1870

WATER-DEER   One species *Hydropotes inermis,*
two subspecies

Flerov (1952) disregards a separate subspecies *H.i.argyropus* for Korea.

Hydropotes inermis Swinhoe, 1870
    Hydropotes inermis inermis Swinhoe, 1870   Chinese Water-deer
    China
    Hydropotes inermis argyropus Heude, 1884   Korean Water-deer
    Korea

Sub-family MUNTIACINAE

Genus MUNTIACUS Rafinesque, 1815

MUNTJAC   Five species (a) *Muntiacus muntjak*
                                      fifteen subspecies
                      (b) *Muntiacus reevesi*
                                      two subspecies
                      (c) *Muntiacus crinifrons*
                                      species only
                      (d) *Muntiacus feae*
                                      species only
                      (e) *Muntiacus rooseveltorum*
                                      species only

Lydekker (1915) divided *M.reevesi* into three distinct species, *M.lacrymans,* *M.reevesi* and *M.sinensis* and several subspecies. Flerov (1952) disregards *M.rooseveltorum* but includes *M.lacrymans* in his five species of *Muntiacus*

(a) *Muntiacus muntjak* (Zimmermann) 1780   Indian Muntjac
                                              (Barking deer)

    Muntiacus muntjak muntjak (Zimmermann) 1780
    Java and south Sumatra
    Muntiacus muntjak vaginalis (Boddaert) 1785
    Northern India, Burma to south-west China
    Muntiacus muntjak aureus (H. Smith) 1826
    Peninsular India
    Muntiacus muntjak curvostylis Gray, 1872
    Thailand
    Muntiacus muntjak pleiharicus (Kohlbrugge), 1896
    South Borneo
    Muntiacus muntjak grandicornis (Lydekker), 1904
    Burma

      Muntiacus muntjak bancanus Lyon, 1907
        Billiton and Banka Islands
      Muntiacus muntjak rubidus Lyon, 1911
        Northern Borneo
      Muntiacus muntjak malabaricus Lydekker, 1915
        Southern India and Ceylon
      Muntiacus muntjak robinsoni Lydekker, 1915
        Bintan Island, Linga Archipelago
      Muntiacus muntjak peninsulae Lydekker, 1915
        Malaya
      Muntiacus muntjak montanus (Robinson & Kloss) 1918
        Sumatra
      Muntiacus muntjak annamensis Kloss, 1928
        Indo-China
      Muntiacus muntjak nigripes G. M. Allen, 1930   Black-footed or Black-
        Vietnam and Hainan Island   legged Muntjac
      Muntiacus muntjak nainggolani Sody, 1932
        Bali and Lombok Islands
(b) *Muntiacus reevesi* (Ogilby), 1839   Reeves's Muntjac
      Muntiacus reevesi reevesi (Ogilby), 1839
        South-eastern China
      Muntiacus reevesi micrurus (Sclater), 1875
        Formosa
(c) *Muntiacus crinifrons* (Sclater), 1885   Black Muntjac or
        Eastern China   Hairy-fronted Muntjac
(d) *Muntiacus feae* (Thomas & Doria), 1889   Fea's Muntjac
        Tenasserim and Thailand
(e) *Muntiacus rooseveltorum* Osgood, 1932
        Indo-China

Genus ELAPHODUS Milne-Edwards, 1871

TUFTED DEER   One species *Elaphodus cephalophus*,
                      three subspecies

    Lydekker (1915) included *E.c.fociensis* as a fourth subspecies, but this has been considered a synonym of *E.c.michianus*.

    Elaphodus cephalophus Milne-Edwards, 1871   Tufted deer
      Elaphodus cephalophus cephalophus Milne-Edwards,
        1871
      South China, northern Burma
      Elaphodus cephalophus michianus (Swinhoe) 1874   Michie's Tufted deer
      South-east China
      Elaphodus cephalophus ichangensis Lydekker, 1904   Ichang Tufted deer
      Central China

Subfamily CERVINAE

Genus DAMA Frisch, 1775

FALLOW DEER   One species   *Dama dama*
                          two subspecies

Dama dama (Linnaeus), 1758	Fallow deer
Dama dama dama (Linnaeus), 1758	Fallow deer
Europe and Asia Minor	
Dama dama mesopotamica (Brooke), 1875	Persian Fallow deer
Iran (Persia)	

Genus AXIS H. Smith, 1827

AXIS DEER   Four species, the last three being
                     subgenus *Hyelaphus*

(a) *Axis axis*
    two subspecies
(b) *Axis porcinus*
    two subspecies
(c) *Axis kuhlii*
    species only
(d) *Axis calamianensis*
    species only

Subgenus AXIS H. Smith, 1827

(a) *Axis axis* (Erxleben), 1777	Chital, Axis deer, Spotted deer
Axis axis axis (Erxleben), 1777	
India	
Axis axis ceylonensis (Fischer), 1829	
Ceylon	

Subgenus HYELAPHUS Sundevall, 1846

(b) *Axis porcinus* (Zimmermann), 1780	Hog deer (Para)
Axis porcinus porcinus (Zimmermann), 1780	
Northern India, Burma and Ceylon	
Axis porcinus annamiticus Heude, 1888	
Thailand and Indo-China	
(c) *Axis kuhlii* (Müller and Schlegel), 1844	Kuhl's deer, Bawean deer
Bawean Island	
(d) *Axis calamianensis* Heude, 1888	Calamian deer
Calamian Islands	

Genus CERVUS Linnaeus, 1758

There has always been considerable doubt as to whether Red deer and Wapiti should be treated as one species *Cervus elaphus,* or a separate species, *Cervus canadensis,* be given to the Wapitoids.

Both Ellerman and Morrison-Scott (1951) and Flerov (1952) favoured the former treatment, whereas Hall and Kelson (1959) followed Miller and Kellogg (1955) and Lydekker (1915) in treating these two deer as separate species, and with this latter view I concur. Dr Anton B. Bubenik (in *lit* 14.3.1970) is of the same opinion.

Nine species	(a) *Cervus albirostris* species only	Thorold's deer
	(b) *Cervus duvauceli* two subspecies	Swamp deer, Barasingha
	(c) *Cervus elaphus* twelve subspecies	Red deer
	(d) *Cervus canadensis* thirteen subspecies	Wapiti
	(e) *Cervus eldi* three subspecies	Thamin, Eld's deer
	(f) *Cervus nippon* thirteen subspecies	Sika deer
	(g) *Cervus schomburgki* species only	Schomburgk's deer
	(h) *Cervus timorensis* six subspecies	Rusa deer
	(i) *Cervus unicolor* sixteen subspecies	Sambar

Subgenus PRZEWALSKIUM Flerov, 1930

(a) THOROLD'S DEER   One species *Cervus albirostris*

Cervus albirostris Przewalski, 1883   Thorold's deer
   Tibet

Subgenus RUCERVUS Hodgson, 1838

(b) SWAMP DEER   One species *Cervus duvauceli,* two subspecies

Cervus duvauceli Cuvier, 1823   Swamp deer, Barasingha

   Cervus duvauceli duvauceli Cuvier, 1823
      North of Ganges, Assam, India
   Cervus duvauceli branderi (Pocock), 1943
      North-central India

Subgenus CERVUS Linnaeus, 1758

(c) RED DEER   One species *Cervus elaphus,*
                                twelve subspecies

Cervus elaphus Linnaeus, 1758   Red deer, Shou,
                                                         Hangul, etc.

   Cervus elaphus elaphus Linnaeus, 1758
    Sweden
   Cervus elaphus hippelaphus Erxleben, 1777
    Europe
   Cervus elaphus corsicanus Erxleben, 1777
    Corsica and Sardinia
   Cervus elaphus wallichi Cuvier, 1823   Shou, or Wallich's
    Tibet   deer
   Cervus elaphus barbarus Bennett, 1833   Barbary deer
    North Africa
   Cervus elaphus hanglu Wagner, 1844   Hangul, Kashmir deer,
    Kashmir   Barasingha
   Cervus elaphus maral Gray, 1850   Maral
    Asia Minor
   Cervus elaphus yarkandensis Blanford, 1892   Yarkand deer
    Chinese Turkestan
   Cervus elaphus bactrianus Lydekker, 1900   Bactrian or Bukharian
    North Afghanistan and Russian Turkestan   deer
   Cervus elaphus atlanticus Lönnberg, 1906
    Norway
   Cervus elaphus scoticus Lönnberg, 1906
    Great Britain
   Cervus elaphus hispanicus Hilzheimer, 1909
    Spain and Portugal

Subgenus CERVUS Linnaeus, 1758

(d) WAPITI   One species, *Cervus canadensis,*
                                thirteen subspecies

Cervus canadensis Erxleben, 1777   Wapiti, 'Elk' (North
                                                         America)
   Cervus canadensis canadensis Erxleben, 1777   American Wapiti
    Eastern North America, extinct
   Cervus canadensis xanthopygus Milne-Edwards, 1867   Manchurian Wapiti
    Manchuria and Mongolia
   Cervus canadensis songaricus Severtzov, 1873   Altai Wapiti
    Tien Shan Mountains, etc.

Cervus canadensis roosevelti Merriam, 1897   Canadian or Roosev-
Western North America   elt's Wapiti,
Olympic Elk

Cervus canadensis asiaticus Lydekker, 1898
Altai to Transbaikalia
Cervus canadensis wachei Noack, 1902
Western Mongolia
Cervus canadensis merriami Nelson, 1902   Merriam's Elk or
Arizona, now extinct   Wapiti
Cervus canadensis nannodes Merriam, 1905   Tule Elk or Dwarf
California   Wapiti
Cervus canadensis macneilli Lydekker, 1909   M'Neill's deer
Szechwan border of China to Tibet
Cervus canadensis kansuensis Pocock, 1912   Kansu deer
Kansu, China, etc.
Cervus canadensis manitobensis Millais, 1915
Saskatchewan and south-west Manitoba
Cervus canadensis alashanicus Bobrinskii and   Ala-Shan Wapiti
Flerov, 1935
South-east Mongolia.
Cervus canadensis nelsoni V. Bailey, 1935   Rocky Mountain
Western North America, except coastal regions   Wapiti

Subgenus PANOLIA Gray, 1843

(e) THAMIN or ELD'S DEER   One species *Cervus eldi*,
three subspecies

Cervus eldi M'Clelland, 1842   Thamin, or Eld's deer
Cervus eldi eldi M'Clelland, 1842
Manipur
Cervus eldi siamensis Lydekker, 1915
Thailand, Vietnam and Hainan Island
Cervus eldi thamin Thomas, 1918
Burma, Tenasserim and adjacent part of Thailand

Subgenus SIKA Sclater, 1870

(f) SIKA DEER   One species *Cervus nippon,*
thirteen subspecies

Cervus nippon Temminck, 1838   Sika deer, Japanese
deer
Cervus nippon nippon Temminck, 1838   Japanese Sika deer
Kyushu Island, Japan

Cervus nippon pseudaxis Eydoux and Souleyet, 1841
   Vietnam, Indo-China

Cervus nippon taiouanus Blyth, 1860   Formosan Sika deer
   Formosa

*Cervus nippon mantchuricus** Swinhoe, 1864   Manchurian Sika deer
   Manchuria, Korea

Cervus nippon hortulorum Swinhoe, 1864   Pekin or Dybowski's
   Ussuri district, Manchuria   Sika deer

Cervus nippon mandarinus Milne-Edwards 1871   North China Sika deer
   North China

Cervus nippon kopschi Swinhoe, 1873   South China or
   South-eastern China   Kopsch's deer

Cervus nippon grassianus (Heude), 1884   Shansi Sika deer
   Shansi, China

Cervus nippon yesoënsis (Heude), 1896
   Hokkaido Island, Japan

Cervus nippon keramae (Kuroda), 1924   Kerama Sika deer
   Middle Ryukyu Islands

Cervus nippon centralis Kishida, 1936
   Hondo (Honshu) Island, Japan

Cervus nippon mageshimae Kuroda and Okada, 1951
   Mageshima Island

Cervus nippon yakushimae Kuroda and Okada, 1951
   Yakushima Island

Subgenus THAOCERVUS Pocock, 1943

(g) SCHOMBURGK'S DEER   One species

Cervus schomburgki Blyth, 1863   Schomburgk's deer
   Thailand (extinct?)

Subgenus RUSA H. Smith, 1827

Lydekker (1915) divided the subgenus RUSA into five species, *Cervus kuhli, Cervus alfredi, Cervus timorensis* (*timoriensis*)*, Cervus tavistocki* and *Cervus unicolor.* In this work *C.timorensis* and *C.unicolor* have been retained, *C.kuhli* (*kuhlii*) has been considered a species of genus AXIS, with *C.alfredi* a subspecies of *C.unicolor.* *C.tavistocki* has been omitted, for Lydekker had no knowledge of the type locality in the Philippines of this deer, and expressed doubt as to whether it was a valid species or race, or merely a sport or hybrid.

* *C. n. mantchuricus* considered a synonym of *C. n. hortulorum* in *Checklist of Palaearctic and Indian Mammals,* Ellerman & Morrison-Scott, 1951.

(h) RUSA DEER   One species *Cervus timorensis*,
                                    six subspecies

Cervus timorensis Blainville, 1822   Rusa deer
  Cervus timorensis timorensis Blainville, 1822   Timor Rusa
    Timor and neighbouring islands
  Cervus timorensis moluccensis Quoy and Gaimard,
    1830   Moluccan Rusa
    Molucca Islands
  Cervus timorensis russa Müller and Schlegel, 1844   Javan Rusa
    Java
  Cervus timorensis macassaricus (Heude), 1896
    Celebes
  Cervus timorensis floresiensis (Heude), 1896
    Lombok and other islands
  Cervus timorensis djonga (Bemmel), 1949
    Muna and Butung Islands

(i) SAMBAR   One species *Cervus unicolor*,
                                    sixteen subspecies

Cervus unicolor Kerr, 1792   Sambar
  Cervus unicolor unicolor Kerr, 1792
    Ceylon
  Cervus unicolor niger Blainville, 1816
    Peninsula India
  Cervus unicolor mariannus Desmarest, 1822
    Guam Island, Marianne Group
  Cervus unicolor equinus Cuvier, 1823
    Sumatra, Malaya, Burma, China, etc
  Cervus unicolor philippinus H. Smith, 1827   Philippine deer
    Luzon, Philippine Group
  Cervus unicolor swinhoei Sclater, 1862   Swinhoe's deer
    Formosa
  Cervus unicolor alfredi Sclater, 1876   Prince Alfred's deer
    Central Philippine Islands
  Cervus unicolor nigricans Brooke, 1877   Basilan or Blackish
    Basilan Island   deer
  Cervus unicolor barandanus (Heude), 1888
    Mindoro Island, Philippines
  Cervus unicolor francianus (Heude), 1888
    Mindanao Island, Philippines
  Cervus unicolor basilanensis (Heude), 1888
    Basilan Island, Philippines
  Cervus unicolor brookei Hose, 1893
    Sarawak, Borneo

Cervus unicolor dejeani (Pousargues), 1896
  South-west China
Cervus unicolor boninensis Lydekker, 1905
  Bonin Islands (extinct?)
Cervus unicolor nigellus (Hollister), 1913
  Mindanao Island, Philippines
Cervus unicolor apoensis Sanborn, 1952
  Mindanoa Island, Philippines

Genus ELAPHURUS Milne-Edwards, 1866

PÈRE DAVID'S DEER   One species

Elaphurus davidianus Milne-Edwards, 1866   Mi-lu or Père David's
  Formerly China (Preserved in zoos and parks only)   deer

Subfamily ODOCOILEINAE

Genus ODOCOILEUS Rafinesque 1832

Two species (a) *Odocoileus hemionus*
                  eleven subspecies
            (b) *Odocoileus virginianus*
                  Thirty-eight subspecies

In considering these New World deer as belonging to the Genus ODOCOILEUS Rafinesque, I have followed Lydekker (1915), Miller and Kellogg (1955) and Taylor (1956), and rejected Hershkovitz (1948) and Hall and Kelson (1959) who have placed these deer in Genus DAMA Zimmermann. This followed the earliest scientific name for the Virginia or White-tailed deer but, in my opinion, is unacceptable, particularly in view of their anatomical disparities, and experiments covering several years to mate an *Odocoileus hemionus* buck with *Dama dama* does all proved sterile. Matings between *Odocoileus hemionus* and *Odocoileus virginianus* have, however, proved fertile (Taylor, 1956, p. 537).

The White-tailed deer of South America – Venado – previously considered a separate species *Odocoileus cariacou* Boddaert 1784 – are now included in *Odocoileus virginianus*.

Subgenus EUCERVUS Gray, 1866

MULE DEER,   One species *Odocoileus hemionus,*
BLACK-TAILED DEER   eleven subspecies

(a) *Odocoileus hemionus* (Rafinesque) 1817   Black-tailed deer,
                                                      Mule deer

    Odocoileus hemionus hemionus (Rafinesque) 1817   Mule deer
      Wide distribution in western and central North
      America

Odocoileus hemionus columbianus (Richardson), 1829 British Columbia to northern California	Columbian Black-tailed or Coast deer
Odocoileus hemionus californicus (Caton), 1876 Mid-California	California Mule deer
Odocoileus hemionus crooki (Mearns), 1897 North Mexico	Desert Mule deer
Odocoileus hemionus eremicus (Mearns), 1897 North-west Mexico and Arizona	Burro deer (Mule deer)
Odocoileus hemionus sitkensis Merriam, 1898 Coastal area and islands off western British Columbia	Sitka Deer (Black-tailed deer)
Odocoileus hemionus peninsulae (Lydekker), 1898 Baja California	Peninsula Mule deer
Odocoileus hemionus cerrosensis Merriam, 1898 Cerros Island, Baja California	Cedros (Cerros) Island Mule deer
Odocoileus hemionus inyoensis Cowan, 1933 California	Inyo Mule deer
Odocoileus hemionus fuliginatus Cowan, 1933 California	Southern Mule deer
Odocoileus hemionus sheldoni Goldman, 1939 Tiburón Island	Tiburón Island Mule deer

Subgenus ODOCOILEUS Rafinesque, 1832

WHITE-TAILED DEER	One species *Odocoileus virginianus*, thirty-eight subspecies

(b) *Odocoileus virginianus* (Zimmermann), 1780	White-tailed deer
Odocoileus virginianus virginianus (Zimmermann), 1780 Virginia and adjacent States	White-tailed deer
Odocoileus virginianus mexicanus (Gmelin), 1788 Central Mexico	Mexican White-tailed deer
Odocoileus virginianus cariacou (Boddaert), 1784 or 1785 French Guiana and north Brazil	Venado
Odocoileus virginianus macrourus (Rafinesque), 1817 Kansas and neighbouring States	Kansas White-tailed deer
Odocoileus virginianus leucurus (Douglas), 1829 Oregon and western coastal area	Columbian White-tailed deer
Odocoileus virginianus gymnotis (Wiegmann), 1833 Venezuela and Guianas (Dutch and British)	Venado

Odocoileus virginianus goudotii (Gay & Gervais), 1846
Colombia (Andes) and west Venezuela — Venado

Odocoileus virginianus toltecus (Saussure), 1860
Southern Mexico — Rain Forest White-tailed deer

Odocoileus virginianus yucatanensis (Hays), 1872
Yucatán to Honduras — Yucatán White-tailed deer

Odocoileus virginianus peruvianus (Gray), 1874
Peru and marginally — Venado

Odocoileus virginianus couesi (Coues & Yarrow), 1875
Santa Cruz, Arizona — Coues White-tailed or Fantail deer

Odocoileus virginianus acapulcensis (Caton), 1877
Southern Mexico — Acapulco White-tailed deer

Odocoileus virginianus osceola (Bangs), 1896
North-western Florida — Florida Coastal White-tailed deer

Odocoileus virginianus truei Merriam 1898
Nicaragua and adjacent States — Nicaragua White-tailed deer

Odocoileus virginianus texanus (Mearns), 1898
Texas and adjoining States — Texas White-tailed deer

Odocoileus virginianus thomasi Merriam, 1898
South-eastern Mexico — Mexican Lowland White-tailed deer

Odocoileus virginianus nelsoni Merriam, 1898
Southern Mexico and Guatemala — Chiapas White-tailed deer

Odocoileus virginianus borealis Miller, 1900
South-eastern Canada and north-eastern USA — Northern Woodland White-tailed deer

Odocoileus virginianus rothschildi (Thomas), 1902
Coiba Island — Coiba Island White-tailed deer

Odocoileus virginianus sinaloae J. A. Allen, 1903
Mid-western Mexico — Sinaloa White-tailed deer

Odocoileus virginianus chiriquensis J. A. Allen, 1910
Panama — Chiriqui White-tailed deer

Odocoileus virginianus ustus (Trouessart), 1910
Ecuador (Andes) — Venado

Odocoileus virginianus margaritae (Osgood), 1910
Margarita Island — Venado

Odocoileus virginianus tropicalis (Cabrera), 1918
Western Colombia — Venado

Odocoileus virginianus clavium Barbour & G. M. Allen, 1922
Florida Keys — Florida Key White-tailed deer

Odocoileus virginianus mcilhennyi F. W. Miller, 1928
Louisiana — Avery Island White-tailed deer

Odocoileus virginianus ochrourus V. Bailey, 1932   Northwest White-
  North-western United States and Canada   tailed deer
Odocoileus virginianus dacotensis Goldman &   Dakota White-tailed
  Kellogg, 1940   deer
  Alberta to northern Dakota
Odocoileus virginianus taurinsulae Goldman &   Bulls Island White-
  Kellogg, 1940   tailed deer
  Bulls Island
Odocoileus virginianus venatorius Goldman &   Hunting Island White-
  Kellogg, 1940   tailed deer
  Hunting Island
Odocoileus virginianus hiltonensis Goldman &   Hilton Head Island
  Kellogg, 1940   White-tailed deer
  Hilton Head Island
Odocoileus virginianus nigribarbis Goldman &   Blackbeard Island
  Kellogg, 1940   White-tailed deer
  Blackbeard Island
Odocoileus virginianus seminolus Goldman &   Florida White-tailed
  Kellogg, 1940   deer
  Florida
Odocoileus virginianus carminis Goldman &   Carmen Mountain
  Kellogg, 1940   White-tailed deer
  Northern Mexico
Odocoileus virginianus miquihuanensis Goldman   Miquihuan White-
  & Kellogg, 1940   tailed deer
  Central Mexico
Odocoileus virginianus veraecrucis Goldman &   Northern Veracruz
  Kellogg, 1940   White-tailed deer
  Eastern Mexico
Odocoileus virginianus oaxacensis Goldman &   Oaxaca White-tailed
  Kellogg, 1940   deer
  Southern Mexico
Odocoileus virginianus curassavicus (Hummelinck),   Venado
  1940
  Curaçao Island

Genus CAPREOLUS Gray, 1821

ROE DEER   One species *Capreolus capreolus,*
                     three subspecies

Capreolus capreolus (Linnaeus), 1758   Roe deer
  Capreolus capreolus capreolus (Linnaeus), 1758   European Roe deer
  Europe, Asia Minor

Capreolus capreolus pygargus (Pallas), 1771   Siberian Roe deer
   Siberia and northern Asia
Capreolus capreolus bedfordi Thomas, 1908   Chinese Roe deer
   Manchuria, China and Korea, etc.

Genus ALCES Gray, 1821

MOOSE, ELK   One species *Alces alces,*
                                six subspecies

Alces alces (Linnaeus), 1758   Moose or Elk
   Alces alces alces (Linnaeus), 1758
      Northern Europe
   Alces alces americana (Clinton), 1822
      Eastern Canada and north-eastern USA
   Alces alces cameloides (Milne-Edwards), 1867
      Eastern Siberia, Mongolia and Manchuria
   Alces alces gigas Miller, 1899
      Alaska and Yukon
   Alces alces shirasi Nelson, 1914
      Wyoming
   Alces alces andersoni Peterson, 1950
      Western Canada, etc.

Genus RANGIFER H. Smith, 1827

REINDEER, CARIBOU   One species *Rangifer tarandus,*
                                nine subspecies

Banfield's *A Revision of the Reindeer and Caribou, Genus Rangifer* (1961) has been followed. Ellerman and Morrison-Scott (1951) included *R.t.sibiricus* Murray, 1866 and *R.t.pearsoni* Lydekker, 1903 as subspecies, but these have been considered synonyms of *R.t.tarandus* by Banfield. Ellerman and Morrison-Scott also give subspecific rank to *R.t.phylarchus* Hollister, 1912; *R.t.angustirostris* Flerov, 1932; *R.t.valentinae* Flerov, 1933, and *R.t.setoni* Flerov, 1933 but these are all treated by Banfield as synonyms of *R.t.fennicus* Lönnberg, 1909 – a subspecies Ellerman and Morrison-Scott consider a synonym of *R.t.tarandus.*

Among the North American forms of *Rangifer tarandus* Hall and Kelson (1959) include the following, all of which Banfield treats as synonyms of *R.t.caribou*: *R.t.terraenovae* Bangs, 1896; *R.t.caboti* G. M. Allen, 1914; *R.t.fortidens* Hollister, 1912; *R.t.sylvestris* (Richardson), 1829; *R.t.montanus* Thompson Seton, 1899; *R.t. osborni* J. A. Allen, 1902 and *R.t.stonei* J. A. Allen, 1901. Hall and Kelson (1959) also give subspecific rank to *R.t.arcticus* (Richardson), 1829 but Banfield considers this Reindeer to be a synonym of *R.t.groenlandicus.*

M

Rangifer tarandus (Linnaeus), 1758	Reindeer, Caribou
Rangifer tarandus tarandus (Linnaeus), 1758 Norway to Russia	Eurasian Tundra Reindeer
Rangifer tarandus groenlandicus (Borowski), 1780 Greenland and Canada	Greenland or Ameri- can Tundra Caribou*
Rangifer tarandus caribou (Gmelin), 1788 Canada and south-east Alaska	American Woodland Caribou
Rangifer tarandus platyrhynchus (Vrolik), 1829 Islands of Spitsbergen archipelago	Spitsbergen Reindeer
Rangifer tarandus dawsoni Thompson Seton, 1900 Queen Charlotte Islands (probably extinct)	Queen Charlotte Island Caribou
Rangifer tarandus granti J. A. Allen, 1902 Alaska Peninsula	Grant's Caribou*
Rangifer tarandus pearyi J. A. Allen, 1902 Ellesmere, Melville and other islands of Canadian Arctic archipelago	Peary Caribou*
Rangifer tarandus fennicus Lönnberg, 1909 European Russia from Karelia to the Ural Mountains, including Sakhalin Island	Eurasian Forest Reindeer
Rangifer tarandus eogroenlandicus Degerbøl, 1957 East Greenland (extinct since *c.* 1900)	East Greenland Caribou*

* A. W. Barfield (1961) prefers to call these deer Reindeer.

Genus BLASTOCERUS Wagner, 1844

MARSH DEER	One species *Blastocerus dichotomus*
Blastocerus dichotomus (Illiger), 1815 Central Brazil to north Argentina	Marsh deer

Genus OZOTOCEROS Ameghino, 1891

PAMPAS DEER	One species *Ozotoceors bezoarticus,* three subspecies
Ozotoceros bezoarticus (Linnaeus), 1766	Pampas deer
Ozotoceros bezoarticus bezoarticus (Linnaeus), 1766 Brazil	
Ozotoceros bezoarticus leucogaster (Goldfüss), 1817 Paraguay, N. Argentina, S. Bolivia and W. Brazil	
Ozotoceros bezoarticus celer Cabrera, 1943 Argentina (Pampas)	

Genus HIPPOCAMELUS Leuckart, 1816

HUEMUL or GUEMAL   Two species (a) *Hippocamelus bisulcus*
                                                (b) *Hippocamelus antisensis*

(a) *Hippocamelus bisulcus* (Molina), 1782   Huemul or Guemal
    Andes of Chile and Argentina
(b) *Hippocamelus antisensis* (d'Orbigny) 1834
    Andes of Ecuador, Peru, Bolivia and
    north-west Argentina

Genus MAZAMA Rafinesque, 1817

BROCKET DEER

Four species (a) *Mazama americana*   Red Brocket
           Fourteen subspecies
       (b) *Mazama gouazoubira*   Brown Brocket
           Ten subspecies
       (c) *Mazama rufina*   Little Red Brocket
           Two subspecies
       (d) *Mazama chunyi*   Dwarf Brocket
           Species only

Lydekker (1915) divided the genus MAZAMA into the following eleven species:

Mazama americana with two subspecies
Mazama superciliaris
Mazama zetta
Mazama sheila
Mazama tema with three subspecies
Mazama bricenii
Mazama rufina
Mazama simplicornis with three subspecies
Mazama tschudii
Mazama pandora
Mazama nana

Data on the genus MAZAMA is incomplete, but in this work the number of species has been reduced to four by considering *M.zetta*, *M.sheila* and *M.tema* as subspecies of *M.americana*; *M.superciliaris*, *M.tschudii* and *M.pandora* as subspecies of *M. gouazoubira* of which *M.simplicornis* is a synonym; and *M.bricenii* as subspecies of *M.rufina*. *M.nana* is probably a synonym of *M.simplicornis*, now replaced by *M.gouazoubira*.

Cabrera and Yepes (1960) also reduce the number of species to three, retaining

M.simplicornis in place of *M.gouazoubira*. In correspondence with the former author, however, *M.gouazoubira* is preferred.

(a) *Mazama americana* (Erxleben), 1777   Red Brocket
    Mazama americana americana (Erxleben), 1777
        South-east Venezuela into northern Brazil and
            the Guianas
    Mazama americana temama (Kerr), 1792
        Mexico
    Mazama americana rufa (Illiger), 1815
        Paraguay and Argentina
    Mazama americana jucunda Thomas, 1913
        South Brazil
    Mazama americana zetta Thomas, 1913
        North Colombia
    Mazama americana reperticia Goldman, 1913
        Panama to South America
    Mazama americana sheila Thomas, 1913
        North Venezuela
    Mazama americana cerasina Hollister, 1914
        Guatemala to Costa Rica
    Mazama americana trinitatis J. A. Allen, 1915
        Trinidad Island
    Mazama americana gualea J. A. Allen, 1915
        West Ecuador
    Mazama americana zamora J. A. Allen, 1915
        From south-east Colombia to north-east Peru
    Mazama americana rosii Lönnberg, 1919
        Northern Argentina
    Mazama americana sarae Thomas, 1925
        Bolivia and extreme north-west Argentina
    Mazama americana carrikeri Hershkovitz, 1959
        Northern Colombia

(b) *Mazama gouazoubira* (Fischer), 1814   Brown Brocket
    Mazama gouazoubira gouazoubira (Fischer) 1814
        Paraguay and northern Argentina
    Mazama gouazoubira nemorivaga (Cuvier), 1817
        South-east Venezuela and Guianas
    Mazama gouazoubira superciliaris (Gray), 1850
        Brazil
    Mazama gouazoubira tschudii (Wagner), 1855
        Peru
    Mazama gouazoubira whitelyi (Gray), 1873
        Peru

Mazama gouazoubira pandora Merriam, 1901
    Yucatán, Mexico
Mazama gouazoubira mexianae (Hagmann), 1908
    Mexiana Island
Mazama gouazoubira citus Osgood, 1912
    Venezuela
Mazama gouazoubira murelia J. A. Allen, 1915
    South-west Colombia and Ecuador
Mazama gouazoubira permira R. Kellogg, 1946
    Isla San José

(c) *Mazama rufina* (Bourcier and Pucheran), 1852   Little Red Brocket
    Mazama rufina rufina (Bourcier and Pucheran) 1852
        Ecuador, south-east Brazil and adjacent
        republics
    Mazama rufina bricenii Thomas, 1908
        North Venezuela

(d) *Mazama chunyi* Hershkovitz, 1959   Dwarf Brocket
    Andes of northern Bolivia and southern Peru

Genus PUDU

Subgenus PUDU (Molina), 1782

PUDU DEER   Two species (a) *Pudu pudu*
                 species only
              (b) *Pudu mephistophiles*
                 two subspecies

(a) *Pudu pudu* (Molina), 1782   Pudu
    Chile and Argentina
(b) *Pudu mephistophiles* de Winton, 1896
    Pudu mephistophiles mephistophiles de Winton,
    1896
        Ecuador and Peru
    Pudu mephistophiles wetmorei Lehman, 1945
        Colombia

Cabrera (1961) considers the last named a synonym of *Pudu* (*Pudella*) *mephisto-philes* de Winton, 1896. (Catalogo de los mamiferos de America del Sur, *Revta Mus. argent. Cienc. nat. Bernardino Rivadavia*, Serie Ciencias Zoologicas, *4*, (2): p. 344

Bibliography

Included in this bibliography are only those works to which direct reference has been made in the text. For a more complete bibliography, reference should be made to the bibliographies in the books listed below, which have been marked with an asterisk*.

AITCHISON, JAMES (1946), 'Hinged Teeth in Mammals: A Study of the Tusks of Muntjacs (*Muntiacus*) and Chinese Water-deer (*Hydropotes inermis*)'. *Proc. Zool. Soc. London.* Vol. 116, part II. pp. 329–38.

ALLEN, G. M. (1930), *Pigs and Deer from the Asiatic Expeditions.* Am. Mus. Novitates No. 430.

—— (1939), 'Zoological Results of the Second Dolan Expedition to Western China and Eastern Tibet, 1934–1936.' Part III – Mammals. Philadelphia: *Proc. Acad. Nat. Sci.* Vol. 90. pp. 261–94.

—— (1940), *The Mammals of China and Mongolia,* Part 2. New York, The American Museum of Nat. Hist. (Bibliography in Part 1 – 1938).*

—— (1942), *Extinct and Vanishing Mammals of the Western Hemisphere.** Pennsylvania, The Intelligence Printing Co. Am. Com. for Int. Wild Life Protection.

BANFIELD, A. W. F. (1951), *The Barren-Ground Caribou.* Ottawa, Dept. of Resources and Development.

—— (1961), 'A Revision of the Reindeer and Caribou. Genus *Rangifer.*' Ottawa, *Nat. Mus. of Canada Bulletin No. 177.* Biol. Series No. 66.

BANWELL, D. BRUCE (1966), *Wapiti in New Zealand.* Wellington, Auckland, Sydney, A. H. & A. W. Reed.

—— (1968), *The Highland Stags of Otago.* Wellington, Auckland, Sydney, A. H. & A. W. Reed.

BANWELL, D. BRUCE (1970), *The Red Stags of the Rakaia.* Wellington, Auckland, Sydney, A. H. & A. W. Reed.

BEDDARD, F. E. (1902), *Mammalia,* London, Macmillan & Co. Ltd.

BENTLEY, ARTHUR (1967), *An Introduction to the Deer of Australia,* Melbourne, John Gartner.

BLANFORD, W. T. (1891), *The Fauna of British India, including Ceylon and Burma. Mammalia.* London, Taylor & Francis.

BOND, J. (n.d.), *The Mule Deer.* Oregon, Conger Printing Co.

BOONE and CROCKETT CLUB (1964), *Records of North American Big Game* (Various contributors.) New York, Chicago and San Francisco, Holt, Rinehart & Winston.

BRANDER, A. A. DUNBAR (1923), *Wild Animals in Central India.* London, Edward Arnold & Co.

BROCK, S. E. (1963), *Hunting in the Wilderness.* London, Robert Hale, Ltd.

CABRERA, DR ANGEL and YEPES, DR JOSE (1960), *Mammiferos Sud Americanos.* (2nd edn.) Laminas Originales del Artista Pintor Carlos C. Wiedner, Ediar.

CAHALANE, V. H. (1939), 'Deer of the World.' *The National Geographical Magazine.* Oct. 1939. Vol. LXXVI. pp. 463–510.

—— (1961), *Mammals of North America.* New York, The Macmillan Co.

CAMERON, A. GORDON (1923), *The Wild Red Deer of Scotland.* Edinburgh & London, William Blackwood & Sons.

CARHART, A. H. (1946), *Hunting North American Deer.* New York, The Macmillan Co.

CARRUTHERS, D. (1913), *Unknown Mongolia.* 2 Vols. London, Hutchinson & Co.

CATON, J. D. (1877), *The Antelope and Deer of America.* (2nd edn.) New York, Forest & Stream Publishing Co.

COWAN, I. MCTAGGART (1936), 'Distribution and Variation in Deer (Genus *Odocoileus*) of the Pacific Coastal Region of North America.' *California Fish & Game.* Vol. 22 (3). pp. 155–246. July 1936.

DANSIE, DR OLIVER and WINCE, DR WALTER (1968–70), 'Deer of the World.' Supplement in *Deer,* Journal of the British Deer Society. Vol. 1. Nos. 7, 8 and 10; Vol. 2. Nos. 1 and 2.

DARLING, F. FRASER (1937), *A Herd of Red Deer.* London, Oxford University Press.

D'AZARA, FÉLIX (1801), *Essais sur l'Histoire Naturelle des Quadrupèdes de la Province du Paraguay.* (2 vols.) Paris, Charles Pougens.

DONNE, T. E. (1924), *The Game Animals of New Zealand – an Account of their Introduction, Acclimatisation and Development.* London, John Murray.

DRIMMER, F. (1964) (Editor), *The Illustrated Encyclopaedia of Animal Life.* (Vols. 6 and 7.) London, Odhams Books, Ltd.

ELLERMAN, J. R. and MORRISON-SCOTT, T. C. S. (1951), *Check List of Palaearctic and Indian Mammals, 1758 to 1946.* London, British Museum (Natural History).

FLEROV, K. K. (1952), *Fauna of U.S.S.R. Mammals – Musk Deer and Deer*. (Vol. 1. No. 2.) Moscow, Published by the Academy of Sciences of the USSR and translated from the Russian by the Israel Program of Scientific Translation.

FOWLER, G. HERBERT (1894), 'Notes on some specimens of antlers of the Fallow deer, showing continuous variations, and the effects of total or partial castration', London, *Proc. Zool. Soc. London*, pp. 485–94.

FRITZ, GRANCEL (1964). See Boone and Crockett Club.

GAUMER, G. F. (1917), *Mamiferos de Yucatán*. Dept. Talleres Gráficos, Secretaria de Fomento, Mexico.

GEE, E. P. (1964), *The Wild Life of India*. London, Collins.

—— (1965), 'Report on the Status of the Kashmir Stag: October 1965.' *Journ. Bombay Nat. Hist. Soc.* 62, No. 3.

GLOVER, R. (1956), 'Notes on the Sika Deer.' *Journ. of Mammology*. Vol. 37. No. 1. February 1956. pp. 99–105.

GRZIMEK, B. (1966), *Wild Animals, White Men*. Great Britain; André Deutsch and Thames and Hudson.

HALL, E. RAYMOND and KELSON, K. R. (1959), *The Mammals of North America*. Vol. 11. New York, The Ronald Press Co.

HARPER, FRANCIS (1945), *Extinct and Vanishing Mammals of the Old World*.* New York, Spec. Pub. No. 12. Am. Committee for Int. Wild Life Protection.

—— (1955), *The Barren-Ground Caribou of Keewatin*. Kansas, University of Kansas.

HEPTNER, V. G. and TSALKIN, V. I. (1947), *Oleni S.S.R.* (Deer of the U.S.S.R.). Moscow, New Series Zoological Division No. 10.

HERSHKOVITZ, P. (1948), 'The Technical Name of the Virginian Deer with a List of the South American Forms.' *Proc. Biol. Soc.* Washington, Vol. 61, pp. 41–8.

——(1958), 'Technical Names of the South American Marsh Deer and Pampas Deer, *Proc. Biol. Soc.* Washington, Vol. 71, pp. 13–16, April 11, 1958.

——(1959), 'A New Species of South American Brocket, Genus *Mazama* (*Cervidae*)', *Proc. Biol. Soc.* Washington, Vol. 72, pp. 45–54, May 1, 1959.

——(1959), 'A New Race of Red Brocket Deer (*Mazama aməricana*) from Colombia', *Proc. Biol. Soc.* Washington, Vol. 72, pp. 93–6, July 24, 1959.

HOLTEN, N. E. (1970), *Hjortevildt i alverdens lande*. Denmark, H. P. Hansens Bogtrykkeri AS.

KELLER, W. P. (1966), *Under Wilderness Skies*. London, Jarrolds Publishers (London) Ltd.

KURODA, NAGAMICHI (1955), 'The Present Status of the Introduced Mammals in Japan', *Journ. of Mammological Society of Japan*, Vol. 1, No. 2, Feb. 1955.

LAURIE, E. M. O. and HILL, J. E. (1954), *List of Land Mammals of New Guinea, Celebes and Adjacent Islands* (*1758–1952*). London, British Museum (Natural History).

LEOPOLD, A. STARKER (1959), *Wild Life of Mexico – The Game Birds and Mammals.* Berkeley and Los Angeles, University of California Press.

LINSDALE, J. M. and TOMICH, P. Q. (1953), *A Herd of Mule Deer.* Berkeley and Los Angeles, University of California Press.

LOWE, W. P. (1932), *The Trail that is Always New.* London, Gurney & Jackson.

LYDEKKER, R. (1893), *Horns and Hoofs, or Chapters on Hoofed Animals.* London, Horace Cox.

—— (1898), *The Deer of All Lands.** London, Rowland Ward, Ltd.

—— (1900), *The Great and Small Game of India, Burma and Tibet.* London, Rowland Ward, Ltd.

—— (1901), *The Great and Small Game of Europe, Western and Northern Asia and America.* London, Rowland, Ward, Ltd.

—— (1915), *Catalogue of the Ungulate Mammals in the British Museum* (Natural History). Vol. IV. Artiodactyla Families *Cervidae* etc. London, Trustees of the British Museum.

—— (1924), *The Game Animals of India, Burma, Malaya and Tibet* (2nd edn). London, Rowland Ward, Ltd.

MACEWEN, WILLIAM (1920), *The Growth and Shedding of the Antler of the Deer.* Glasgow, Maclehose, Jackson & Co.

MILLAIS, J. G. (1897), *British Deer and Their Horns.* London, Henry Sotheran & Co.

—— (1906), *The Mammals of Great Britain and Ireland.* Vol. III. London, Longmans, Green & Co.

MILLER, G. S. & KELLOGG, REMINGTON (1955), 'List of North American Recent Mammals.' Washington DC Smithsonian Institution, *US Nat. Mus. Bulletin* 205.

MURIE, O. J. (1935), 'Alaska-Yukon Caribou.' *N. Am. Fauna* No. 54 (June, 1935). Washington DC, US Dept. of Agriculture.

—— (1951), *The Elk of North America.* Pennsylvania, The Stackpole Company, and Washington DC Wild Life Management Institute.

—— (1951), 'Contribution to New Zealand–American Fiordland Expedition.' Compiled by A. L. Poole, Wellington, *N.Z. Dept. of Scientific & Indust. Research Bulletin* (*see below*).

NAZÁROFF, P. S. (1932), *Hunted Through Central Asia.* Edinburgh & London, William Blackwood & Sons, Ltd.

OSGOOD, W. H. (1943), *The Mammals of Chile.* Chicago, Field Museum of Nat. Hist. Vol. 30 (28 December, 1943).

PEACOCK, E. H. (1933), *A Game Book for Burma and Adjoining Territories.* London, H. F. & G. Witherby.

PENNANT, T. (1784), *Arctic Zoology.* Vol. I. London, Henry Hughes.

PETERSON, R. L. (1955), *North American Moose.* University of Toronto Press.

POOLE, A. L. (1951), 'Preliminary Reports of the New Zealand–American Fiordland Expedition, 1949.' Wellington, *N.Z. Dept. of Sci. and Indust. Res. Bulletin* 103.

PRATER, S. H. (1965), *The Book of Indian Animals* (2nd rev. edn) Bombay, Nat. Hist. Soc. (1st edn) 1948.

PYCRAFT, W. P. (n.d.), *The Courtship of Animals*. London, Hutchinson & Co. (Publishers) Ltd.

RED DATA BOOK (1966), Volume 1, *Mammalia*. Published by International Union for Conservation of Nature and Natural Resources, Survival Service Commission, Switzerland.

RITCHIE, J. (1920), *The Influence of Man on Animal Life in Scotland*. Cambridge University Press.

ROOSEVELT, THEODORE (1914), *Through the Brazilian Wilderness*. London, John Murray.

SANBORN, C. C. (1952), 'Philippine Zoological Expedition 1946–1947.' Mammals. *Fieldiana, Zool.* Vol. 33, No. 2, November 28, 1952.

SCLATER, P. L. (1871), 'On Certain Species of Deer now or lately living in the Society's Menagerie.' London, *Trans. Zool. Soc.* Vol. VII. Pt. V (January, 1871).

SETON, E. THOMPSON (1910), *Life Histories of Northern Animals*. Vol. I. London, Constable & Co. Ltd.

—— (1953), *Lives of Game Animals*. Vol. III. Part 1. Boston, Charles T. Brandford & Co. (3rd edn) (1st edn 1909).

SEVERINGHAUS, C. W. and CHEATUM, E. L. (1956), 'Life & Times of the White-tailed Deer.' Contrib. to *The Deer of North America*. (See TAYLOR, W. P.)

SMITH, R. V. FRANCIS (n.d.), *Rifle Sport in the South Island*. Christchurch, The Pegasus Press.

SOWERBY, A. de C. (1914), *Fur and Feather in North China*. Tientsin, The Tientsin Press, Ltd.

—— (1918), *Sport and Science on the Sino-Mongolian Frontier*. London, Andrew Melrose, Ltd.

STOCKLEY, LT. COL. C. H. (1936), *Stalking in the Himalayas and Northern India*. London, Herbert Jenkins, Ltd.

STOREY, H. (1907), *Hunting & Shooting in Ceylon*. London, Longmans, Green & Co.

TAYLOR, W. P. (Edited by) (1956), *The Deer of North America*.* Pennsylvania, The Stackpole Co., and Washington DC, The Wildlife Management Institute.

THOMSON, G. M. (1922), *The Naturalisation of Animals and Plants in New Zealand*. Cambridge University Press.

TOMICH, P. QUENTIN (1969), *Mammals in Hawaii*. Honolulu, Bishop Museum Press.

VAN BEMMEL, A. C. V. (1949), 'Revision of the Rusine Deer in the Indo-Australian Archipelago.' Buitenzorg, *Treubia*. Vol. 20. Pt. 2, pp. 191–262 (October, 1949).

—— (1952), 'Contribution to the Knowledge of the genera *Muntiacus* and *Arctogalidia* in Indo-Australian Archipelago.' Amsterdam, *Beaufortia*, No. 16 (May 7, 1952).

VAN BEMMEL, A. C. V. (1953), 'One of the Rarest Deer in the World.' Amsterdam, *Beaufortia, Zool. Mus.* No. 27 (February 18, 1953).

WALDO, C. M., WISLOCKI, G. B. and FAWCETT, D. W. (1949), 'Contribution on the Blood Supply of Growing Antlers.' *Am. J. Anat.* Vol. 84, No. 1. January (*see also under* WISLOCKI).

WALKER, E. P. (1964), *Mammals of the World.* Vol. II. Baltimore, The Johns Hopkins Press.

WALLACE, H. F. (1913), *The Big Game of Central and Western China.* London, John Murray.

WALLACE, H. F. and EDWARDS, L. (1927), *Hunting and Stalking the Deer.* London, Longmans, Green & Co.

WARD, ROWLAND (1928), *Records of Big Game.* (9th edn.) London, Rowland Ward, Ltd.

WHITAKER, J. (1892), *A Descriptive List of the Deer-Parks and Paddocks of England.* London, Ballantyne, Hanson & Co.

WHITEHEAD, G. KENNETH (1950), *Deer and Their Management in the Deer Parks of Great Britain and Ireland.* London, Country Life, Ltd.

—— (1964), *The Deer of Great Britain and Ireland.** London, Routledge & Kegan Paul.

WISLOCKI, G. B. (1942), 'Studies on the Growth of Deer Antlers.' *Am. J. Anat.* Vol. 71. No. 3. November 16.

—— AUB, J. C. and WALDO, C. M. (1947), 'The Effects of Gonadectomy and the Administration of Testosterone Propionate on the Growth of Antlers in Male and Female Deer.' *Endocrinology,* Vol. 40, No. 3. pp. 202–24. March, 1947 (*see also under* WALDO, C. M.).

WODZICKI, K. A. (1950), *Introduced Mammals of New Zealand, An Ecological and Economic Study.* Wellington, New Zealand; Dept. of Scientific and Indust. Research.

General Index

For Index of Countries, Islands and Localities, etc., mentioned in the text, see pages 187–90.

For Index of Latin Names of genera, species and subspecies, see pages 191–4.

NOTE: Page numbers in *italics* denote principal description of the species.

Index of Countries, Islands and Localities, etc.

For General Index, see pages 177–86.

For Index of Latin Names of genera, species and subspecies, see pages 191–4.

Index of Latin Names of Genera, Species and Sub-Species, etc.

For General Index, see pages 177–86.

For Index of Countries, Islands and Localities, etc., see pages 187–90.

Page numbers in *italics* denote principal reference to the Genus.